FEMINIST STAGES

Kir.. A!£

2009

Contemporary Theatre Studies
A series of books edited by Franc Chamberlain, Nene College,
Northampton, UK

**Please see the back of this book for other titles in the Contemporary Theatre
Studies series.**

FEMINIST STAGES

INTERVIEWS WITH WOMEN IN CONTEMPORARY BRITISH THEATRE

Lizbeth Goodman
The Open University, Milton Keynes, UK

Jane de Gay
Research Assistant
The Open University, Milton Keynes, UK

harwood academic publishers
Australia • Canada • China • France • Germany • India
Japan • Luxembourg • Malaysia • The Netherlands • Russia
Singapore • Switzerland • Thailand • United Kingdom

Emmaplein 5
1075 AW Amsterdam
The Netherlands

British Library Cataloguing in Publication Data
Feminist stages: interviews with women in contemporary
    British theatre. – (Contemporary theatre studies; v. 17)
    1. Women in the theater – Great Britain 2. Theater – Great Britain – Interviews
    3. Feminist theater – Great Britain 4. Women in the theater – Ireland
    5. Theater – Ireland – Interviews 6. Feminist theater – Ireland
    I. Goodman, Lizbeth, 1964 –   II. de Gay, Jane, 1966 – 792'.082

    ISBN 3-7186-5872-0 (hardcover)
    ISBN 3-7186-5882-8 (softcover)

Cover photograph: Deborah Baddoo, *In Defence of Identity* (1993); photo credit:
State of Emergency.

This book is dedicated

to the continuing spirit and talent of
Joan Littlewood

whose work in British theatre
has inspired and encouraged so many

and to the memory of
Ruth Elizabeth Hess Harrington,
1902–1994,

one of my personal sources of inspiration
world's best grandma,
feisty to the end.
L. G.

CONTENTS

Contents

INTRODUCTION TO THE SERIES

Contemporary Theatre Studies is a book series of special interest to everyone involved in theatre. It consists of monographs on influential figures, studies of movements and ideas in theatre, as well as primary material consisting of theatre-related documents, performing editions of plays in English, and English translations of plays from various vital theatre traditions worldwide.

Franc Chamberlain

LIST OF ILLUSTRATIONS

ACKNOWLEDGEMENTS

This book was made possible by a generous grant from the Open University Arts Faculty Research Committee for The Gender, Politics, Performance Research Project: an ongoing initiative exploring international connections between gender, race, class and representation in the theatre and arts (Project Director: L. Goodman). A British Academy Personal Research Grant provided funds for follow-up research in late 1995.

Thanks to: Franc Chamberlain (Harwood Series Editor) and Judy Collins, Mags Noble, Angela Jamieson, Jenny Bardwell, G. D. Jayalakshmi, Carole Brown, Jill Tibble, Amanda Willett, Jayne Ellery and Tony Coe at the OU BBC for assistance in recording and transcribing some of the interviews printed here; Juliet Cunliffe, Todd Woodard, Jonnie Leger, Alex Slee and Kristi Street, production assistant/interns; Valerie Bishop, Julie Dickens, Susan Gallagher, Jo Biggs, Tony Coulson, Trevor Herbert, John Wolffe, Gerrylynn Roberts, Wendy Stainton Rogers, Nick Wagstaff, Dennis Walder and Stephen Regan at the Open University; and Richard Adams, Simon Rae Selina Devereux and all their colleagues at Academic Computing Services for technical assistance and trouble-shooting.

Thanks are also due to the many colleagues and students who wrote over the years asking for these interviews, suggesting that such primary source material was indeed of interest and of academic value.

Special thanks to all the women and men who took part in the collaborative process of making this book — especially Jane de Gay, Bryony Lavery, Gabriella Giannachi and Mary Luckhurst.

* * *

The interviews were conducted by Lizbeth Goodman unless otherwise indicated (individual interviewers are credited in the text). All interviews were framed by questions set by Lizbeth Goodman, with the exceptions of the interview with Louise Page by Elizabeth Sakellaridou and of the interview with Deborah Levy by Irini Charitou.

Permission to reprint some of the interviews was kindly granted by *New Theatre Quarterly*, Cambridge University Press, with thanks to Clive Barker and Simon Trussler.

L. G.

INTRODUCTION: FEMINIST STAGES

An Introduction to the Introduction (or Why This Book)

The project of putting women's theatre work centre stage is exciting and frustrating at the same time. The theatre event is live, fantastically organized and also rather arbitrary, interactive and ephemeral. Books such as this one can only attempt to put down some ideas and images on paper, to make them last. Perhaps this book may offer a spotlight for the women who speak in it and through it. But the spotlight keeps changing focus.

The nature of theatre transforms and is transformed by each generation, each culture. One 'angry young generation' of playwrights instills expectations in its audiences, who become the theatre makers of the next generation, faced with the demands and possibilities of developing work not only in 'theatre' but also in multi-media and inter-disciplinary forms. Creative development, however, does not always go hand in hand with economic development. In the 1990s, with Arts funding devolved to the regions (whereas The Arts Council once funded from its central London location), much theatre is truly out of the 'arm's reach' of funding bodies. Theatre administrators may find employment possibilities developing, even as theatre companies continue to shrink and close; or theatre practitioners may become administrators in the effort to secure a financial base to support their creative work. Meanwhile, today's critics have still to review something — and so some set of 'standards' for funding and evaluating theatre will continue to be applied, even as values shift and work which falls into the margins, or which attempts to redefine the nature of theatre, may continue to be overlooked, or may be condemned outright.

So, in the 1990s, many theatre makers work without financial support, looking for our own ways of deviating constructively and artistically from an ever-changing 'norm' for theatre. Some have been successful, tracing the paths of those who have gone before, attempting to overturn the values of traditional theatre (aesthetics, production values, content, intent, politics and performance). Such creative individuals may be ridiculed for their enthusiasm, style, methodology or approach — for the effort to trace new paths in darkness is never easy, and always easy to criticise. Sometimes we — all of us who make and write about women's theatre in Britain — get tired or, like the proverbial light bulb, 'burnt out': it is difficult to maintain staying power and to keep a theatre company running with no funding for more than a few years without feeling tempted to take a break from theatre work, to look on from the audience and to ponder the nature of theatre, the attraction of the spotlight, the meaning of it all....

This book offers space for such existential and even theoretical searching, not only to academics and students but also to women active in making theatre. Some of the contributors argue that what a woman will find when she looks at theatre may be quite different from what a man will see, because of a 'gendered way of seeing'. Others disagree, sometimes vehemently. But nearly all agree with the more general point that what a woman will find in any theatre piece will differ in intriguing ways from what the woman next to her will see. Her profession will influence her perspective: a playwright might pay particular attention to the language of the piece; an actor to the characterization; a working woman in the audience worried about her ride home alone on the tube after a late night show may be more distracted by the time on her watch. So it goes.

A woman making theatre, but not necessarily aiming to make either 'great drama' or 'well made plays', will need to be tough, determined and have a good sense of humour. She will need to redefine terms, decide what she wants to make and show to the world, struggle to let the light shine strongly enough on the work to allow people to see it. Of course, this may also be true of men working in theatre today — no doubt about it. But women are the concern of this book.

In the 1990s, theatre makers have to be open to all eventualities; funding influences the very survival of theatre as a form, so women (and men) making theatre must consider a range of survival tactics. Sometimes, survival depends on blending in — which, unfortunately, often seems to translate into a hesitation about being identified as 'feminist', since the 'F' word is still considered 'dirty' in many parts of Britain, due primarily to 'bad press' created by and through the media. Perhaps one day it will be OK to be Feminist. Or at least, perhaps in the next decade or so, the ranks of theatre critics may open further to women, in the paying sector as well as the small women's periodicals (which have, to date, been a powerhouse of support for women making theatre, though they have often worked in danger of closure as well). Maybe one day in the mythical but entirely possible future, women's work in the theatre may be a different animal altogether: British culture may have opened its doors to include women working in newly-lit spaces illuminating all kinds of new work and new ways of writing about that work. But meanwhile, this book is intended to help shed some light on a breed of work, an unusual animal, rarely seen: women theatre makers, some of whom playwright Bryony Lavery has 'sighted' as 'guerillas in the mist' (see her Afterword to this volume, p. 303).

For now, while all the women who speak out in this book are still active in the theatre (and the theatres aren't yet all 'dark'), let's acknowledge that over the past few decades, women making theatre in Britain, and the work they have produced, have varied tremendously. It is not only difficult, but positively unhelpful to try to find one way of discussing women's work. It is not all feminist. It does not all mean to be feminist. There are so many definitions of feminism that application of the term sometimes seems ludicrous. Yet women have helped each other out, often behind the scenes, and have also competed with each other in unhelpful ways. All is not rosy for women working in theatre today. Some will say things have improved, others will cry woe, destruction and despair. It's not just a matter of perspective: there are of course 'real' issues and implications to working at any job in the UK in the 1990s, let alone as women, in an industry where it is still not at all uncommon for people with many years professional experience to work for low pay or even for nothing, with few or no job benefits, in order to keep working and keep the theatre alive.

The women interviewed in this book have performed on and within three major 'stages' in the development of British theatre: the 1960s, the 1970s, the 1980s. Now we're all looking hard at the 1990s, when women making theatre must find new ways of working, and of writing about our own work. Feminist or not, political or not, whatever kind of theatre we make, and whether or not we find it valuable to publish books about it, we are all part of the same project, the same dialogue with culture.

Now for the Introduction 'Proper'

This introduction so far has not, obviously, been typically 'academic', either in tone or in content. Like much women's work, this book does not fit traditional categories. It is not purely academic, but it should be quite useful to students and to those who want to add to the (still meagre) list of published materials on the subject of women's theatre. Nor is it purely practical: it is not a guidebook or handbook for actors. Nor is it merely polemical. This Introduction, like many of the contributions in the book, will use humour to convey serious messages, partly in the hope that the more readable this text is, the more it may be read. Now, of course, I realize that I enter here the dangerous terrain of categories: is it a Research publication? Yes. It is the result of over eight years of research, writing, analysis, feedback and dialogue with women across generations and cultures, disciplines and languages. Is it a general market book, of value to people in the theatre and in the 'real world' as well? It is intended to be, and the process of revising this material for publication has involved demystifying the academic jargon, clarifying definitions, and engaging in 'reality checks' with the women whose voices and ideas it represents. It has also been designed to illuminate and frame the plays selected for publication in a new anthology: *Mythic Women/Real Women: Plays and Performance Pieces*, ed. and introduced by L. Goodman (forthcoming from Faber and Faber in 1997).

　　　Now, I hear the critics saying, one book can't be all things to all people. But, I'd argue, the boundaries between research and practical theatre documentation have been far too stringently defined in the past: the voices of the women included in this volume contribute to a collective statement about just how limiting and counter-productive such clinging to artifical boundaries and definitions can be. Just as each play and performance piece can be 'autobiographical' and general, humorous and serious, enjoyable and political, so one book can be a contribution to the academy and to the theatre, pedagogic and practical. Women's performance work since the 1960s, and most published writing about it, has crossed just these borders, over and over again with or without passports, green cards or 'landing forms for aliens'.

Background

In the five years of research which led to publication of *Contemporary Feminist Theatres* (Routledge, 1993), I conducted an extensive survey of theatre companies and practitioners, interviewed a wide range of women working in theatre and writing about the theatre, and dug through all the available published accounts of women's theatre work in Britain. This research was telling in several ways: it showed how little serious academic research had been conducted on the subject, suggesting that I would have to learn the hard way that women's theatre, much less feminist theatre, is still not considered a 'serious' area of inquiry. I also became aware of a considerable difference between the definitions of feminism among women making theatre: it was nearly impossible to conduct a survey, as respondents wouldn't respond unless the definition of terms was clarified to the point of absurdity. The learning process described above is what inspired publication of this book of interviews, but paradoxically, also what has made the process of collecting and updating and editing the interviews so difficult. In the three years since completion of the first book, I've worked on updating these interviews and collecting the body of material which might make the work more accessible to theatre makers as well as to academics. I published the results of my 'Feminist Theatre Survey' (Cambridge University Press: *New Theatre Quarterly*, vol. IX, no. 33, February 1993) and collected feedback and further information as it became available. I've begun an extended analysis of this work for a new book (*Sexuality in Performance*: forthcoming from Routledge in 1996), and have also revised and updated the interviews in this volume. Still, there are significant gaps and silences which are informative in and of themselves.

Some women who contributed significantly to the development of women's work in theatre as practitioners did not want to be interviewed, or to have their interviews published. There are many reasons why practitioners may hesitate to give interviews: the popular press often misrepresents women's work, or draws inappropriately on their life experiences; the tabloid press invents misinformation about their lives; practitioners may be understandably suspicious about an academic project which seeks to examine the feminist politics and cultural impact as well as the artistic importance of theatre work. There are also logistic reasons why collections of interviews may not be as inclusive as the editors and readers might wish. In preparation of this volume, for instance, it proved impossible to reach a number of women due to their busy schedules and distant locations; Joan Littlewood and Emma Thompson could not be interviewed for these reasons. Tilda Swinton has moved on mainly to film work and did not, therefore, feel it would be appropriate to have an earlier interview we conducted updated for inclusion here (see *New Theatre Quarterly*, vol. 6, no. 23, August, 1990). But some of the women I had hoped to include had strong views about the nature of interviews, 'feminist' or not. For instance, Caryl Churchill hesitates to give interviews as a general rule. She was kind enough to grant me an interview, recorded for an Open University BBC video on *Top Girls* (1995 — producer: Mags Noble). But she did not want that or any other interview material published in a book, not even an updated version of her interview with Geraldine Cousin (printed in *New Theatre Quarterly*, vol. 4, no. 13, February, 1988), or the one printed in the collection of interviews — mainly with North American women, in Kathleen Betsko and Rachel Koenig, eds. *Interviews with Contemporary Women Playwrights* (Beech Tree Books, 1987). While Churchill's work is undeniably feminist in impact, editors and readers must respect her wish not to be labelled as a 'feminist playwright' or to have her spoken words committed to print. So be it.

To the women who consented to be interviewed for this book, I owe a debt of gratitude on several counts. It serves the theatre community and the academic community (students and teachers and theorists) to have access to the words of these women. But the debt is also material; no one was paid for their contribution to this book. As the state of academic publishing parallels that of theatre funding in many respects, it is regrettable that so many women (and men) continue to volunteer their time and energy and ideas and talents, for the 'greater good'. I can only hope that this book will be an acceptable form of payment...

In conducting and editing the interviews collected here, I got around the problem of defining 'feminism' by offering each respondent the chance to define the term for herself, and to answer accordingly. This led to an interesting variety of answers and a unique dialogue with the 'British' culture — and its use of languages, regional and 'central' — as well as a dialogue across generations of women. The Index to this book grew and grew as a result — it seemed that one of the most significant 'academic' and 'practical' contributions the book might make would be provision of an easy way of indexing all kinds of terms and names. This is intended to allow the reader (and all the contributors) to cross-refer to these interviews, in order to find out what many different women have said about, for instance, the definition of 'feminism', or about the contributions and inspirations of other women working in the theatre. Yet of course, the flexibility of the term 'feminism' means that the book can not be easily used as a source for sociological or any other form of empirical analysis. Again, so be it. The field of feminist theatre studies falls between disciplines, between the boundaries and forms of standard methodological analysis. I hope the book will be of wide interest, will provide inspiration to women working in the theatre and studying theatre, may inform those who don't believe there is such a field as 'feminist theatre', or who have latched on to the idea that so-called 'post-feminism' has eliminated the need to consider women as a special interest group.

The interviews included here vary tremendously in many ways, yet they also share some very important similarities: however the terms are defined, all these women see factors and considerations (financial, political, social, personal) which distinguish the career development and ways of working for women in the theatre, as opposed to men in the theatre. Some argue that things are getting better, some not. Some describe the frustration of not being taken seriously, missing out on promotions while men moved up beyond the 'glass ceiling': that invisible barrier to promotion against which so many women continue to hit their heads. Some describe their frustrations with younger women who don't always seem to appreciate the efforts made by women who came before. Some offer thanks, through generations and cultures. Others describe feelings of frustration with a lack of role models, a lack of 'sisterly' support for newcomers. Most describe a feeling of solidarity with other women, and a preference for working collaboratively with women — suggesting that generational frustrations may be a by-product of cultural non-representation of women's issues and concerns in the mainstream. Perhaps this book may function as a bridge between generations, and across the disciplines which sometimes divide women who might otherwise work together. I hope it may at least be one plank in that footbridge...

Mainstream Feminist Theatre: 'Alternative' to what?

In discussion with Franc Chamberlain, Commissioning Editor for Harwood, and with Jane de Gay, Research Assistant, and others, I decided to include as wide a range of voices as possible in this book: women of different generations, educational and practical experiences, cultural backgrounds, working methods. I also chose to include some 'big names' or established personalities in the theatre world, as well as a number of lesser known women and groups. The comparison works to show that the concerns are the same across the boundary of 'stardom', though funding is an inevitable problem for newer groups and young women, particularly those working in experimental forms or in expressly political ways.

Again, the illumination of certain areas of experience shared by contributors is diffused by dispute about the definition of 'feminism' in relation to theatre work. The term 'feminist' has taken on new meanings and connotations in the past few years, particularly with the increasing influence of academic feminism and feminist theory. As a result, some women are wary about applying the term 'feminist' to themselves or their work because they are not sure what it has come to mean. Playwrights such as Caryl Churchill, Pam Gems and Louise Page can be labelled 'feminist' according to their own definitions, or because some of their work has helped to focus attention on the situation of women's lives, and women's work in the theatre. Yet their focus in the work, and their life circumstances and ways of representing themselves in the public domain, differ significantly from a range of younger women as such as Sarah Daniels, Jackie Kay, Emilyn Claid, Deborah Baddoo. The experiences of actors obviously differs from that of directors and designers and playwrights. Direct comparison of such a wide variety of women is not particularly helpful, but consideration of their perspectives across generations and within their own definitions of 'feminism' is enlightening.

The work of the many companies included here also differs significantly, on many and varied fronts. Political theatre companies are included, as well as experimental companies which begin with an awareness of and interest in feminist theory, as well as political action groups focused on 'women's issues', as well as solo performers exploring the possibilities and limitations of bodies in performance spaces, as well as women who have collaborated in collective groups, as well as actors working in mainstream theatre. Despite the range of work experiences, it is striking that so many of the interviews touch on issues of gender in relation to class, race, power and communication. Neti-Neti Theatre, for instance, works in English, Bengali and Sign Language to produce original plays which include positive female characters and multi-racial themes. Anna O begins with the notion of the woman silenced by patriarchal ideas about femininity and 'hysteria', while Theatre of Black Women and Talawa both describe work which has explored the role of black women in positions of power despite racial prejudice.

The focus on 'feminism' becomes better illuminated as we grow closer to an understanding of the tremendous diversity of interpretations, approaches, working methods and styles of the many women who 'speak' in this book.

The title: Feminist Stages

First things last: the title is at one level a simple pun on the word 'stages' to designate theatrical performance spaces, and stages of development in a more general sense. Feminism has developed in stages, though these are not easily divisible or definable, just as theatre has grown and developed from generation to generation. But the intersection of feminism and theatre has been particularly problematic.

I argued in *Contemporary Feminist Theatres* (1993) about the differences between 'women's theatre' and 'theatre by women' and 'theatre about women' and 'feminist theatre'. These differences have developed and become, in some ways, even more extreme in the past few years, with the development of Queer Studies — drawing some lesbian feminists into a closer working relationship with gay men in a joint project dedicated to cultural and sexual/political agendas not confinable within the term 'feminist' — as well as with the many factors mentioned above, including the continual undermining of women's theatre work by cuts to arts funding across the UK. The debate will continue, as the terms change meaning from person to person, generation to generation, culture to culture. But the idea that there is an entity which can be called 'feminist theatre' holds. Whether or not we include men, or insist on specific sets of theoretical views, we can identify a body of performance work influenced by the thoughts and actions of a generation of people thinking about 'feminism'.

In these pages, a wide range of definitions of the term are offered. Were other women interviewed, the definitions would be different still.

In one book, it was only possible to include so many voices, so many perspectives. A great deal of editing had to done. Some of the interviews printed here represent months and months of discussion and considered thought, while others were conducted hastily over the telephone or in rehearsal rooms or tube (subway) stations. Some have been previously published, some not. Some are with very well known figures, while others are with young or 'new' women in British theatre. What is written between the lines and the pages of this book is a dialogue, a range of perspectives offering some representation — however partial — of the diverse and fragmented and remarkably visionary views which illuminate both the making and the study of contemporary British theatres.

The interviews have been divided into three sections according to a loose organisation based on generation, rather than on the age, political views, working methods, sexual orientation, cultural identity, or profession of interviewees or their theatres. This seemed the most interesting way to allow voices to speak to each other, with less mediation and no pretense of a uniformity of views. Of course, each contributor has something to say which transcends the limits of a decade. But in speaking to a decade, it becomes possible to speak to an issue — such as feminism and theatre — with some sense of context, artificial though it may be. And once the discussion is underway, it could (and does) lead in all kinds of interesting directions.

Each of the women's voices included in the volume has its own rhythm: something which often seems to be edited out in collections of interviews and articles. I have tried, in so far as is possible, to retain the distinct rhythms and speech patterns of all the women interviewed. So, while the editing process has inevitably involved some rewording for the sake of clarity — we all express ourselves more clearly in print, after repeated revisions, than we do in unrehearsed conversation and interviews — I have tried to avoid putting words into anyone's mouth. Each woman interviewed was sent the first draft of her transcript and given the chance to revise it as much as she liked; even to change her mind, or delete entire sections of an interview if this was the best way to represent her views. Most contributors chose to check and revise a second draft as well, and some checked and revised up to eight drafts, using this opportunity to develop their ideas with feedback and editorial support. The editing process was, therefore, a lengthy one, but I hope also a fruitful one. Though this manner of interviewing and collecting feedback on various drafts is time-consuming for all involved, it also leads to the most informed discussion of key issues. In addition to extensive dialogue between the editorial and artistic contributors to this book, interviewees often contacted each other to compare notes. Dialogue began in 'real life' beyond the covers of the book, and I hope that something of the process of recording that evolving dialogue is captured here.

The styles and formats of some of these interviews also varies; everyone has their own way of speaking, listening and communicating, and it seemed too heavy-handed an editorial policy to insist upon complete reformatting of interviews for the sake of superficial appearances. Instead, I have done my best to collect a readable body of material which is roughly similar in format across the book, but which also reflects some of the ways in which individual contributors felt most confident responding. While most of the questions have been edited right down, there are a few interviews which include the full text of questions because some interviewees preferred more of a two-way conversation — including explanation and contextualization of ideas — than an 'interview' proper. Others hardly needed prompting, and were most comfortable when left to dig right into the issues themselves. I have, wherever appropriate, edited my questions and preamble down to the minimum, but in some cases (for instance, in the interviews with Gillian Hanna, Bryony Lavery, Nancy Diuguid and Sarah Daniels) the interview included in this book is the latest version of a series of interviews and conversations held over the past six or seven years. The status of these interviews as records of ongoing dialogues is reflected in the format of the printed interviews.

I'm reminded here of an anecdote which may seem minor, but which was critical in my impetus to develop this book. Sarah Daniels, as is well known, is one of the UK's leading playwrights. The term 'feminist' is often applied to her and her work, though she does not embrace it for herself. Daniels has expressed the tension between being labelled a 'feminist playwright' and being a playwright who is feminist. In the Introduction to her first collection of plays, she explained that she did not "set out to be a 'Feminist Playwright'..." but is nonetheless proud if some of her plays "have added to its influence" (*Plays One*, Methuen, 1991). Always captivated by her combination of wit and wisdom, I have followed Daniels' work closely for many years. When I first began research on women's theatre as a graduate student in Cambridge in 1987, I quickly found that the academic setting would simply not support the kind of work I needed to do. I needed to talk to people who wrote plays, and not only the 'classics' but feminist plays in particular. I also wanted to talk to feminist directors, designers, dancers, choreographers, performance artists, musicians and comedy performers. When I couldn't find many of these people in Cambridge, I worked up the courage to write to a few of the practitioners whose work I most admired, starting with the playwrights. I wrote to Caryl Churchill, Pam Gems, Bryony Lavery, Michelene Wandor and Sarah Daniels, among many others. They replied, and indeed some of the interviews in this book were begun as far back as 1987. But I kept up the communication with Sarah Daniels in particular, as I was interested in her explicitly feminist approach to 'issue plays' about women. I sat in on the rehearsed readings of *Beside Herself* (directed by Jules Wright for the Women's Playhouse Trust, at the Royal

Court Theatre Upstairs, in 1990). Not much later, I wrote to give Sarah my feedback on the play, and she responded with a postcard: one I've kept since (and which hangs on the side of the wardrobe, 'arm's length' to my right, as I write). The postcard features a cartoon by Angela Martin, and its feminist message is both comic and clear: 'Post-Feminism: Keep Your Bra, Burn Your Brain'.

While Sarah Daniels does not embrace the term 'feminist', she does not deny it either. Indeed, she is well aware of the power of the term, and of the strange status of the term 'post-feminist' to undermine and even ridicule women's achievements of the past few decades.

I record this personal anecdote because it has political significance as well as comic effect. Many of the women in this volume have tried to embrace the varied differences of perspective which the wild wacky mix of a heterogeneous group called 'women' might conceivably include. Many of the interviews record a sense of belonging and not belonging simultaneously — to the club called 'feminists', and also to the ambiguous entity called 'culture'. Some of the voices included are deliberately provocative, others deliberately diplomatic. I have not edited out either the most controversial or the most cautious statements, as it is not my job to agree or disagree or impose a party line, but rather to offer a full account of the state of play for women in British theatre today. In addition to reading the statements and views of each woman interviewed, we can of course also read between the lines, considering the employment contexts and material conditions for each woman, as these will inevitably affect what each feels free to say, and in what terms. It is also intriguing to read sideways through the interviews, using the extensive Index to highlight the mention of individuals, companies, venues (all across the UK), and themes which recur in feminist performance work of all kinds. It is interesting, for instance, that the Index includes so many men's names: mainly playwrights from the past and directors working today (influencing women's work and working opportunities in important ways). But of course, the number of women's names and women's companies is far greater, and is testament to the sheer variety of the work women do in contemporary British theatre.

The interviews form a collective story, told and retold in and through many voices which sometimes overlap (as in Caryl Churchill's play *Top Girls*). The voices sometimes contradict each other and sometimes hit on the same themes in strikingly similar ways, even across generations. Collectively, these voices tell of some women who've learned to succeed in the 'dark' of contemporary theatre production, while others have stumbled along blindly until deciding to create a new light source. The interviews show how things have improved for some and not for others, while 'talent' has not been so

1. Post Feminism postcard by Angela Martin (Leeds Postcards, 1990); courtesy Leeds Postcards.

weighty a factor at times as sexuality, race, class, nationality. They tell a story of generations who have listened to the early cries of the 'third wave' feminist movement, had our consciousnesses raised, and then our hopes dashed as terms like 'post-feminist' and 'politically correct' slipped into common usage. And through it all, the interviews reveal a sense of determination.

The women interviewed in this book, and many others not included here too, have made a real impact on contemporary British theatre, and culture more generally. Despite problems and set-backs of many kinds, they have kept on making theatre, defining and redefining theatre, defining and redefining feminism. Just as importantly, they have kept on going to the theatre, to see each other and create a sense of community, varied and occasionally short-sighted though it may be. These women have made and performed on and taught about a whole range of feminist stages, recognizing and appreciating the contributions of women who worked against greater odds so that others, myself included, could work against fewer. They've taken control of their own spotlights, sometimes turning them to illuminate the areas behind the scenes, and sometimes on the audience. The wonders of modern science; the wonders of modern feminism(s); the wonders of modern theatre.

Lizbeth Goodman
Oxford, July 1995.

Futher Reading on British Women's and Feminist Theatres
Ferris, Lesley. Acting Women. *(Macmillan, 1990).*
Goodman, L. Contemporary Feminist Theatres: To Each Her Own. *(Routledge, 1993).*
Goodman, L. and J. de Gay. 'Voices of Women/Languages of Theatre: Magdalena 1994', a special theme issue of Contemporary Theatre Review *(1996).*
Keyssar, Helene. Feminist Theatre. *(Macmillan, 1984).*
Rutter, Carol. Clamorous Voices: Shakespeare's Women Today. *(The Women's Press, 1988).*
Todd, Susan ed. Women and Theatre: Calling the Shots. *(Faber and Faber, 1984).*
Wandor, Michelene. Carry On Understudies. *(Routledge, 1986).*
Wandor, Michelene. Look Back in Gender. *(Methuen, 1987).*
Woddis, Carole, ed. Sheer Bloody Magic: Conversations with Actresses. *(Virago, 1991).*

Gender and Performance Videos Now Available from Routledge (OU/BBC Approaches to Literature Series) *A Doll's House, Top Girls, The Rover, As You Like it* and the audio cassette on Gender and Drama on the Series features the work of and interviews with many of the women in this book.

PART I

FEMINIST STAGES

FROM 1968 INTO THE 1970s

INTRODUCTION

'Feminist theatre' in Britain came into its own in the late 1960s. Theatre censorship was abolished by Act of Parliament in 1968, and the first British National Women's Liberation Conference was held in Oxford in 1969. Such cultural, political and social changes influenced the formation of what is now often called the 'second wave' of modern feminism, with the development of consciousness raising groups, and feminist activism in the form of political protests for women's rights. This same period saw the formation of women's theatre companies dedicated to producing work by women, or to dealing with issues of particular importance to women's lives. The rise of the women's movement in this period influenced the first specifically gender-oriented political demonstrations since the era of the suffragists. Important demonstrations against the Miss World and Miss America Pageants were staged in 1969–71; these questioned long-accepted stereotypes of women as sexual objects by denouncing such forms of representation on both personal and political grounds. Early feminist activists discovered the effectiveness of public performance as a form of political communication and persuasion. So, many feminist protests were staged as theatre performances, on the streets and on (and in) many different stages.

Demonstrations such as the beauty pageant protests can be seen, in retrospect, as the first stage in a clear progression from early feminist consciousness to organized feminist theatre. The next stage in this development was the emergence of early feminist agitprop groups such as The Women's Street Theatre Group. The development of feminist theatre from street demonstration to 'theatrical production' was contingent upon the development of 'fringe' theatre. The emergence in 1968 and after of fringe theatre companies allowed for the subsequent development of splinter groups with particular allegiance to women's issues. For instance, fringe companies such as Portable Theatre, The Pip Simmons Group, The Warehouse Company, The Brighton Combination, Welfare State International, and Incubus Theatre were instrumental to the development of The Women's Street Theatre Group (which sometimes performed in theatre spaces), Monstrous Regiment and Mrs. Worthington's Daughters.

Red Ladder produced *Strike While the Iron is Hot* in 1972, and Women's Theatre Group produced their first show, *My Mother Says I Never*

Should, in 1974. Playwrights including Ann Jellicoe, Jane Arden, Margaretta D'Arcy, Shelagh Delaney and Doris Lessing, who were among the first women to write for the British stage in the 1950s and 1960s, were followed in the late sixties and seventies by a second generation of feminist playwrights including Caryl Churchill, Maureen Duffy, Pam Gems and Louise Page. Ann Jellicoe's early plays for the Royal Court are, perhaps, what earned her reputation as one of the UK's leading playwrights, but her recent work in community theatre is also important. As her interview in this book reveals, the role of women in contemporary community drama — as in contemporary communities — throws a new light on the subject of 'women in theatre'.

Funding was also a factor in the development of women's work in the theatre. Women's Theatre Group was funded by the Arts Council of Great Britain, but The Women's Company was not. Monstrous Regiment of Women received some funding, as did Gay Sweatshop (a mixed company of lesbians and gay men), but Siren (an explicitly lesbian theatre company) struggled to find financial support. The women interviewed in these pages give a personal account of the impact of arts funding on the development of women's theatre work.

The Conference of Women Theatre Directors and Administrators (CWTDA) was founded in this period. Sue Parrish, Sue Dunderdale and Sarah Daniels, among many others, published important articles in CWTDA's papers. (See *Contemporary Feminist Theatres* for details).

Perhaps most importantly, some — though only a precious few — of the companies founded in the 1970s are still producing feminist theatre today. The women who give voice to this crucial period in feminist theatre 'history' are also leading lights in contemporary (1990s) theatre practice.

Lizbeth Goodman

ANN JELLICOE

During her long and varied career in the theatre Ann Jellicoe has been actress, stage-manager, director, producer, literary manager (Royal Court Theatre) and teacher (Central School of Speech and Drama, RADA, etc.). But, she is probably best known as a playwright and as the innovator of community plays. Her plays include: The Sport of My Mad Mother *(1958),* Shelley; or The Idealist *(1965) and* The Knack *(1961). Translations include* Rosmersholm *(1959) and* The Seagull *(1964) and an opera* Der Freischütz *(1964). She has also written plays for children. Since the late 1970s, she has concentrated on producing, and in most cases writing and directing, community plays — fourteen in all — from* The Reckoning *(Lyme Regis, 1978) to* Changing Places *(Woking, Surrey, 1992).*

Are you aware that the position of women in the theatre has changed during the time that you have been in the profession?

When I started at the Royal Court in 1956, it was still very unusual for women to work there. You weren't even a token woman; they didn't think in terms of token women. You were expected to think of yourself as 'privileged' to be there. There was no thought for women's issues or women's place. The curious thing is that, at the time, one just accepted that: it was absolutely bred into one. It's very hard to imagine now. In the 1970s, I went back to the Royal Court as Literary Manager. I was the first woman Literary Manager, although I don't think they thought of me as a woman: they knew my work very well, and so they probably regarded me as an 'honorary man'.

By the 1970s, I could see the balance changing. I remember going to a woman's theatre season at the Round House in 1970–1, and seeing a play by Pam Gems, and I suddenly felt that something had changed, the balance had tipped. For one thing, I almost always used to go to the theatre alone. Theatre-going was not a social event to me, but part of my job. I always felt that there was a certain *frisson* about a woman being there on her own. But when I went to that season, I felt that I had a perfect right to be there. It didn't matter that I was alone, that as a woman I was in my right place.

Of course since then there have been so many women directors in the provincial theatre, that it's no longer possible for men to say they can't appoint a woman director for the National Theatre because women haven't got any experience. Women directors are clocking up experience like mad. And it's the provincial theatres which have done it. Jane Howell, at Exeter, was one of the first, then there were Annie Castledine, Clare Venables, and more recently Jude Kelly to name a few, coming up through provincial theatres[1]. Not through the Royal Court. Not through the National. But we've now got women in the position where they can seriously be considered as possible directors of the National Theatre.

Why did that change happen first in the provincial theatre?

Because there is less money, less power, fewer resources, it's not so important and not so enviable. I'm awfully conscious that men are aggressive. I've noticed that in any group or workshop, if you call for volunteers, the men rush forward pushing women aside. So until now, women have always had to work with less money, less power. The interesting thing is: Jude Kelly was appointed specifically to work in tandem with the (male) administrator (just as Elisabeth Esteve-Coll was appointed to the V & A because she was willing to play by rules set by the Governors — whose Chair, Sir Robert 'Economical with the Truth' Armstrong, was Mrs Thatcher's Cabinet Secretary). These arrangements have apparently proved satisfactory. Clearly men think that women are more biddable, more easily managed, more practical and realistic as to where power lies and what is actually possible. The men may well be right. But I wonder what are the implications in terms of women's art?

When you think about the changes which you have described over the last three decades, what do you think has contributed to that process: have changes within or outside the theatre been more important in shifting the balance?

Changes outside the theatre have been most important: political education and political awareness. That's what happened to me: one realises that one may have been brought up to accept things in a certain way, but that's not necessarily how things need to be.

I'd always wanted to be in the theatre ever since I can remember. I just floated along: I started out as an actress, director, even playwright of sorts. Then I taught at drama school, then I became a 'real' playwright. For a long time, I was politically blind. Looking back, I realize that people patronized me, but it's only when you're politically aware that you realise what's happening.

I sometimes wonder if being a woman held me back and I'm pretty certain it did, but I wasn't aware of it at the time. I was the woman who had broken through — people produced my plays (there were plenty of women novelists but not many women playwrights in the fifties and sixties). I never consciously sought to gain power. It came without my noticing it.

---

[1] Betty Caplan discusses the importance of regional theatres, page 183.

Did the feminist movement ever become important to your work?

Hardly. I'm very much aware of women's interests, women's points of view, but I have never engaged in the struggle, it's not in my nature to be aggressive in that way.

Would you say that you were a feminist?

I fight my own way. I write some plays about women but they are hardly political plays except insofar as everything we do is political.

Thinking about the development of theatre over this period, do you think that feminism has had an impact? You say that people have become more politically aware: do you think that feminism has been an important element?

Oh yes, incredibly important, because it has aroused people like me who are not particularly political. In a sense we owe them a great debt. They made me politically aware of the issues, of what was going on, aware of the arguments. They educated me, made me aware that I was being patronized, that men take all the big jobs and block the road.

When you write plays about women, are you conscious of writing as a woman, from a woman's perspective?

I have written two kinds of plays: community plays and 'ordinary' plays. In the community plays women's interest is forced on you because there are always more women than men who are interested in being in the play. So you are always looking for a story which is based on women — to which women are fundamentally important and not peripheral. So that naturally means you take women's stories. In my other plays, the women are always, I hope, interesting, but the plays aren't specifically about women, though they are about the relationships between men and women.

Do you think that the theatre can affect social change?

Yes. For example — John Osborne's *Look Back in Anger*. I was brought up in the North of England and I thought that nothing ever happened there, that nobody was interested in the accent or wanted to see a play about the area. *Look Back in Anger* re-started the movement which Annie Horniman had begun with the Manchester Rep by transforming public opinion of provincial plays. However, theatre is not as powerful as television, which can speak to more people.

What about your community plays — can they affect social change? Do you find that people can be changed by participating or by watching?

Oh yes. I've said a lot about this in my book, *Community Plays*, (Methuen, 1987). One example that springs to mind is a housewife in

Dorchester, who had little confidence and a part-time job as a school secretary. That woman, after two plays, is now chairman of the Dorset Arts Group which is a big organization with its own premises. Other women may say to me 'I lost my husband just before I joined in the show, but through this everybody has been so nice to me and looked after me and I've made so many friends'. These experiences are duplicated literally hundreds of times. Astonishing things happen to people.

I suppose that ties in with what you were saying about Look Back in Anger *making the northern character more acceptable in the theatre. Do you think that maybe community theatre similarly elevates people's local characteristics and interests?*

Yes, but the two processes are different. *Look Back in Anger* was a conventional play which struck a public nerve. Whereas community plays involve many individual experiences through which people may change and develop and at the same time, through local audiences, a validation and celebration of a particular place or community.

Do you get many local political issues being raised?

This is the great controversy about community plays. There is a tremendous debate: should we take the burning political issues either in the town or nationally, and *reveal* the differences in the community? I work the other way: I don't go for political issues because they're divisive. I believe it is possible to make friends across the political divide and so help close the divide. Community theatre is riven by this controversy as to whether to be political or not, and they use a lot of energy arguing amongst themselves.

We have talked about community theatre, now what has been your personal involvement in other forms of theatre?

Very little for the last fifteen years really. Occasionally I take part in productions of my own work, but I haven't written any new small-cast plays. I've rather slowed down even on community plays in the last two years.

What's your perspective on the state of contemporary theatre?

The whole theatre is in a dire state: losing confidence and money. Maybe that's why I'm not in it. Even the finest playwrights find it difficult to get their plays produced; all the main writers are trying to take their plays out into the sticks because the big theatres have cut down on production.

Is the funding situation bad at the moment?

It's not the main problem but it is bad, although I sense things are getting better. The other day I had a meeting with some people I am helping with another community play in Dorchester, and one of the local organizers, a shop-keeper and local politician, said that money is getting easier to obtain, that businesses have more money to spend on these ventures.

How do you see women within that situation: is their future in the theatre looking up?

Oh yes! it is much, much changed. Women are much more confident and assertive. To a certain extent they are more accepted. There will always be trouble: men are aggressive and fairly ruthless when their interests are challenged, they may or may not be blind to their own motives. But by and large women are much more aware of what's going on and that's a great source of strength.

Jane de Gay
Interview conducted on audio tape, London, December 1994.

PAM GEMS

Pam Gems, one of Britain's leading female playwrights since the 1970s, served in the Armed Forces before taking up writing for the stage. One of the first women to have plays performed at the Almost Free Theatre, and then at the King's Head lunchtime series, she was one of the founders of The Women's Theatre Group. Her many plays include: Dusa, Fish, Stas and Vi *(1976),* Guinevere *(1976),* Queen Christina *(1977),* Piaf *(1978),* Ladybird, Ladybird *(1979),* Aunt Mary *(1982),* Loving Women *(1984),* Camille *(1985),* Pasionaria *(1985),* The Blue Angel *(1991) and* Deborah's Daughter *(1993/4). She has also produced her own adaptations of* A Doll's House, Uncle Vanya, The Cherry Orchard *and* The Seagull.

Does gender matter in the theatre?
　　　Yes.

In what way?
　　　Well, think of the obverse — if there were not men or women, simply people of one sex, it would be a different kind of theatre. To put it cheaply, *vive la différence.* Certainly gender matters particularly at the moment because women have a great deal to say and this is really the first time they have been able to say it.

Are you aware that the position of women in the theatre has changed in any way?
　　　Réluctantly I'd say yes, it has in the many years that I've been around. There's a lot more lip-service paid to the position of women in the theatre and although it isn't what we hoped for in the seventies, the heady days of neo-feminism, there are more women directors, a few more women writers in live theatres, but many more women writers in television where you can actually make a living. As far as acting goes, I do think that female actors are very badly done by, mainly because we live in an Anglo-Saxon country where you're not allowed to be a woman after the age of forty, and we the women are going to have to change that.

With plays such as Queen Christina *and* Piaf, *and now with your new play* [The Seagull] *you've done a great deal in terms of creating strong female characters, and recreating historical characters, on stage. Has this been a conscious aim in your writing?*
　　　Yes. I was trained as a psychologist and I came into the theatre at the age of 45 after I had had, and partly reared, four children, including a

handicapped child. I had always been stage-struck and loved the theatre but I had to find a way of justifying something that I loved so much but which at the same time seemed to me to be frivolous. When I came to London looking for some education for my kids, and started to go to lunchtime theatre when I had free time, I found that there were no parts for women. I used to count up every week in the *Radio Times* and the *TV Times* and there was twice the amount of work offered to the men, so that five years out of drama school, a boy would be doubly skilled, and I thought: now I can justify sitting at home and writing. I'll write parts for women. It was just as simple as that.

Are you aware of writing as a woman? Do women write differently or write about different subjects when creating parts for women?

Well I would have said 'absolutely' once, but I'm not so sure now, perhaps because I'm getting older. I recently wrote a play, for example, about Stanley Spencer, the painter, of whom I'm a devotee like many other people. The fact that I'm a woman trying to enter into the consciousness of a man didn't cause me any trouble at all — I've had uncles and brothers and sons — and I didn't find that it was bothersome. I didn't find I was any harder on Stanley, who behaved appallingly to his wife — well, ineptly anyway. I found I was Stanley, with no problem. So, I'm less clear-cut than I used to be. I want to write a play about Garibaldi who is a great hero of mine. An unambitious man — that rare thing. I'm not at all daunted by the fact that I'm a woman and he's a chap. So I think that we have to be careful about drawing hard lines.

Now that you are also writing plays about men, do you think that a man might be able to write about strong female characters as well as you did in, for instance, Queen Christina *and* Piaf?

No, in both of those plays. Piaf was right at the bottom of the well as it were, as far as class and privilege was concerned, and doubly so by being female. Because if you're female, especially if you're four foot eleven, anybody can beat you up. You have got no power at all. On the other hand, what interested me about Christina was that here was a woman who was so powerful by accident of birth that they brought her up as a man and thoroughly messed her up. And I really cannot see that a man's consciousness could have dealt with that. I'm not saying that I dealt with it well, but I don't think it's a subject that a man would have taken on.

What is the story of Queen Christina?

Well, Christina's mother had 16 children, and Christina saw her mother destroyed by that. She became a hysterical and sickly woman. Christina was the only survivor. Her father went to battle and was killed, leaving instructions for her to be brought up as a man in order to rule: to be taught politics, taught to hunt, to fight, taught languages, to be trained as a man. So she became the queen of Sweden at 25 and then they say 'Oh there's just one thing, if you wouldn't mind marrying, and breeding an heir'. And she said more or less 'No, I'm a fella, I despise women: all that stuff about having babies. Look at Queen Elizabeth: she was sharp, she didn't marry. It kills you and in any case once you've got an heir, you've got a rival'. And in fact in real life she decamped — she abdicated. She went to Rome because at that time Catholicism was the trendy thing — it was like being a hippy then. And she thought she was going to a lovely free life, but she wasn't. So she made another mistake. But it was an interesting thing — at the end of my play she discovers that she's a woman and she doesn't know what that means and she is determined to find out: what that should probably mean, what her contribution should properly be, and what her demands should be. And I thought that although the play is set in the 1600s, Christina's dilemma is totally modern.

It's fascinating that a historical 'real-life' story, adapted for the stage, can say so much about contemporary ideas relating to feminine roles, and what it means to be a 'woman'...

Absolutely. I wrote the play in the seventies for the Royal Court, who turned it down by telling me that they thought it would appeal more to women than to men (I have the letter still). The seventies was a time when the cry was: 'Yes, girls, you can join. Find your shoulder-pads, we'll let you in'. But we didn't want to be let in, as I tried to say in *Christina*. I wrote another play, called *Guinevere*, in which I did try to deal with redefining the rules so that we might contribute relevantly to society.

Has that play been published?

No, it's never been published. It's a short play, and it's very hard to get short plays published. The Royal Shakespeare Company produced *Guinevere* in 1976, and after that I wrote a second act (in which Arthur also features), in order to help get it published. It didn't seem that publishers were interested in one-woman plays, or short plays, so I thought they might be more interested if I added a man. But they weren't.

Do you feel strongly either for or against working collaboratively with other women in the theatre?

I did work in groups in the seventies. I started the Women's Theatre Group. It was because of me — I did two plays and Ed Berman liked them so much that he asked us in for a season of plays by women. That was at the Almost Free Theatre in London. We demanded to choose the plays and direct them ourselves. He said 'OK, in that case you can paint up the theatre'. So we did.

That split into the Women's Theatre Group and the Women's Company. We had a stand-off because we had people coming in who were not theatre people — nurses, secretaries — and they would say: 'sorry, I can't rehearse tonight, I'm going out with my boyfriend'. And some of us felt that actors, who tend to be out of work ten months of the year, had a case for saying: 'Look, this isn't respectful to our penury'. Then there was a split.

Then I was a member of the Women's Playhouse Trust for a while and I did do collaborative work: a show about abortion, which toured. But in regard to collaboration, I think it's a double-edged thing. Some of Caryl Churchill's recent work is less good because it was done collaboratively. At its worst, collaboration can be when people don't want to write. I used to find, partly because I was older than everybody else, that people love to throw in all their ideas but in the end you the writer have to find a structure, and the reason, and a subtext, a text. This can be hard. If you're doing something like a play about abortion, and you've got one good strong theme, you need all the contributing ideas you can get, so that you can't be second-guessed. But there's another side to writing, and it's the side which is mysterious in all arts — painting or music or writing — and that tends to be disregarded in collaborative work.

What side of writing is that?

That impulsion, that deep, passionate energy which comes from one head. This became unfashionable because it was seen as too egoistic, particularly in the pseudo-Marxist days of the seventies, but it should be respected. Whatever your skill is, if you're an actor or a set designer or a clothes designer or a writer, there should be respect for your skill. And if you're a writer then you're not just a typist. You are bringing something else and what you're bringing may not always be what people want. Ibsen upset first the left and then the right with his plays.

You write from your preconscious. You don't know what you're doing. Often I write and I think 'oh why didn't I think of that?', because I don't think it, it's this man or woman that I'm writing about. And you have to transpose. Then you have to use your theatrical taste, your consciousness as a civic person, and you bring all of that to bear when you're actually writing collaborative work.

What's the state of play for you in terms of collaborative theatre work in the mid-1990s ?

Fashion has changed and I've got older. I don't get about as much as I did, so that I don't do as much topical or overtly political writing. I would say that in any production you collaborate totally because you are so mutually dependent, but I don't find that heady, lovely certainty that was there — we started to run out of everything so that we had to go right-wing. Of course we've got raised hopes after the last election!

But nowadays I get very depressed about it. You see young writers coming on — they get a couple of things put on and then they get pulled by television because they can make a living and they are lost to the live theatre. It's very sad. My own son is in Hollywood making vast sums of money as a script-writer. He worked as a fringe playwright in London for ten years but if you don't want to write for subsidized theatre, if you just write for the 'off-West End' (for the Bush in Hampstead or the Gate in Notting Hill), you're not going to make any money. He was working as a night porter at Portobello Hotel. So money is a problem in all kinds of theatre writing, especially collaborative work, and perhaps even more so for women.

Sometimes, what gets lost in interview questions about writing is the fact that people might write something one day or one year and something very different the next; that people are not definable or fixed. Your voice as a playwright has developed over the years; how does it feel to be seen as a kind of role model for younger women playwrights?

It's true. We all change, but the work is published and that gives you a 'date'. The word that comes to mind is authenticity. I was talking to the fine woman playwright Anne Devlin recently about the burden of being asked to be a voice for feminism. You cannot be that, and be an artist. Polemic belongs on the public platform. Brecht said 'Unhappy the land that needs heroes.' I hate the way that certain women have been forced into the role of icon. I find it improper, foolish, lazy and destructive to look for 'leaders'. You lead yourself. If you are an artist you have to trust the talent, you have to work hard, you have to stop your line as best you can, and then you have to trust the dream. We've all woken up the next morning and found that the problem has been solved for us. You have to trust that what comes through is of value to other people. And then the proof of the pudding: for instance the play that I have just done in Manchester, *Deborah's Daughter*, was received passionately by the audience. It was about a very rich woman going to Northern Africa to donate $20 million in memory of her oil-tycoon husband who has just been killed. So you get a collision between the first and third world. I had two male critics from London who said these were the most embarrassing moments that they had ever witnessed. And I wanted to say to them, you've obviously never been a woman, and you've never been subject to the kind of gallantry which actually can be extremely woo-some. So, I was insulted, not for the first time, by the ignorance of the reviewers.

It's now a commonplace to point out that the majority of theatre reviewers in the UK are men. Do male reviewers — depite the advances of feminism in so many other areas — persist in 'insulting' or over-simplying or missing the point of much women's work?

Yes, they do. They're often dismissive, with the attitude of 'it's just a little woman'. (Recently I was criticized as arrogant for a new version of *The Seagull*. Baffling. Then it clicked. How can a mere woman translate Chekhov? 'Arrogant', you see.) Or they're deeply affronted, as though you are going to cut off their... you know. Either way they're on the turn. To some extent, I can understand it in as much as throughout history men have had mothers and then wives to see to them as a back-up system, and things have changed radically. I think it was Ian McEwan who did a television play (*The Imitation Game*) about a woman who wasn't allowed to do secret work during the war because she was a woman. She saw something she shouldn't have seen and ended up in prison. Deeply inauthentic.

During the war, we women did everything. We parachuted into foreign countries, women died for the cause, women ferried liberator aeroplanes across the Atlantic, there wasn't a job we didn't do. Dangerous work with chemicals. These kids have got it all wrong. It's after the wars when their jobs are at risk that men think this.

I have to say that I would like more women critics, except that the few women critics I have read disappoint me utterly. I think it's partly that when you become a journalist you become a hack. The other thing is, I was talking to a very nice woman from the BBC who was interviewing me once who said, 'Look, I have to say at the outset, I'm terribly sorry, I haven't been to a play for a year because I was on the Olivier Awards Panel last year and I had to go to the theatre two or three times a week, and honestly, I never want to enter a theatre again.' And you realize that you cannot go to the theatre two or three times a week, see things which are not to your taste, simply to make money. It isn't like doing a job on the factory floor where you can put your head to sleep. I've seen the critics asleep many times. You can hardly blame them — it's their job to sit there and be tortured. Yet you *can* blame them, because if they don't pay attention, who will? If there should be a rule, it is that nobody should be a critic for more than a year at a time. It is not fair on them, on the reader, or on the potential theatre-goer.

I'm interested in the idea that there might be a feminist way of reviewing. Obviously, female critics face a dilemma: how to be critical enough to have their work taken seriously, when male-defined ways of valuing work don't often fit with feminist aims and objectives, or alternative aesthetic criteria and priorities. Would you agree that this is a problem?

I certainly would. I would love to see virtuous women reviewing, that is, women who are up to date in their thinking, but with the same proviso that intelligent women should be asked not just to comment on plays by women or plays about so-called female subjects, but across the board — *Julius Caesar*, plays about the power games women have to play in the modern world, the whole lot. But not for too long.

I'll follow that up with a huge question: how would you define 'feminism'?

It's quite simple for me really, it's friendliness. I come from the lower working class and I have all the class loyalty that I don't see in the middle class — boy, do they fall apart when the wind is blowing! Although, a good middle class usually sees stability in the country.

For me, with feminism, one isn't asking for a special privilege, but for relevant privilege. For instance, when a woman is heavily pregnant, she needs support from those around her and from her community because she is vulnerable and she's carrying something vulnerable. I have been knocked off a pavement when I was heavily pregnant and it's saddening — it's less than human. All women are asking for now is fair dues — a rate for the job, equal opportunities — what else can you ask for? We've had equal pay and the Sex Discrimination Act, but they are not enforced, partly through exigency. Women sometimes gain employment in this world in part because they accept the rate for the job, especially if they head single-parent families, and have to take what they can get. That situation angers women, understandably. And it affects men too; it's putting men out of work, and putting up a terrible wall between the sexes, an awful resentment. At the same time, men are resentful anyway because they have lost their female support system. For instance, Ron Atkinson, who [was] manager of Aston Villa was saying recently that women should not talk about football — that it's none of women's business. That's the old show. I tried to deal with this attitude in my play *Guinevere*.

Gender and power. But it all gets complicated quickly, if you try to look for patterns. Of course there are areas of separation: possibly more women like knitting than men, possibly more men like rugby, etc. But the key is having a mutual regard, a mutual respect. There has been a lot of disrespect of women because both men and women are frightened, because the mother is the first human being you are frightened of, normally speaking.

If the father raises you from babyhood, then it's him, but that's unusual. So men and women are both frightened of women under some circumstances. And as a result, we women have a big fight on our hands every time we do anything — a fight from all sides. That's normal. We have to be aware of it.

There's so much division. And the question of feminism does tend to divide us rather than unite us, which is sad. But there is hope. I used to play devil's advocate in the days when 'feminism' tended to mean, or at least include, some degree of man-hating. But today that kind of polemic is unusual, and what is most disturbing is the reality of women's situations in this world. If you go to a battered women's home and see a woman with a broken nose, you can understand feminism. And you have to try and embrace all the aspects of unfairness and exploitation and out of that try and build a structure for survival, for progress, even for creativity.

Do you think that kind of structure — a mutually supportive structure — can develop in the theatre?

I like to think so, though I have my days of despair on that account. For feminists working to revise the way we all see things (including each other), it's hard. It's as hard in the theatre as anywhere. And of course, with theatre funding what it is today, it's hard to work in the theatre, full stop. Partly the problem for all of us working in the theatre is our very weak union. We've always got over 80% unemployment among theatre workers. So there's not a lot of protection.

What's the future for women in the theatre?

Anything is possible. Everything is possible.

Can theatre affect social change?

Of course it can. It must. Theatre should change things. There is a common but specious belief that art changes nothing. Of course art changes things: society, people, art itself. One man stepping off a train can change everything. One woman can make tremendous changes. Artists are very important. We can affect social change, and fashion shows this. Clothes are a very good indication of what happens at a very deep level, a psychological level, in society. As fashion changes, people's ways of thinking change as well.

If we, as women, can pervade with our nobility, forgiveness and wit we can change everything.

Lizbeth Goodman
Interview conducted on audio tape, London, October 1994.

GILLIAN HANNA

Gillian Hanna is an actress and translator. She has worked with the 7:84 company and with Belt and Braces from 1971 to 1975 before co-founding the Monstrous Regiment theatre group in 1975. Hanna worked exclusively within the Regiment from 1975 to 1981/2, and was one of the three original members who actively participated in Regiment management, production and performance until the ACGB (Arts Council of Great Britain) withdrew funding in 1993 and the company was forced to stop working. Since 1982 she has also worked extensively outside the group, winning several awards (1989 Time Out/01 for London, 1990 Manchester Evening News Best Actress for Juno and the Paycock at the Contact Theatre, 1991 Martini/TMA Regional Theatre Awards, Best Actress for Beatrice in Arthur Miller's A View from the Bridge at the Royal Exchange, Manchester). Her translations of Dario Fo's Elizabeth: Almost By Chance a Woman and Franca Rame's collection of one-woman plays A Woman Alone are published by Methuen. Her history of the company, Monstrous Regiment, A Collective Celebration is published by Nick Hern Books. In 1994 she toured in the Out of Joint/Royal Court/West End production of Sue Townsend's The Queen and I.

You gave an interview to Peter Hulton entitled 'Feminism and Theatre' which was published in 1978[1] and is still widely quoted, sometimes to your consternation, since the material is often quoted without reference to the fact that the information is now 16 years out of date. This is your chance to set the record straight on some of the things you said in that 1978 interview, and our chance to hear what you have to say, both in response to that interview and more directly on the subject of feminist theatre today.

That interview is often quoted, and I am concerned because it was so long ago. What I think about things has changed quite a lot, and it's odd to see myself quoted as believing something I no longer believe, or at least that I wouldn't any longer say without qualification. In fact, I can't believe that people are still *reading* that interview!

Of all the material written on feminist theatre, the 1978 interview is one of only a very few items which have been entered into computer files and cross-referenced in the major libraries; thus, the interview is visible, accessible, in a way in which many other materials on feminist theatre are not. Though this does not in any way detract from the considerable impact of the information the interview provided, it does seem to me to be typical of the arbitrary nature of much of the selection and distribution of

---

[1] Published in *Theatre Papers* (Dartington College, Second Series, no. 8).

materials made available for study in any given discipline, and especially in a contemporary and 'alternative' discipline like feminist theatre.

The lead-up to the 1978 interview wasn't quite as arbitrary as it sounds. At the time, Monstrous was one of the most visible of the women's groups and was doing some of the most exciting work. So we were the group to whom any interviewer would naturally have gravitated, and my knowing Peter made me the natural individual to single out for the interview. But I do agree that some of the most valuable material written to date is not generally available. (The Monstrous Regiment book, for example, is almost impossible to find though it is still in print)[2]. I think we have a responsibility to make the ideas and events of women's theatre as visible as possible. Otherwise, it will all sink out of sight and be 'hidden from history' again.

Were there men involved in the Regiment in 1978?

Yes. There always had been, right from the beginning. It was only in 1980/81 that we became an all-women's group, and then it wasn't because we sat down and decided we were separatists; it wasn't that simple. The shift from a mixed to an all-women's group was more of a process than a decision; it was something that evolved.

And yet, men included, the Regiment was clearly thought of as a feminist group. Does that imply a consensus that the men involved were, in their own way, feminist? Or did the Regiment's relatively positive representations of women earn it the feminist label?

It's hard to say, looking back. What people tend to forget is that, in the late 1970s, feminism was the most exciting thing going, especially for people interested in politics.

I want to be very careful about discussing the 'men and feminism' issue in relation to our theatre. In the early years, there were a lot of men who claimed to be feminist, who wanted to be a part of the movement because (a) it looked exciting; and (b) it looked progressive. Some self-consciously left-wing, progressive men wanted to be part of that, but it didn't mean that in their heart of hearts they really believed in what feminism stood for or that their commitment would withstand the pressure when they were called on to abandon some of their patriarchal privileges.

As I recall it, there was no question of *not* having men in the group at the beginning. It wasn't that as women we felt unable to operate without the sanction of male presence. It was that the kind of plays we wanted to do —

---

[2] *Monstrous Regiment: Four Plays and a Collective Celebration*, ed. Gillian Hanna (Nick Hern Books, 1991).

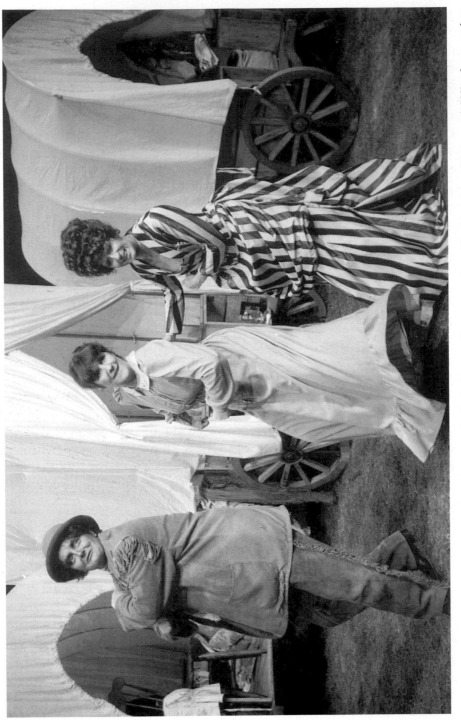

2. Gillian Hanna, Jane Cox and Mary McCusker in *Calamity* by Bryony Lavery, produced by Monstrous Regiment (1983); photographer: Diane Gelon.

the subjects we wanted to tackle at that time — required having men on the stage. We never sat down and decided not to work with men, but after the men involved left for various reasons, we could see no reason to take on any others. The projects we were planning at that time were shows with no male characters in them. And in time we found that it was easier. In the end we just had to organize ourselves autonomously and to work in women-only situations.

When you talk about us as a feminist group, you have to make a distinction between the organizational structure of the company and the work that appeared on the stage. The Regiment was established on the basis of feminist principles. It was crucial that it was run by women, that its commitment was to women... good stage-parts for women (where women could take centre-stage, and not be relegated to the sidelines), jobs for women technicians, writers and directors; child-care provision written into the budgets... It didn't all come together at one moment. We were a disparate group of people who came together and we had to establish our rules through the collective process as we went along.

In the 1978 interview you emphasized the importance of forwarding a feminist consciousness in your work, of trying 'to ally (your perceptions of the world, the need for social change) in some way with those inner needs you have, and those talents you've got...' Does this hold true in the same sense today?

The idea holds true: what has changed is that it is becoming harder and harder for most people to find ways of allying those inner needs and their talents. There are certain places where women's issues are taken seriously these days — mostly in colleges and universities is where 'women's studies' are now an accepted part of the curriculum. But we mustn't assume that we've achieved all our goals. If anything, we have to shout louder than ever, otherwise we will be buried under the backlash.

Considering that Monstrous Regiment has now closed, how much impact did Conservative economic policies have on the group?

Well, it was not so direct that you could blame them for the closure of the company. The fact is that the Arts Council withdrew support: we had had a very rough patch when they made the continued receipt of subsidy dependent on our appointing an Artistic Director. Although we were loathe to do that in some ways, in other ways we recognized that it was a sensible move for us, because, as we were all working more and more outside the group, it became impossible to organize things as well as they should have been organized. So we appointed an Artistic Director, but it was a disaster. All I can say is that values and beliefs were at odds in ways that we had

never envisaged. We started out with a great deal of good will and it just
didn't work. The work that year was not wonderful and I think that the Arts
Council saw that we were in difficulties, and whereas perhaps 15 years ago,
they might have offered help, in 1993 it seemed to us that they were glad of
the opportunity to cut us off. I see no reassurance whatsoever that the money
that was taken away from us has gone back to funding any other women's
projects at all. Maybe they have, but I haven't seen them.

I should add, we haven't completely wound the company up. We are
inactive because the Arts Council withdrew our grant, but we are still
registered at Companies House — just in case.

Was sponsorship a viable alternative to an Arts Council grant?

The way it is sometimes talked of you'd think public support for the
Arts is some kind of charity. It isn't. Fay Weldon says that public subsidy of
the Arts is a benchmark of a civilized society. I agree with her. I'm committed
to the idea of public subsidy. Conservative government is opposed to it
because subsidy is an attempt to take art out of the marketplace (and this
government is Hell-bent on turning everything into a commodity). Art is not
a commodity. It is a vision of possibilities. It's very difficult to create
theatre/art in a society that doesn't believe in anything but acquisition.

Do you believe that the theatre can affect social change?

An artist should be working at the edge of consciousness. As an
artist, you should be able to articulate, not necessarily what everyone else is
thinking, but what is in the air: you should be on the crest of the wave. It is
true that a lot of women over the years have said things to us like 'I saw
Scum[3] and it changed my life', but I don't believe that we change people's
lives with our theatre in the same way that, for instance, political action can.

Theatre, our theatre, was activist and theatrical. In the seventies, we
were truly at the edge of consciousness; we were riding on the crest of the
post-1968 feminist wave. Women recognized themselves in our work; just as
many women will cite books like Kate Millet's *Sexual Politics* or Germaine
Greer's *The Female Eunuch* as transformative forces in their lives, so our
theatre was such a force. It wasn't that the books or plays themselves affected
change, but rather that the act of reading or watching them coalesces
something within ourselves. A work of art or a book or a play can act as a
catalyst. In other words, you can read something or see something which
makes things click into place for you, but if those things hadn't been in your
consciousness already, the new perspective wouldn't change your life.

---

[3] 1976, by Claire Luckham and Chris Bond.

But it may lead to recognition, which can support and encourage change?

Or you may realise that while your feet have been walking in one direction, your head has all the while been turned the other way. And so you'll realign yourself, re-define your situation and direction. That's not to say that our work wasn't exciting. At the time, our work was thrilling beyond belief because there was such a strong sense of being part of an important movement. That's the difference between women and men in relation to the 'political theatre' label, and even in relation to the more general notion of revolutionary politics. Women get excited by being part of a larger movement, while men like to think they're acting independently (and I don't mean this in an essentialist way, but rather in a positive, choice-oriented way). Conscious women who were working in certain areas found that their excitement, their sense of purpose, came largely from feeling themselves to be, possibly for the first time in their lives, part of a larger group, a larger movement, as actors in the world, and not as isolated individuals. The sense of connections was terribly important is when Monstrous Regiment started: connections across race, across class, across all kinds of boundaries. That's what the Women's Movement was about.

Are we dealing with the same kinds of connections, or is that what is lacking today?

What is lacking today is one united feminist theatre, or one unified feminist movement, for that matter. We seem to have lost that sense of connection. When the wave of feminism hit us in the seventies we were individual women, mostly isolated with our individual strengths and weaknesses, but in the main lacking in confidence when it came to expressing our ideas. We discovered our confidence and power through collectivity: consciousness-raising groups or rent strike support groups or theatre companies or whatever. And we all gained immeasurable strength from that. And young women have inherited that strength. We created a point on which they can stand and expect their voices to be heard. I see a lot of stroppy young women now which is great. But at the same time they have experienced the Thatcherite eighties, the worship of individualism and the demonization of collectivity. Collectivity is *so* unfashionable, so *uncool*. So it seems to me we've arrived at a situation where you have a lot of tough sassy young women who are wonderfully 'in your face' about their ideas and opinions but who in many ways are as isolated as we were. If only they could experience and understand the power that's unleashed when you act together, what a change they could bring about.

What would you say to the idea that the word 'feminism' — which seems to be a dirty word in England — has cut off the women associated with it in terms of their careers and opportunities for personal and professional advancement, thereby effecting another split between women so affected and younger women who are fresh to the struggle?

Of course, many of these young women I'm talking about would rather jump out of a moving train than acknowledge that word. Nothing makes me madder than women who say: 'I'm not a feminist, but...' That's exactly what we've been fighting against: it signals a cutting off of your own experience from women's collective history. After all, what is feminism, except a belief that women matter?

The tragedy is that so many women seem to have been alienated from the word, largely because the patriarchs and old fogies (especially in the media) have so debased and besmirched it, held it up to so much derision and ridicule. So a situation has developed in which we find many women back-peddling to avoid any association with the terrible word. It's the same old cycle. We have to reclaim the word just as other generations of women have done.

In the 1978 interview, you were asked to discuss the new 'vistas of material' suddenly opened to women in the theatre. Have those vistas stayed open? Were they really so open (accessible) to begin with?

We were referring to 'vistas' of subjects for women to write about, and those haven't closed; there's still the experience of 51% of the population that rarely gets put on the stage. But if you're talking about access to resources, then one difficulty is that women meet with a lot of resistance when they move into the mainstream... Even ten or fifteen years since 'alternative' theatre came into being, it seems that if you're asking for anything more than the norm, you're in trouble because it's still perceived as a threat to that norm. I think that women working in the mainstream are pressured to try to conform to the norm while maintaining an image of the lone genius woman in the men's club. There are so few women working in the mainstream, I don't know any of them very well, but I would love to talk to them about how they see themselves. It seems from an outside perspective that they feel a need to sidestep feminism because it makes life too difficult. Or, perhaps, they are simply striding forward on what gains have been made in the last fifteen years.

In the 1978 interview, you were asked to describe your vision of 'the possibility of a feminist consciousness pushing towards a new form'.

Yes, I still think the question of form is fascinating. And I think it comes not just from a view of history, but from the different ways the sexes experience their lives... I think I said a lot of this in the original interview, but

I haven't really changed my belief in this. In fact, looking at what many women are writing now, I see it even more clearly. Men's plays tend to be strong on forward moving narrative whereas women's tend towards the episodic, the circular. That's a reflection of how we experience ourselves. I once heard a Canadian playwright describe it also as a reflection of the difference in our sexual experience: men's plays build singlemindedly and inexorably towards one big climax, whereas women's plays have more side-steps and many climaxes along the way. Of course there's a continuing struggle to get this form accepted as legitimate, because as ever, the way men write is accepted as the norm and anything else is a deviation or an aberration.

Lizbeth Goodman

The full version of this interview was published in New Theatre Quarterly, *volume VI, No. 21, February 1990 pp. 43–56. The original version was compiled from taped and untaped interviews held from April to August 1989 and edited with collective input from the Monstrous Regiment. It should be noted that the views expressed are those of Gillian Hanna, and do not necessarily reflect those of the Regiment as a whole. Thanks are due Rose Sharp (who was Company Administrator in 1989), and to the Monstrous Regiment Management Collective and Advisory Committee for their valuable criticisms and comments. This interview was updated in January 1995 by Jane de Gay, following a further interview and telephone discussions with Gillian Hanna.*

BRYONY LAVERY

Bryony Lavery has been involved in the development of British alternative theatre since the 1970s, and has taken part — as a performer and as a writer — in productions with many key women's groups including Monstrous Regiment and Dramatrix, the group which produces the hugely successful annual lesbian feminist pantos at the Drill Hall in London. Her recent plays include Her Aching Heart, Two Marias, Wicked *and* Origin of the Species. *Her interview here is best read in conjunction with the 'Afterword' printed in this volume.*

In January 1991, two of your plays were produced in London: Kitchen Matters *(for Gay Sweatshop) and* Her Aching Heart *(for Women's Theatre Group), both of which received rave reviews, and both of which deal with domestic, as well as political issues. Neither of these plays is about war: that is, about men in uniforms killing each other. But both deal brutal blows to the idea of a safe, predictable theatre tradition. Are these feminist plays, and are they political?*

Are they feminist? Are they political??? Is the Pope Catholic? Do bears shit in the woods? Yes! Yes!

In Kitchen Matters, *the stage directions include 'miracles occurring' and 'a Bumpity-Bump from a dramatically different musical tradition than ours'. With such directions, you seem to poke fun at the idea that any version of theatre history records the values of an age or society, and suggest that instead, history is composed of a composite of reviews, written mostly by men with interests and values of their own. In other words, theatre history — like all history — is biased. What was the 'history' or aim of the play,* Kitchen Matters?

Kitchen Matters was written partly as a response to the Arts Council's attempt to close down Gay Sweatshop because there were 'other groups doing gay work'. The implication of the Arts Council's threat was that Gay Sweatshop itself might become 'history'. Theatre is so ephemeral — theatre history never seems to me to capture the 'word of mouth' feeling of a play at its time, never to capture the excitement! So in both senses, the play was intended to keep the company alive, by showing the excitement of live theatre. Also, to return to your question, funny stage directions make me laugh!

In Women and Theatre: Calling the Shots *(ed. Susan Todd, Faber and Faber, 1984), you drew an analogy between theatre history, and a museum run by male curators. In your words: 'At the moment the theatre seems too much like a great museum run by male curators. The glass exhibition cases are opened up and historic exhibitions taken out and shown to us all, if we can afford the entrance fee... I am tired of my role as cleaner in this museum. Most of the rubbish is dropped by men.'* Are you still tired of that 'role as cleaner' in 1995, or has the role of women in the theatre changed?

Yes! I'm desperately tired of that role as cleaner. And, to expand the metaphor, I'm an increasingly *aged* cleaner: more crotchety about the aching joints, with housemaid's knee from the bending, lifting, scrubbing, etc. So, the role of women has not changed nearly enough: there are still 'writers', and 'women writers'.

Your eye for the comic in the mundane, the absurd in the average and the truth behind all the wearisome statistics is what keeps your writing fresh. Would you agree that what translates your writing into successful plays is observational detail and your focus on believable characters: not politicians or superwomen, but shop assistants and home-makers; not queens, but cleaners?

Yes, I do think my unusual focus and use of language help to keep my writing fresh. Also, I have two assets — a good brain and a fine pair of 'comedy feet' — and I understand and explore the relationship between them! I think when I die, most of my form there on my deathbed will excite tears, sadness, but my feet will be sticking straight up in comic fashion, and everyone will laugh. Believable characters are always both tragic and hilarious.

Some of your earlier work contains the germs of the ideas which are developed so successfully in both Kitchen Matters *and* Her Aching Heart. *At the core of much of that early work is the developing awareness and articulation of women's place in society: you recall with amusement your debut in an experimental play (by a man) called* Furniture Revolts, *in which you were cast as the left arm of a sofa: '...it was a three seater... we were all female...' In the early 1980s, you formed your own group, without a home venue let alone furniture, and called it 'Female Trouble' followed by 'More Female Trouble.' Since then, your work has developed ideas and images of class consciousness, the sexual division of labour, sexuality and sexual orientation as weapons effectively used in society to keep women down (or treat them as furniture). Do those kinds of ideas still inspire you in 1995?*

I think those kinds of ideas still swirl about my consciousness — but what I think *inspires* me (breathes new life into me) are the new stories and ways of constructing dramatic presentations of the old horrors .

Your 1987 play Witchcraze *is an allegory of the witch trials, in which (in your own words): 'three theatre cleaners play nineteen parts to illustrate the history of witch-*

burning'. Is the repeated use of the women-as-domestic (or cleaners) metaphor deliberate?

Actually, I never consciously made the link between the play and the essays. But yes, the subconscious must have been at work: it's a very real image. In *Witchcraze*, the characters wore masks because faceless people, expressionless people (like women in a male world) tend to be losers. Very often my characters are low characters: cleaners, losers. It's all part of my unstated operational job-creation scheme for all the good women actors out there ... Come to think of it, my later play, *Puppet States* (1988), is subtitled *Waiting for the General*. I guess it was about three cleaners again...

In much of your work the history of war, like theatre history, is depicted as primarily focused on what goes on behind the scenes: it is about the women who do the waiting and the cleaning up. Kitchen Matters *is billed as Epic Comedy. Yet it is no less than a revised version of Euripides'* The Bacchae *set in 'AN EPIC BLASTED KITCHEN WITH MODERN APPLIANCES.' Is the play comedy, tragedy or a new genre of your own devising?*

The play is serious as well as comic. I wanted to write a comedy based on Greek tragedy.

Kitchen Matters *depicts ordinary characters, in an ordinary environment. But it also depicts gods: one goddess in particular: Trixia, described as 'a cross between a sad goddess and a gangster's moll.' She has make-up, long cigarettes and divine power' (in that order). In this version, it is a female power which is most dangerous, when the issue is sexuality and the sphere for the conflict is both cosmic and domestic. A woman is torn apart in this truly Epic version of the story, while the mother reaffirms her sexuality and the Chorus, in true EPIC style, 'WATCH WITH GROWING CONCERN', Agawe makes an anachronistic entrance — presumably from the set of* The Bacchae *— to deposit body parts and polish the taps (this is a bit of KITCHEN SINK DRAMA). In what way does this comic epic represent women and men of the 1990s?*

It showed our 1990s gods and mortals and their interchangeability. We carry our gods in our mortality.

The sink is an appliance in a kitchen which is a battle zone in a war fought between gods and mortals, over the issue of sexuality, and — in the real world — in the face of financial ruin for Gay Sweatshop. The theme of the play is doubly ironic as a statement about the anonymous powers playing with the lives of ordinary people, when we remember that the theatre itself is seriously under threat at this particular point in history, and that Gay Sweatshop has had more than its share of problems in securing adequate funding. War and recession have very immediate effects. So do other anonymous powers: funding bodies, the gods, and critics (not necessarily in that order). How did Kitchen Matters *fit in with Sweatshop funding plans?*

The chorus (i.e ordinary folk) feel frightened, helpless and drained of the ability to effect change. They feel impotent but are actually capable of making history (the show and its financial collections, petitions and *bothering* of the Arts Council of Great Britain actually reversed the decision to cut the company's funds). The 'Leading Parts' — i.e. the Establishment figures — had to yield, give up privilege to change the world. Very political, huh?

Her Aching Heart *is another story altogether. Actually, it is two stories at once. A two-hander featuring Nicola Kathrens and Sarah Kevney, this 'lesbian historical romance' is set in the present, and also in a mock Gothic past, or fantasy/romantic world. The play deals with issues as varied as friendship, love, sex, desire, gender roles, the function of romance, and the influence of stereotype and expectation (i.e. past precedent) on forming and informing the present. In one memorable scene, a deer's death in the forest, by the hunter's gun, is described as a 'cooking accident.' The line is extremely funny and in this particular context, is also chillingly ironic and deeply political: particularly in the post-Gulf climate, with history so directly informing economic and domestic concerns, fuelling military action, and with the nightmare of environmental disaster simply coming true. How do you go about dealing with such serious issues in such an enjoyable, comic manner?*

I think it's back to the pair of good comedy feet again! Also for some reason, my personality has copious amounts of Rage, rather than Despair. Rage is a hot, vibrant fuel for inspiration....

In the author's note published with Origin of the Species, *you wrote: 'The history of evolution is a glorious soup of assumptions and guesses. It is written largely by men and is as riddled with male chauvinism as is our later history.' Would you say the same in 1995?*

Yes. Fortunately, as a result of feminist thought effecting an enormous paradigm shift in our consciences — male chauvinism is now riddled with feminist challenges.

In 1988, you wrote a play called Puppet States. *What was that piece and how does the title describe the position of women?*

It's a feminist statement, and a strong one. We don't realize how furious we are until we write and try to represent through words and images exactly what we are perceived as — how we perceive ourselves, from the outside, as objects. The puppets in *Puppet States* appear when we try to represent ourselves in this way: it's part of a source of rage at the way women are treated. I think it's equivalent to the way men tend to portray a lot of wars, violence and soldiers: that's the parallel fascination in men's theatre.

In 1991/2, you co-wrote a new version of Peter Pan, *and performed in it as Tinkerbell. Pantomimes obviously offer up rich veins for the exploration of lesbian performance dynamics and the power implications of cross-dressing. But why the panto,* Peter Pan, *and why Tinkerbell?*

I co-wrote this version of *Peter Pan* with Nona Shepphard. Our reasons were quite simple, initially. The main fun in *Peter Pan* is that you get to fly! We really wanted to have a Panto with flying in it. When we settled down to the original text, we found it such a *boy's* story. We hated Wendy, so we made her the villain, plus the nasty rich boy brothers and made everyone else secretly female. So we could do a great transformational 'Pantomime Reveals' at the end. What? Captain Hook — a Woman? We had two mothers in the Darling household, who flew after their children. We just brazenly kind of 'femaled' the whole thing. Our family was a real family, but not a nuclear unit.

Tinkerbell had always been a small green light in the theatre. We, carried away by our brazen approach throughout, made her a big green fairy. We wrote the part for Rose English, who unfortunately (for us) went off to play a Champagne bottle at the English National Opera instead. So I got the part of Tinkerbell by default. The comedy feet were a considerable asset here.

In an essay full of wonderful advice for women writers, you wrote: 'Alfred Hitchcock said that actors were cattle. Wrong, Alfred. They are people who have read a lot, done a lot, been through a lot. They don't just roam around and moo'. Have you any further gems to share with aspiring women writers?

Yes. I have a quote, and it's from a man. I can paraphrase and interpret for this context at the same time:

> *Keep me up till five only because all your stars are out, and for no other reasons.... Were most of your stars out? Were you busy writing your heart out? Before ever you sit down to write (remember) you've been a reader long before you were ever a writer. You simply fix that fact in your mind, then sit very still and ask yourself, as a reader (play-watcher/audience-member), what piece of writing in all the world Buddy Glass would most want to read, if he had his heart's choice. The next step is terrible, but so simple I can hardly believe it as I write it. You just sit down shamelessly and write the thing yourself.*

That — more or less — is taken from 'Seymour: An Introduction', by J. D. Salinger. The message: write what you need to write, what you'd like to read.

3. Bryony Lavery as Tinkerbell in *Peter Pan* by Nona Shepphard and Bryony Lavery (1994); photo credit: Dramatrix.

In our conversation in 1988, you argued that: 'We need to get angry again about the number of plays by women which get produced, and the constant negative criticism we get from the Michael Coveneys of this world, who of course want to see plays about them.' In 1995, what's your view on male criticism of women's work? Have things changed?

No. I gave a paper at a conference in Germany about this (that paper is printed as the 'Afterword' to this volume). I was supposed to talk about feminist playwrights but I tore up my paper and talked instead about the need for critics to alter *their* 'gaze' — to take off the spectacles and lenses and just look at the plays they go to see. If they did this wholeheartedly and honestly — they would not always link Sarah Daniels with Caryl Churchill with etc., etc. ... Whenever I read most books of criticism, I see sets of very neat but very dull filing cabinets of categories. I think I have more links with, say, Alan Bennett, than with a lot of other playwrights.

Feminist theatre of the past few decades has exploded stereotypes and myths, eliminating the NEW WOMAN (in the upper case, of course) and introducing some more believable and likeable characters to the stage. Now we have the so-called NEW MAN to worry about as well. But where are your cleaners? Has the role of women in theatre changed in the past few decades?

In some ways. But the cleaning roles haven't been grabbed up by men. In my latest theatre work, *Nothing Compares to You* for Birmingham Rep (April 1995), I've got some characters, at the moment called 'Creatures', who assist in our deaths. Oh dear, celestial cleaners!

With its magical element, Peter Pan *seems quite appropriate to the rest of your work. As you wrote in* Kitchen Matters, *'we could all use a bit of divine intervention on our side once in a while.' Would divine intervention help improve the state of women in theatre today?*

Yes. And so would an improved understanding between playmakers and audience, critics and people with money to fund theatres.

Now for the grand prize: are you a feminist theatremaker?

Yes. But lately I find myself redefining and reconsidering that term. I'd say my views are best represented in mixed metaphors, as in my paper 'Guerillas in the Mist' (see 'Afterword' to this volume).

Lizbeth Goodman

This interview is compiled from a series of interviews recorded on audiotape in 1988, and for BBC Radio (as part of the course 'Issues in Women's Studies') in 1992, and from telephone and postal correspondence in December 1994. An earlier version of this interview was published in Everywoman *magazine, December 1991/January 1992.*

ELIZABETH MacLENNAN

Elizabeth MacLennan acted in the West End, TV and film, before co-founding the 7:84 Theatre Company with her husband, John McGrath. She recently published a book about 7:84, The Moon Belongs to Everyone *(Methuen, 1990). Her recent projects include a one-woman show, based on the story of Rigoberta Menchu (the Quiché Indian Guatemalan indigenous peoples' activist, who won the Nobel Peace Prize in 1992), writing a TV comedy series on women's issues, and teaching at Columbia University Drama Department in New York.*

Do you feel strongly either for or against working collaboratively with other women in the theatre?

I feel strongly *for* in that all work in the theatre that's any good is by its very nature collaborative — but I don't feel impelled to work exclusively with women.

How would you define 'feminism'?

Very simply. In my definition it's mostly about advocacy. I think that the most useful contribution that I can make to the advancement of feminism is by advocating equal political, economic and social rights for women — for all women in all situations.

Do you feel that the word feminism has shifted in meaning — do you feel that it means different things in different countries?

Yes, clearly it does have a historical basis and it has developed at different rates in different countries according to the extent of economic deprivation in different countries. If you talk about feminism, for example, in the light of the struggle of indigenous peoples in the 1990s — which I think and hope is a struggle that a lot of young people are concerned about — then you are clearly talking about something different from what you would be talking about in the context of the relatively affluent western European countries, or in a North American context. But then in the broad sweep I don't think it is important to be confused by differences. What is interesting is that in all cases women are still not equal. It's the extent to which they are not equal that varies.

According to your own definition, would you call yourself a feminist?

Yes, hopefully. I'm not backward in speaking out about it, so in that sense I am an advocate of equality in my work, and I always have been.

Have you always felt this way?

My mother was a feminist, that was important. She involved me at a very early age and her most important book was Virginia Woolf's *A Room of One's Own*. Yet her feminism was more than *that*. It was not just an intellectual idea: it was a practical one. It was not something I discovered in the 1970s. It was something I grew up with and am still growing up with. Obviously, there were certain writers who influenced me at different stages and they weren't all women.

Would you say that feminism has affected the theatre in any major way? If, so, in what way?

Most dramatically, most effectively, in the 1890s. Sadly I don't feel that anything that has happened within the last 20 years in the theatre can equal the astonishing impact on life — on women's status — that happened in the theatre in the 1890s.

How would you describe what happened in the theatre in the 1890s?

The first thing that 'happened' was the work of Ibsen, which had a huge impact on the way women were perceived. Their economic political and social status. He closed down theatres. There were riots and unfortunately I haven't seen this yet as a result of Caryl Churchill! Ibsen and his work were taken up both theatrically and in the political sphere by George Bernard Shaw to extraordinary effect. That was the first really sensational outburst of feminism in the theatre.

I suspect that the equivalent impact now is very necessary but unfortunately theatre — and feminist theatre in particular — has become more marginalized. And until it gets itself that kind of prominence it will not have the same influence on people's thinking.

Why do you think theatre, and feminist theatre, have become marginalized?

It has been government policy for the last 15 years to under-fund anything which is critical of the status quo. Particularly if it is articulate. The fashion is now for what is called 'non-verbal' theatre.

Do you believe that the theatre can affect social change?

Well, obviously I do, or else I would not have spent the majority of my life working and acting in that glow of hope. There are many concrete examples of the success of theatre in affecting social change. I suppose you could regard the closure of so many socially aware and political theatres in the past 15 years as concrete evidence of the fact that they disturbed the government. That's in Britain alone. Of course in France there is a more liberal, let's say left, consensus and there they have not closed down theatres... yet.

They are closing down there too.

Yes they are, now that the consensus in France is moving to the right. So there is a direct relationship between closures and social effectiveness.

What is the future for women in the theatre in the UK?

The UK sounds a bit token. Speaking as a person who centres her activities in Scotland, far be it from me to pontificate about England.

I think that the theatre in Scotland has got a great deal more going for it at the moment than the theatre in England. Although it has a great deal less money it has got a lot more will-power and equality of poverty than in the 'UK' as a whole. So in that sense it's not so marginalized.

Interestingly in the last few years there has been quite a strong development of women working in isolation because they feel they have been marginalized; and because in Scotland there is a very strong chest-thumping machismo and we are very opposed to this and in small ways, but effectively, becoming vociferous.

I've worked in popular theatre with a strong Scottish identity and a strong working-class audience so most of my relationships with women in the theatre have been with very loyal female audiences and many of the plays that we did in 7:84 reflect their situation often using broad comedy and ridicule while being very identifiable to most of the audience. So a lot of people quite consciously saw me as an advocate and were expecting me to speak up for them. And when I did so, in plays like *Blood Red Roses* they would vociferously agree with it and continue the argument after the performance, hopefully strengthened by the sense that they were not on their own. This was a pattern which emerged through a lot of our plays in 7:84.

Blood Red Roses *had a powerful impact on audiences. Could you describe the play? And would you call it feminist, or pro-feminist, in any way?*

It was the story of a fighting woman from the highlands, who became an industrial activist in East Kilbride, and as convenor at a large plant led a successful multi-national strike. It followed her development and that of her daughters, her subsequent victimization and black-listing. Her struggle goes on all over our 'post-industrial' areas. Waste and managerial terrorism are now institutionalized.

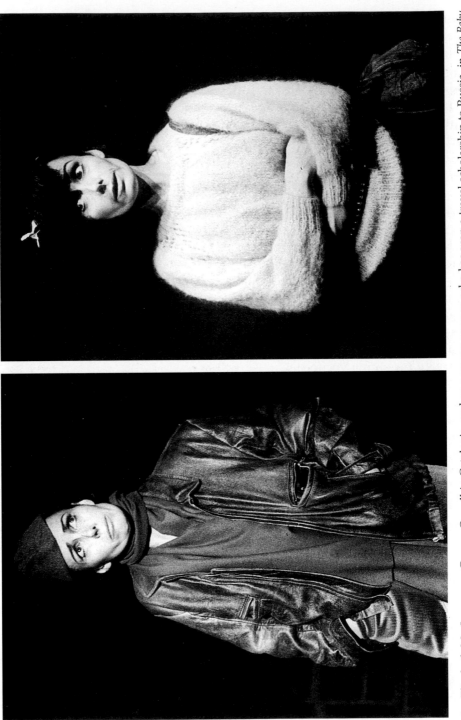

4. Elizabeth MacLennan as George Orwell in Catalonia, and as a young woman who has won a travel scholarship to Russia, in *The Baby and the Bathwater* (a one-woman show) by John McGrath for 7:84 Scotland Tour (1984–7); photographer: Anthony Brannon.

The Baby and the Bathwater *was also particularly relevant to women, and a political play. What was the most important contribution which that play made?*

It showed how political paranoia develops and produces wars, ignorance and misery. But it was also, believe it or not, very funny. I played seven different characters — including George Orwell and the Pope — but my favourite was a 16-year-old schoolgirl who is terrified of going to Russia, because of what she has been led to believe.

What can live theatre achieve, artistically and politically, which is different from other media, such as television or film?

The most powerful weapon for change is speaking your mind. Society these days is organized mainly for people to listen, and to do what you're told, to accept the words of politicians. So until theatre-makers are actually physically silenced they can't take away that power from the theatre. Since audiences are predominantly made up of women, women can contest and challenge the status quo and its values in theatre like nowhere else. Women decide what show to go to and what they will do for a night out. Equally, more decisions about what is going on in the theatre should be taken by women. Although at the moment, producer power is largely male-dominated, many women have assumed control of the administration of theatre in Britain — but they seem less than preoccupied with breaking new ground and opening up our society to scrutiny. They are all too busy trying to stay alive at all, and in a way are experiencing a very effective form of economic censorship. But happily of course there are some exceptions — Jude Kelly, director of the West Yorkshire Playhouse in Leeds, is one. And times change, don't they?

Gabriella Giannachi and Lizbeth Goodman
Interview recorded on audiotape by Gabriella Giannachi in May 1994, revised by Lizbeth Goodman with Elizabeth MacLennan, December 1994 and February 1995.

KATHLEEN McCREERY

Although she was born in Canada and did not come to Britain until the age of 23, Kathleen McCreery has been deeply involved in political theatre in the UK. She was a member of Red Ladder from 1969 to 1974, went on to help found Broadside Theatre, and co-authored the book Theatre as a Weapon *(Routledge, 1986). She began her career as an actor, but has also worked as a radio journalist and lecturer. She now concentrates on writing, with occasional forays into directing.*

Does gender matter in the theatre?

Of course. Theatre reflects, or wrestles with, what is going on in the broader society, and it certainly matters there. Gender has always been a major source of conflict.

I can't leave it alone in my work, even when it's not the main subject of a script. The central characters in my plays are usually female and always restless. My male characters are uncertain too. I am interested in the shifting relations between them, and between women.

As far as the industry itself goes, the theatre is still dominated by men. I have only worked professionally with two female directors, Vicky Featherstone and Claire Grove, if you exclude the times I have directed myself. All the rest have been male. Annie Smol directed my play *The Chambermaids* with an amateur company, and film-maker Penny Woolcock directed a seven-minute video for which I wrote the script. Ava Hunt is about to do an abridged version of my *Ballad of Mary Barton* with an adult education class. That's it. In 34 years as a professional actor and writer! Is my experience exceptional?

In the North-East we used to have five county companies. Until recently all the artistic directors were men, and their record of commissioning plays from women was, on the whole, pretty poor. It's getting slowly better. Northumberland Theatre Company is now directed by Gillian Hambleton, and they have won one of the Northern Arts franchises, but staging more plays by, about and for women doesn't appear to be one of her priorities.

Are you aware that the position of women in the theatre has changed in any way over the years?

Things have changed in the rest of the country, but in the North-East we have a lot of catching up to do. Northern Stage put on a fairly traditional production of *Gentlemen Prefer Blondes* at Newcastle Playhouse. After that, perhaps they felt the need to provide an antidote to what is, after all, a pretty sexist tale (yes, I know, it was penned by a woman!), so they commissioned a designer and nine northern women, including me, to write ten-minute plays, and staged them all at the much smaller Gulbenkian Studio Theatre under the title *Women Prefer...*

It was a runaway success. They were turning people away at the door, there was a real buzz in the air, audiences rocked with laughter. The quality was uneven, but some of the plays were very funny. The reviews... well, surprise surprise, most male reviewers were critical, the few female reviewers loved it. I met an actress, who is well-known here in the North-East, and she was railing. 'Didn't you like it?' I asked. 'Of course, but it makes me so angry! There should have been nine commissions for *full-length* plays by you lot, yet we're supposed to be grateful for ten minutes, why are we *always...?!'*

The North-East was an area of heavy industry, coal, shipbuilding, steel. This was reflected in the subjects playwrights chose. Now those industries are virtually gone. The biggest employer in Sunderland is the local authority, and that means a work-force with a lot of women. But there has been little recognition on the part of theatre boards and directors of the need for plays that deal with the lives and concerns of these women, with the changes that are taking place for them. That means they are losing potential audiences, the kind of people who packed out the Gulbenkian for *Women Prefer...*

A few years ago, I took part in an extraordinary discussion evening under the aegis of Northern Playwrights. It was my turn to introduce it, and I decided to talk about the plight of women playwrights. For various reasons, none of the women in the organization could make it that night. I was on my own with nine or ten men. Predictably, it was a disaster. They began to nit-pick about the statistics I used, objected to my trying to put the argument in context by using everyday examples from my own experience of discrimination and sexism outside the theatre. One kept saying, 'It's not that bad, there's Caryl Churchill and Pam Gems and...' At the end of the evening they went to the pub. I was not invited!

'Next Stage' was an attempt to raise funds to commission and produce women's plays. A number of us were involved in an *ad hoc* committee. It got as far as rehearsed readings. There was an informal, wonderfully gossipy and boozy women's discussion group, a quarterly that managed five issues and workshops. It felt hopeful for a while. Now I get the impression that most of us are plugging away on our own, developing our work, trying to earn a living, raising children.

Are you conscious of writing and performing as a woman?

Of course. When I direct, I think less of gender, I just do it as well as I know how. But I have qualities that many of the male directors I've worked with don't have, such as a real desire to find the key that will help actors unlock their potential. I get such pleasure from their discoveries! I am also very concerned that they should feel secure and confident when they go out to perform. And I don't like it when a production is taken over by the technical elements. They are there to support the play and the actors. I see it as my job to provide an overall, coherent vision, without imposing it. But I am good at coming up with conceptions which express visually what is essential in a play. I am logical as well as emotional. People still tend to think of these as male attributes.

To some extent, this is true in my writing as well. My plays have rarely been rooted in personal experience. I am attracted to epic stories and themes, huge issues, complex content, the broad historical sweep, perhaps because of my years spent in political theatre and journalism. I love researching.

Mind you, this is changing. The farce I wrote for *Women Prefer...* was called *9 ¹/₂ minutes* and it was so domestic! It was about my house — everybody was in it, my daughter (to her great embarrassment), husband, lover, a composite lodger, the window cleaner, the cat... And these days I notice that a lot of personal feelings and experiences are surfacing in my work.

Do you feel strongly either for or against working collaboratively with other women in the theatre?

Women Prefer... was great, there was a workshop with the other women writers, Vicky Featherstone was a challenging director. But in the end it was my script. I did so much collaborative work in the sixties and seventies, and I am frequently asked to lead workshops and teach now, often with others, which I do enjoy, but... I feel the need to write as an individual. Successful collaboration is very difficult, dependent on personalities hitting it off, on knowing each other very well, and it takes time to get it right.

Example? OK. A mixed team of Marion Sedley, Steve Trafford, Glen Park and myself, wrote *Strike While the Iron is Hot* with Red Ladder. It was a lengthy process which developed over many months in 1973–4. We read a lot of theory, interviewed a wide range of women, and then for the first time we sat down as a group, and instead of grappling with issues that primarily affected other people, like productivity and new technology and unemployment and rent strikes, we explored our own histories, our own feelings as men and women.

The women in the group became more confident and the men had to listen more and became less authoritative, less strident(!) It wasn't plain sailing, there were tears shed, fierce arguments. All worth it though, the play made a big impact. Our audiences were affected in a way that rarely seems to happen now, except perhaps in TIE — Theatre in Education — (which is one of the reasons why I like working with and for young people!).

Collaboration can be enormously helpful in unleashing talent, building confidence, giving newcomers a start. But also for us old hands: we're all insecure, we crave confirmation that what we're doing is on the right track. I compulsively read my plays aloud as I'm writing, to whoever I can buttonhole, demanding feedback. I'm so glad when rehearsals begin and I can work with directors, actors, designers and MDs [Musical Directors]. Unlike some writers, I am not precious about altering the script if the changes they suggest will improve it. So, in that sense I still need collaborators. I would love to work with a women's company. But it would be a big mistake to think that working with women solves all your problems… Oh, no!

How would you define 'feminism'?

I can say what I *think* it is about. Feminism is about what is happening to all of us now, the rights we have and don't have. It is about the past: uncovering what really did happen, celebrating the contributions we've made, grieving for our losses, licking and binding up our wounds, not forgiving and forgetting, but trying to heal ourselves. And it's about the future: about what could happen, our potential for power, both as individuals and *en masse*.

According to your own definition, would you call yourself a feminist?

Yes.

Would you say that feminism has affected the theatre in any major way?

Yes. But it's hard to pin down, I don't know if the women whose work I have admired like Timberlake Wertenbaker, Caryl Churchill, Peta Lily, Pip Broughton, Liz Lochhead who have helped make the changes would call themselves feminist. Groups like Scarlet Harlets, Spare Tyre, Resisters certainly affected their audiences! I believe that there is greater awareness, less of a tendency for the subjects we write about to be ghettoized. A few months ago, a male director asked me to adapt *Frankenstein* on the grounds that it was written by a woman and that all the adaptations to date have been very masculine. I think that's progress.

Do you believe that theatre can affect social change?

Oh, yes. Certainly there are many examples in the history of workers' theatre, some of which we dealt with in *Theatre as a Weapon*. Red Ladder and Broadside occasionally inspired audiences to take action. A performance by Broadside of *The Big Lump* on a building-site in Scotland led to the ending of lump labour (heavy manual labour) on that site; a Broadside play *Apartheid: The British Connection* led to photography students deciding not to boycott Kodak film, but to use the film to mount an exhibition about the racist system in which Kodak was investing. I'll never forget the trade union school where the polite veneer was blown away by our play on racism, and the hotel and catering workers, who were mostly immigrants confronted the white water workers. We had men standing up in our audiences saying 'I've been a cabbage all my life and your play has showed me that'; a woman hitting her husband over the head with her handbag.

Mind you, the effect we had was dependent on a number of factors: we rarely performed in theatres, we invariably had discussions which carried on the process begun in the plays, we involved people at the sharp end in the making of our plays, and we often performed for them when they were in crisis, when their lives were turned upside down and they were open to new ideas.

Perhaps the most poignant example of a cultural event changing hearts and minds was when Broadside organized a benefit for the Grosvenor House Hotel chambermaids who were on strike. As the benefit was about to start, the union called a meeting in a room just off the hall and bullied the chambermaids into calling off the strike. The women fled to the toilets, some had to be physically restrained, because they were so angry with those who'd voted in favour. We coaxed them out, we performed our *Working Women's Charter Show*, which helped ease the tension, and then Isabel, a Portuguese maid, got up to sing. Her songs spoke so powerfully, so honestly of the experience of immigration, of the exploitation in the hotels that when she had finished, they looked at each other and one said, 'We need another meeting'. They went back into the room and wouldn't let the male official in, and voted the strike back on! I wrote about it years later in *The Chambermaids*.

Is 'feminist theatre' different in Northern and Southern England?

There's less of it up here. A lot of my work has been outside the area. There's this heavy weight of industrial history, and the problem of communities under attack where women can find it difficult to be critical of the men who oppress them everyday because of the perceived need to close ranks against the enemy both are facing...

Based on your experiences of both North America and Britain, is 'feminist theatre' different in these two cultures (allowing for the vast regional differences within each culture)?

I have lived away so long and when I get back it's for short periods, so I can only give my impression. There were terrific groups springing up in the sixties and seventies in the States, such as the Alive and Trucking Theatre in Minneapolis. I look back with fond nostalgia on the talks I had with women's theatre groups in New York then — they were way ahead of us here in England. It was such a relief to find out that there were other women who had problems like mine, and that maybe *we* weren't the problem…

I've noticed recently that Canadian women are good at revues, very funny, and can be very overt about sex. I know this goes against every stereotype the 'Brits' have ever held about us 'Canucks', but it isn't always 40 below!

My mother is a member of the Raging Grannies, a movement of older women who use songs and street theatre to campaign on everything from the environment to US domination, and of course the situation of women, especially older women. I was asked to do a workshop with them in Vancouver a few years back. The oldest participant was 87 and I don't think she sat down once. Last summer, when my mother had a hip operation, the Grannies organized a rota to visit her, run errands, whatever she needed. They know what the word solidarity means.

Of course in Canada now there is tremendous turmoil as Native writers, women and men, begin to occupy some of the space they have been denied. And that's different from the situation here, because their ancestors were never immigrants.

What advice would you give to young women who are aspiring to work in the theatre today?

I'm faced with this now. My 14-year-old is in her first year of GCSEs, doing drama and media studies, and thinking about a career in one or the other. When she first told me, I must admit my heart sank. I guess I wanted to protect her from all the rebuffs, the heartache, the insecurity, the poverty.

I think you must have a passion. At the same time you shouldn't take yourself too seriously — you aren't the centre of the universe. And I think it helps to acquire as many skills as you can, to get work. But you should hang on to your integrity. I'm not sure the compromises and sacrifices are worth it if you end up doing work you are ashamed of, or don't believe in. In this respect, I've been very lucky.

What's the future for women in the theatre in the UK?

In reality or in dreams? This is an interesting question in the light of discussions I took part in recently in South Africa. A lot of revivals were being staged, people were unsure what to write about, now that apartheid is over. The mass audiences that responded to agitational theatre have, according to some, melted away. It struck familiar chords, for very different reasons.

I think we have to remind ourselves of the importance of the audience. That doesn't mean 'giving them what they want', so-called 'popular entertainment'. It does mean shedding light on what really concerns them. I hope we can become less Eurocentric, and feel freer to mix media and forms. I trust that we are moving away from the stultifying political correctness that has led to new stereotypes, superficiality and inhibitions. That doesn't mean going back to the way things were!

I expect we will have to continue to pound on the doors, and to push the power-brokers into funding our work. The inequalities are still profound.

Mary Luckhurst and Jane de Gay
Interviewed by Mary Luckhurst; revised by Kathleen McCreery; edited by Jane de Gay, 1995.

NANCY DIUGUID

Though born in the USA, Nancy Diuguid has contributed to British theatre for many years, mainly through her work as a director for theatre, opera and film. She came to Britain in 1972 and trained as an actress at the Central School of Speech and Drama. Her acting experience ranges from Jerzy Grotowski's Polish Laboratory Theatre to Warren Beatty's Reds. *Her career has followed a trajectory from women's and gay theatre to the mainstream. As a director she has worked in numerous London theatres including: the Royal Court; Hampstead Theatre where she was an Associate Director; and the English National Opera; and she has worked extensively abroad. She has twice won the Time-Out 01 for London awards plus Munich and Edinburgh Festival awards for her theatre productions. Productions have included such classics as* Twelfth Night, A Streetcar Named Desire, *Goldoni's* Il Campiello, *and the operas* Woyzeck *and* A Masked Ball, *plus premieres of new work by Timberlake Wertenbaker, Louise Page, Howard Brenton, Noël Greig and Franz Xavier Kroetz. She has also written and directed her first drama for film,* Aftermath, *funded by the British Film Institute as well as two documentaries for the UK's Channel Four. In 1995, she was at work writing an original screenplay.*

Your career has moved through several phases or 'stages'. What have these been?

My work has changed with the decades, each exploring new forms and media, the overall drive remaining the same. In the mid-seventies to early eighties it aimed to connect art and politics, was issue-based but not agit-prop, and reflected the conditions of women, lesbians and gay men. In the eighties, I expanded my work to include more physical and visual-based theatre as well as the mainstream which, by then, was beginning to legitimize alternative work. I have also worked internationally, and the late eighties and nineties have taken me into opera and film.

But from the beginning my work has been varied. I came from the United States in 1972 and trained at the Central School of Speech and Drama as an actress. We were not supposed to perform outside the school, but I did. In 1974 three Portuguese women, alias The Three Marias, were imprisoned for writing their book *New Portuguese Letters*, which was an indictment of Portugal's policies both towards its women and its colonies. This fuelled an international campaign. Consequently, their writings and their plight were dramatized. I took part with performers from both the National [Theatre] and the RSC. The houses were packed and the audiences electric. Women's theatre took off.

After Central, as part of an ongoing political commitment, I performed in various institutions like prisons and mental hospitals. I felt at the time that it was an important contribution in a neglected area. It's wonderful to see the number of theatre and opera companies doing this work today as it was considered unusual then. I also had the good fortune to work with Jerzy Grotowski's Polish Laboratory Theatre.

And then, in 1976, you joined Gay Sweatshop and performed in their first all-women's play, Jill Posenor's Any Woman Can. *What was this landmark play about, and what did it accomplish?*

There were a number of firsts in *Any Women Can*. It was Jill's first play; a women's company was formed within Gay Sweatshop; a coming-out story was written; and many lesbians were seeing their lives portrayed honestly. We played to women and men who often had no network of support. Or to parents who had no understanding. Our work went beyond the performance. Men and women came to talk with us until four in the morning. We were on marathon radio phone-ins. Some rang to tell us we should be driven over the edge like lemmings. Some said they didn't mind us if they didn't have to see us kissing in the streets. Others remarked 'You sound like such nice young people.' Then there were those who were supportive. But the prejudice was so great we were even threatened in Belfast with a bomb. Along with *Any Woman Can*, the men's and women's company came together for our rendition of Cinderella in the pantomime *Jingleball* with music by Tom Robinson. 'Glad to be Gay' was our closing number, with women in dungarees and all!

In 1977, you initiated and co-ordinated along with Julie Parker the first Women's Festival, attended by some 10,000 people over its three-week run at the Drill Hall.

Yes, the festival brought together a rich mixture of art and politics. It provided a forum for the introduction of writers and theatre companies, for instance, Melissa Murray, Jude Alderson, Beryl and the Perils, The Cauldron Theatre Company, The Sadista Sisters. Susan Griffin's *Voices* opened at the festival and subsequently we performed it at the ICA. We had workshops on every issue under the sun, films, music, a bookshop which later became Sisterwrite, and so on.

Just after the festival, still in 1977, one of Gay Sweatshop's most politically important plays, Care and Control, *was premiered. That play is still considered one of the most important feminist texts ever produced; would you describe the research and writing process?*

Care and Control is about women and the custody of children, the relationship between the nuclear family and the state. I did the initial interviews and research, including actual court cases from the seventies, with Kate Crutchley who directed it. There are three storylines, all based on true stories. The first is about a single mother who loses her child because the father's signature is on the birth certificate. The second — my role — concerns a heterosexual woman with three daughters who becomes a lesbian in the course of the play and loses custody of her daughters because she reads *Spare Rib*. (This shows you how threatening *Spare Rib* was and how ignorant the judiciary were.) The third concentrates on a working-class lesbian couple.

In the play, both the single and the married mother lose their children. Only the lesbian mother is allowed to keep her child 'because of bricks and mortar': she is secure with a home and a job, but her husband is not. If he were, there would be no way she would have been given custody.

The process of creating *Care and Control* was a lengthy one, three months in all. It was a collaborative effort where the characters were drawn from the women we had interviewed. We talked with the women about their lives from the birth of their children. We combined the biographical histories to create the characters and story-lines. We felt a tremendous responsibility to represent the women and their struggle truthfully. We then created the play through improvization and, in the court-room scene in the second act, from the actual court cases. Then Michelene Wandor was invited to polish and write the final script.

When the piece was ready for performance, we invited the women we had interviewed to be the first audience and give their comments. All but one came. We were incredibly nervous, but the feedback was enormously positive.

We are up to 1978, when you moved from performing into directing, with Louise Page's Tissue.

Yes, *Tissue* is about another taboo of the time — breast cancer.

You then moved on to help organize and run the successful Women's Project '78: would you say a bit about that?

The Women's Project opened with Michelene Wandor's *Aid Thy Neighbour* about the new hot subject: artificial insemination. Throughout that year, Kate Phelps and I were researching and co-devising *Confinement*, a piece that had been brewing since my days performing in prisons and my friendships with women ex-prisoners, whose stories had inspired and horrified me. We decided Kate would write the final script and I would direct. It was the second production of the Women's Project. The play was an indictment of the overcrowding, the prison health system and its abuse of drugs, and the complicated question of the rights of pregnant mothers behind bars.

The design was interesting in that it was in the round but with the prison cells thrusting into the audience. The audience and the actors were practically living together in those cells. Grotowski would have gone even further. For instance, he would have had the audience sitting on the bunks. But I wanted the audience not only to identify with the prisoners and to enter their emotional world but also to be able to distance themselves in order to understand and to act. I only understood fully what I was doing then when I was directing Howard Brenton's *Sore Throats* at the Royal Court in the late eighties: it was combining at their extremes an Artaudian approach with a Brechtian one.

Can you explain the differences between those approaches, as you see them?

Artaud called for a theatre which would disrupt the spectators' logically-controlled equilibrium and free their subconscious minds so that they might glimpse once more the mysterious sources of existence. Brecht wanted the spectator to watch critically, to delineate real life and the stage, and to apply what they saw in the theatre to real life and so work actively for social change.

In the alternative scene until the mid-eighties, there were two camps — political theatre on the one hand and performance art on the other. Some of us wanted to synthesize the two approaches. It was the subject of numerous debates. And new approaches began to develop.

Later, I moved into opera because it has a curious way of distancing you and then dropping you straight into the interior realm of a character. Like Greek tragedy. But with music.

All I am saying is that the split in me was between social realism and this person who likes to dream. A friend of mine observed that my *Twelfth Night* was like the Royal Court meeting the English National Opera. An apt observation.

Before we move on, can you pick out and describe some of the most important pieces you did at this time?

Two of Noël Greig's plays, *Dear Love of Comrades* and *Angels Descend on Paris*, were very important to me. Maybe they are also coming up because music was an essential element in both. So I think they were again foreshadowing opera. Besides, I had been brought up on the musical in the US.

Dear Love of Comrades is about Edward Carpenter and his attempts to form a social and sexual utopia in the chilly climate of late Victorian England, while *Angels Descend on Paris* is named after a phrase Sartre uses when describing the Nazi invasion. The play deals with not only the oppression of the Jews but also of the gays. I think for their time these plays were seminal.

Another relevant piece is Timberlake Wertenbaker's *New Anatomies* which I directed for the Women's Theatre Group. It is based on the life story of Isabella Eberhardt who in the late nineteenth century rejected the conventions of her semi-aristocratic upbringing and followed her own intellectual quest for wisdom. She travelled from the salons of Paris to the sands of French colonial Algeria where she dressed as a young Arab and mixed with Sufi followers. Again the theme of colonization and the need to break the shackles of it returns.

Back to 1984 and the production of Patterns. *You formed Changing Woman Theatre Company to produce it. What's in the name, Changing Woman ?*

The Apache called the earth-goddess by this name, for she never grew old. When her age began to show, she simply walked toward the East until she saw herself coming toward herself. She kept walking until her young self merged with her ageing self and then, renewed, returned to her home.

The legend speaks of renewal. It is telling about what I was experiencing. This was a traumatic time.

The company was formed as a direct result of wanting to bring together political theatre and performance art, to create work that was both multi-racial and multi-disciplined. The fourteen women were not only of various nationalities, races and religions, but also from different artistic disciplines.

Patterns explored the links between characters from Greek mythology and contemporary women working in the textile industry. We drew freely from the relevant plays, re-interpreting the roles of the women and their relationships, and continually moving back and forth between the time-frames of ancient and present. Our central theme was theft — of power, both economic and personal.

The production was one of those failures that I can appreciate now. It was one of the more important pieces I have ever done precisely because it did not work. I was told by many that I should try this project again in five years' time. Five years on, I moved into opera which is a complex form that allows issues to be presented in forms of music, poetry, dance and visual arts.

Verdi can hammer out political themes like the Spanish Inquisition in *Don Carlos* and then move into a character's dream landscape. I think the British writer Robert Donnington expresses what opera does most eloquently. He assigned it to that mysterious place 'where the promptings of the irrational imagination are at their most uninhibited and the restraints of naturalism are at their least intrusive'.

I think now there are theatre companies that do combine harsh reality and imaginary worlds. But then it was a different matter. Today I feel we owe a lot to such companies as Theatre de Complicité.

How did you approach other areas of your theatre work?

In the second half of the eighties I directed in Japan, Brazil, Greece, Israel and Holland as well as London. I concentrated on the classics — both period and contemporary. I know what you are going to ask and, yes, all the work was informed by my feminism. But there are two pieces in particular I would like to talk about. They are *Sore Throats* by Howard Brenton and *Request Programme* by Franz Xavier Kroetz.

Sore Throats is a powerful piece about marriage, brutality, survival and friendship. Doing work about people who are at the edge is for me second nature.

Request Programme is a one-woman drama. It is about isolation, loneliness and suicide. Despite this, the work is not without humour. Eileen Nicholas gave a memorable performance. Whoever came was fascinated, whatever their class, experience, age or background. The audience began with the usual anticipation, then it hit them that there was not going to be any dialogue; the only sound for part of the time was that of a radio programme, hence the title of the play. They became uncomfortable, nervous. Then they became transfixed. At a profound level, their thoughts and imaginations were released. They could project their own experiences or imagine that of an aunt or a neighbour. This I am sure was Kroetz's intention, to remind us of a world full of unwillingly lonely people. And his genius was to do it silently.

I would also like to mention Darrah Cloud's *Stick Wife*, which the Gate Theatre produced. It brings me back to the formative influences of my childhood and youth. The play focuses on three women whose husbands are members of the Ku Klux Klan. The women are forced to confront their repressed fears and self-deception about their husbands' involvement in such a violent and racist organization. The inciting incident is the death of three black girls during a church service. The church has been bombed — an incident that actually happened in Mississippi. The husbands are involved. What is to be done? In the actual case, one of the women turned her husband in. He got off scot-free.

I grew up in a small southern town of 400 people in Kentucky. Mark Twain country and not far from where Toni Morrison set her novel, *Beloved*. When I was four I saw my first, and thankfully last, cross-burning.

Is violence a theme you return to often?

Yes, it seems to be. There is so much of it in our society. And still it is too often glorified and distorted. Recently I wrote and directed *Aftermath*, a film about a woman who has been raped. I felt I had not seen anything that dealt with the actual violence of rape without being titillating or presenting the barrage of terrifying images that such a loss of control causes. I wanted to redress this in *Aftermath*. The film has one word, 'No' — the rest is a story enacted through images and sound. The response has been extraordinary. The film has been taken up by International Film Festivals and the Metropolitan Police, who are using it to train all their recruits, and for their sexual offences unit.

What has happened to women's and gay theatres in recent years?

Women have achieved a great deal. Lesbians have become chic. What might win the best play award in the nineties (ie — a lesbian play) was a cause of a bomb threat in the seventies. Undoubtedly things have changed. That's great. That's what we wanted. We had a dream: that there would be no more need for the Gay Sweatshops and the women's companies. That the multiplicity existing in the world would be reflected in the theatre.

Unfortunately, in our so-called 'post-feminist' age that dream is still a dream. If post-feminism means the end of women's struggle for equality, then it has been forgotten that the majority of the world's poor are women.

I would like to think that women of the next generations understand or at least have a sense and appreciation of what the women of the previous generations achieved. And will, on our shoulders, take it further.

Lizbeth Goodman

This piece draws on material from interviews conducted by Lizbeth Goodman in London on 4 and 18 August, 1988; 18 April, 1989, 12 July, 1989 and 29 August, 1989, 13 December, 1989, and January 1990; and on an interview conducted by Jane de Gay in London on 26 January 1995. Revised February 1995.

KATE OWEN

Kate Owen trained at the Central School of Art and Design and began working at the Citizens' Theatre, Glasgow. She became seduced by alternative and experimental theatre, designing the first productions of many new theatre pieces in the 1970s and 1980s. Her theatre designs have included: The Gut Girls *and* Gaslight *(Albany Empire);* Circus Moon *(Half Moon);* The Man Who Lit Up the World *(Hackney Empire/LIFT Festival);* On the Verge, East Lynne, Loot *and* Entertaining Mr Sloan *(Birmingham Rep);* Poppies, This Island's Mine *and* Kitchen Matters *(Gay Sweatshop);* Two *(Not the National Theatre);* Stairway to Heaven *(Shared Experience); and* Betrayal *(Two's Company). Dance and visual theatre designs include:* Labelled with Love *(Albany Empire);* Three Pieces *(Extemporary Dance Theatre);* Dirt, Cold Wars *and* Strokes of Genius *(Blood Group); and* Crazy Daisy *and* Ordinary Lives *(Laurie Booth). She has directed* The Visitor *and* Familiar Feelings *(Theatre Centre); and* More *(Gay Sweatshop).*

Does gender matter in the theatre?

People are still very aware of gender when they employ. It is difficult to answer that in the context of theatre design because there have always been a lot of students of theatre design who were women. However, I was taught mainly by men — there was only one woman who taught me and that was Nadine Baylis. Also, there aren't as many famous women theatre designers as there are men although there are loads of women theatre designers, for example: The Motleys, Jocelyn Herbert, Sally Jacobs, Alison Chitty, Maria Björnson, Jennifer Carey, Sue Blane, Jenny Tiramani and Rae Smith.

Has the position of women in the theatre changed over the past few years?

I work with more women directors now than I used to and I work with more women playwrights than I used to. But that is possibly because I have got a bit typecast as being somebody who sometimes does feminist theatre, so maybe generally things haven't changed a lot. But it feels to me — and I think my writer friends would agree with this — that there has been a swing back to working on the classics again. It feels like there has been less new writing happening and so of course that means that one is tending to design for more male writing again.

Are you aware of designing as a woman?

It depends. As a designer, one's job is broken into lots of different bits. When I am at home designing I am not aware of being any sex at all. The artist part of me is pretty androgynous really. But of course, theatre design is all about how you see the world, and my vision of the world must be different from what it would have been if I had been a chap brought up in the fifties and sixties. Gender affects the way that you talk to people. Making theatre is a collaborative art form, and women have a different way of doing that than men.

Do you feel strongly for or against working collaborating with other women in the theatre?

It depends on what type of theatre you're doing. Making traditional British theatre where you have already got the script, you have a designer, a director, is a very different set-up from when you have a group of people in a room who say 'let's make theatre'.

Sometimes it's easier devising with men because men stick to roles more clearly. I think the edges get blurred with women and that isn't always a good thing. In the end, I prefer whatever makes the best theatre — that's what matters the most.

In your experience of working with different directors, do you find yourself establishing certain kinds of working relations with women and with men?

No. Relationships between directors and designers are very complicated. At best they are equal. It *has* to be that. So it's all about rapport and sharing a 'vision' of the production. You either 'click' or you don't. Each relationship is quite unique.

As a designer, I liaise with everyone in the show — actors, technicians, makers and builders. My working relationships with these people are different from my relationship with the director. So, for example, I sometimes find that male carpenters and stage crew are more likely to be aware that I am a woman.

How would you define 'feminism'?

I would say that feminism was questioning the traditional role of the woman and demanding an equal place in the world. You have to bring your own personal history into that, and a sense of whether you are looking at it in a work situation or a private situation.

Would you call yourself a feminist according to your definition?

Yes. Most women I have worked with in the theatre would.

Has feminism had an impact on the theatre — mainstream and alternative?

Yes, feminism has affected the theatre, but I am sure that many women would say that it has not affected it enough. For example the content of plays: there might still be things in plays that aren't right but we now notice that they are not right. Years ago a lot went unnoticed.

Can you give an example of what you mean by something which 'isn't right'?

Portraying women as victims, neurotics, nymphomaniacs. The same script can be given different meaning with just a different vision and understanding. Women directors are more likely to do this. I'm thinking of plays like *Gaslight* and *Entertaining Mr Sloane*, and especially of adaptations of nineteenth-century novels.

There are lots of forms of theatres now that probably would not have existed without feminism, and these have fed the mainstream. A lot of the visual theatre of the eighties has informed mainstream theatre and a lot of that work was done by women. Pina Bausch and Geraldine Pilgrim with Hesitate and Demonstrate. People like Robert Lepage are doing that work now. There were lots of women experimenting with new ways of presenting theatre which has affected an awful lot of the theatre that is happening now, even if it is text-based.

Can the theatre affect social change?

Yes. I think any theatre that *works* makes people look differently at the world. When I worked with Gay Sweatshop or Blood Group, we used to get hundreds of letters from people who were affected by the work that we did. That was why we did it. There is also a lot of theatre that does not affect people at all. I don't know what the political role of theatre is in the nineties, because people have a different attitude towards socialism than they did in the seventies and the early eighties.

How do you see the future for women in the theatre?

The political theatre movement that I was part of actually began in the seventies and it hung on by its fingernails in the eighties and sort of fizzled out. But at its best there were different groups of people with a common idea that was very anti-establishment. What is ironic is that a lot of those theatre companies, the ones that still exist, have become part of the establishment and are now run by completely different people. There used to be a kind of respect from one company to another. Now that doesn't really fit in with the political agenda of the nineties at all. I can see it in myself: I'm now a jobbing designer. I have had to become ambitious and competitive again. I have had to return to mainstream theatre sort of cap in hand!

One situation which has changed is funding. In the eighties we were desperately trying to keep companies afloat and desperately trying to please funding bodies. That was a real problem — the work suffered enormously as a consequence. A lot of the work that experimented with form was not given the support that it needed because nobody at the Arts Council could decide what department it belonged to and so it slipped through the net. Now, funding guidelines have changed so that it is possible to get funding for work that experiments with form, so there's more of a move towards experimentation.

What would you like to see happening in the future?

In terms of the nineties and British theatre, I would like to see more risks being taken with individual artists. I am very interested in individual artists from other parts of Europe and would like to see more risks being taken here. And it would be great if these risks were taken by women.

What kinds of risks would you like to see being taken?

The kind of risks that artists have always taken. Some people at the moment think that theatre should be healing. Well, I think it has that facility — people are enabled to understand or feel complex things as a consequence of watching theatre. But actually I think art should always move forwards, stirring, shaking, startling, moving people to see things afresh. Theatre should have an expectancy about it. It's form *and* content again...

Jane de Gay
Interview recorded on audiotape, London, July 1994.

LOUISE PAGE

Louise Page was born in London in 1955, but has lived in Sheffield most of her life. She read drama at Birmingham University, and took a postgraduate diploma in playwriting, then returned to Sheffield in 1979 as Fellow in Drama and Television. In 1982–3, she was resident writer at the Royal Court, and in 1985, was awarded the first J. T. Grein Prize by the Critics' Circle. She has a string of widely-produced plays from the early Tissue, *through* Salonika *and* Golden Girls *to* Beauty and the Beast *(for The Women's Playhouse Trust),* Diplomatic Wives *(1987),* Adam Was a Gardener *(1991),* Hawks and Doves *(1992) and* Another Nine Months *(1995).*

How would you define yourself in terms of political ideology? Is there a conscious choice that determines the route of your plays, thematically?

I think if I have to define where I stand politically, I certainly stand to the left. That does not mean that I'm not very critical of the left and certain mistakes that it has made in Britain. In terms of feminism, I can see how one can be a woman in the l990s without being a feminist. So what I think I am is a socialist feminist. One writes from one's point of view: therefore I write about women because I am a woman.

I have to say that when I started writing plays at university, I'd never heard of feminism. We didn't do a course on women writers, and it just never occurred to me that women did not write plays. I'd heard of Shelagh Delaney, but hadn't read anything by a woman playwright or seen anything. It was only later, when I wrote *Tissue*, that everybody started telling me how difficult life was for women as playwrights but until that point it really never crossed my mind. That was when I became politically aware of the injustices done to women rather than thinking that was the way the world was.

One of the popular slogans of feminism is that 'the personal is political'. Now many of your plays seem to fall within this textual politics in the sense that they present domestic scenes and particularized cases and psychological insights that create an atmosphere of emotional intimacy rather than one of rational thinking. How far is this approach a matter of personal preference and how far a compulsion deriving from the financial and other strictures of theatres, for example, limiting the number of actors, offering you small stages, and so on?

I believe very strongly that people's politics tend to come from things that happen in their lives. I know people say that I am a writer who deals with minutiae, but it seems to me that it is those moments that actually do radically affect people. It's things that happen over very small spaces of time, or chance meetings, or suggestions that you read a book, which can, often, set on course that sort of change in somebody's life.

The question of whether what you do is defined by the limitations — well, of course it is but sometimes the limitations can be positive in that you find other ways of doing things. And certainly when I started writing professionally I really did not have the skills to handle huge plays. There is no way I could have written a play with a cast of twenty-two, sustaining character and emotion and plot development, so what it might have been was, say, three main speaking parts and a chorus of extras.

The first big play I wrote, *Golden Girls*, which has a cast of fourteen, was quite difficult because up to that point I hadn't really written for more than about five or six, and suddenly having to deal with fourteen I sort of assumed it was going to be half the number of lines for twice the number of people — but it does not work that way at all! And I had to learn to write exit lines. One of the problems with having a lot of characters on stage is how you get them off again.

I start writing knowing what I have to write about, but without knowing where I'm going to end up. I start writing a play and usually as I write it the play defines itself. I find things out. Plays get defined by all sorts of things, and they can literally change course in the middle because of the things that happen in your life.

There has been a lot of discussion lately about gender politics, and among critics the question of how far a writer can transcend gender in his/her point of view in delineating characters. Now I notice that when you choose to create full-bodied characters as in Salonika, Real Estate, Hearing — *your male portrayals are as credible as the female ones. How do you do this?*

What about *critics* transcending their genders? No. I think you do what any good writer should do, which is to look at the world. You observe people, you see the way in which people behave. I tend to be more sympathetic to men on stage than a lot of women are. But then you have to be if you are writing a play like *Real Estate* and you want to change things.

Very deliberately in *Real Estate* I wrote a scene in the kitchen where the men bake a cake, and cook it properly, so they become positive role models of house-husbands. And there have been huge problems in various places where I've been to rehearse that play or watch that play because the male actors think it's a joke scene. So you get them doing things like dropping eggs on the floor or sieving the flour all over the table. There was one production in which one of the male actors put in swearing because he thought the scene would be more masculine if there was the occasional 'bloody' and that sort of thing, which of course I made him take out.

You write the characters that you need. I don't think you'd ever go out and meet any of the characters that I've written on the street because there's a point where they're not quite characters, they're also metaphors or images.

It's very important now that women write men who are credible, men who can be perceived as patterns, rather than men who aren't credible and men who are two-dimensional. Women know what women's lives are like. We live them all the time. We don't need to be told that there are men who patronize you and pat you on the bottom. What we need to know is that men could change, and men need to see that, too. I think sometimes men need to understand men. I'm afraid a lot of women discuss men very nastily — they tend to laugh at men, whereas when men talk about women they go into the sexual thing. They are both forms of destruction.

I'll talk about John in *Diplomatic Wives*, because he is the most recent man I've created. He is in a sense a slightly externally perceived man. He is based on all the diplomats I've ever met or all the men that I've ever met that work for the British Council, a sort of composite figure of all those. It's how men in those positions of authority do behave. But I don't think that John is a particularly unsympathetic character: he's making hugely wrong decisions, and I understand Christine's frustration with him, but in a sense he is ignorant. He doesn't look. That doesn't mean he is wicked: he is ignorant, and it's the ignorance that has to be changed. Any form of liberation is about education.

I like writing men. There are three men in *Salonika* and I am very proud of scene in the play where the three of them talk together. However, it is the women's play. Men don't actually control the play the way the women do. One of the most pleasing reviews I've ever had was a review of *Real Estate* which said something like 'Louise Page writes such good male characters'. Now this coming from a male reviewer was thrilling: it's my favourite review really. But almost everything I've ever written has been about the lives of women and the world which women inherit.

Diplomatic Wives *reminds me thematically of your radio play,* Housewives. *But that was a much tougher play: this is rather quiet and defeatist. The two women in* Diplomatic Wives *in the end accept the fact that they cannot react to the situation, that most of the times they are forced or led into a decision. There are no other options.*

It's like that because it is true: for those two women because of who they are, there aren't. In the England of today I think it's true of a woman like

Christine who is very intelligent, who has a good job, to find the pressures put on her because she is a woman at times too difficult to take. But she is very clear on why she is frustrated and what the problems are.

In that sense I would hope it is a teaching play, because the lines are very clear, and I would hope in that way that it is a play of internal discussion for the audience, so that men seeing it would say 'yes, I suppose this is true — I do expect a woman to come from the office and to have changed and to look nice.' So it is a play of illustration. You can use the word Brechtian about it — it is one of those plays that sets out very clearly to *show*.

There is also a point for a lot of women in the audience that they would be terrified by the notion of the superwoman: going to the office at eight in the morning, and coming back at seven at night, entertaining their husband's business friends and cooking wonderful meals and having children and driving all the children to their piano lessons and their ballet lessons. It's terrifying, that notion, for a lot of women...

I am very bored with seeing the sort of high-powered, high flying women who seem to be having it all but are cracking up because they haven't had it emotionally. And then there's the other side of the coin, which is the woman who walks out on her husband because she is not intellectually fulfilled. One of the things I was trying to do in *Diplomatic Wives* was to reconcile those two things. I don't think the men have had very pleasant lives either.

It's also a play about the fatigue of the feminist movement. The feminist movement has inevitably become tired of fighting and battling and constantly having to explain. Nothing is more awful than constantly having to explain to people, to men, that this is how life is and that it is unfair because you know half the time they don't listen and then you have to explain it again and they don't actually want to hear.

I think I am becoming more and more interested as a writer in contradictions. Christine is a contradiction: she has changed her mind about certain things very much in the way the feminist movement has. Fifteen years ago children were very unfashionable in the feminist movement: they weren't accepted and they weren't really part of the debate, whereas now they are, because women have realized that having children is very fulfilling and that it's a pleasure they can have out of life. Then there is the frustration about childcare, and the sharing and the fathering.

But that's the strength of feminism — the fact that it changes and regroups and runs constant guerilla warfare. The other great strength of feminism is its contradictions: the fact that there are women who are working through separatist politics and other things is very important, very strengthening, because each area does and should inform the other. The most important thing about feminism is that the debate continues, that it's had to come to terms with its racism, ageism, homophobia and so on.

I am very weary of people who say to you: 'Oh, we would like you to write a play because you are a feminist and we need a play about a woman's issue', because that is ghettoizing feminism, which is a dangerous thing. You end up with men telling you how you should think because you're a feminist! And those men think they are liberated. Certainly in the theatre, feminism is not as popular as it was. There was a sort of fashion, just as there has been a fashion for black writers, Asian writers, and so on.

I don't like it when I go to conferences, and they say, 'Here is so-and-so to discuss his work, and so-and-so is here too to discuss his work, and Louise Page is here to discuss problems of women in theatre.' This says that my work is about a problem rather than it being about my work, and that it is in some ways inferior. Nobody ever says somebody like Howard Brenton or David Edgar 'is here to talk about the problems of being a man in the theatre.' It never gets discussed like that. Constantly talking about the problems like that is a way of censoring the work. If all you can see is the problem, how do you do the work?

There's a problem when women start writing the plays that women are expected to write because many of the issues confronting the world are more frightening than that and they are bigger than just writing about women being oppressed. Things are more desperate. You have to write about big issues, but I don't think in this day and age you can write the plays that were written at the beginning of the seventies, those big agit-prop plays, because there is no point any longer preaching to the converted. We've got to find a way of convincing the people who aren't convinced.

I think it is impossible to explain to all the people unless you take them on an emotional journey. I don't mean the emotional journeys of the late sixties when it was all emotion and that wasn't backed up. We have to find a way of reconciling the two. There is a huge need for plays that are not only about the head but are also about the heart and the things that move people. Emotion is an incredibly powerful weapon and the theatre has to use it.

Have you ever thought of writing a really subversive play, a radical utopian play in terms of a feminist or socialist ideology?

I would hope all the work is in a sense subversive. I certainly think *Real Estate* is a subversive play, in that it says that the mother should be free to live her own life and not to bring up the grandchild. But a lot of people's response to *Real Estate* is 'here is a woman who doesn't support the right of women who don't have partners to have children'. And I support Jenny's right absolutely to do that, but I don't support her right to do it and expect her mother to change the nappies.

I wish I could believe in a theatre where everybody would rush out and start changing the world, but I don't think that's possible, certainly in the theatre in Britain. What theatre can do is act as a catalyst that can influence people — change their lives because they suddenly see that there are other ways of doing things, and then they begin to think, reflect on the world around them.

I've just begun to read feminist science fiction, and I am quite interested in the notion of writing a feminist piece of science fiction. I'm afraid the future is quite bleak — for example, Margaret Atwood's notion, in *The Handmaid's Tale*, that the world is so ecologically polluted that very few women will be able to have children, and therefore the ability to have children becomes again a weapon of oppression.

You have to be very careful about saying, 'well here's an utopia', because it is unfair to give people an utopia without giving them a map. You need also to tell them how the utopia is achievable. It is very important that as a writer you try and point out ways that people can begin to do the changing. You have to know how to achieve the utopia. You have to know what the utopia is in order to be able to find it.

Elizabeth Sakellaridou
Interview recorded in Greece in September 1988 while Louise Page was preparing the film adaptation of
Salonika. Edited in 1995 by Lizbeth Goodman.

ANNIE CASTLEDINE

Annie Castledine was Artistic Director of the Northern Studio Theatre, associate Artistic Director of Theatr Clwyd in Wales, and Artistic Director at the Derby Playhouse. She has also worked as a television producer, and is editor of Volumes 9, 10, and 11 in Methuen's Plays by Women *series.*

Does gender matter in the theatre?

There is no categorical answer to whether gender affects the way that women work and makes their way of working different from men's. Some women, because of their values, beliefs and strong sense of fair play, will work differently from authoritarian, tyrannical males. On the other hand, I have known some women take on what I would call a male persona and work in exactly the same way as men. In fact there are many women, certainly those who began in the fifties and sixties, who have had so few women role-models that they have taken examples of how to behave and how to direct from men.

You mentioned the fifties and sixties. Are you aware that the position of women in the theatre has changed over the past few decades ?

You can't discuss this idea of change in isolation from the society in which we live. One development is that women directors have become more consciously present, but the way in which they are treated is perhaps no different.

Then, I would say that a lot of women collude with men in the way that they allow the status quo to be maintained. I saw a very interesting example of that recently, where a woman in a position of power was talking to a very prominent male director on the telephone, and her role with him was flirtatious, commiseratory, indulgent and enabling. When she put the telephone down, and turned to me, an equally prominent director, but a female, her manner was quite different.

Are you conscious of directing as a woman?

I'm always conscious of being a woman, but I'm not consciously doing things because I'm a woman.

But do you think that in practice you might pick out issues which are important to women, or that perhaps you choose to direct plays by women or about women?

I've always chosen to devote one aspect of my working life to promoting and nursing plays by women through into a major arena, because I believe that if I didn't do that, a lot of women's work would not be produced. I can give examples all the way through my working life: I have promoted work by Maureen Lawrence, Sheila Yeger, Claire Luckham, Jane Beeson, Gerlind Reinshagen, Elfreida Jelineck, Bette Muller, Endesha Ida Mae Holland (a black woman writer from the States) ... the roll-call is endless.

What criteria determine your choices of play to direct?

As a freelancer, I am often *asked* to direct, and what will influence me will be whether I think it is a great play, or has wonderful things to say. Or, it may be a flawed piece, but I will still want to do it because I want to experiment. I am very eclectic and I constantly choose plays which enable me to push the boundaries of form and practice.

You also edit plays. Is that part of your project of promoting women's writing ?

Yes, it is a way of enabling women's writing to be visible and to be *there* so that other people can direct it.

My priorities for my choice of plays are always: are these great plays? And do they withstand the classic tests to which I would subject the work of Ibsen and Shakespeare and other great male writers? Those are the only plays by women that I am interested in directing. I am heartily sick of volumes of plays being called 'Plays by Women', actually. I think we should be reaching a state where we can take for granted that any volume of plays will contain an equal number of plays by men and by women.

What priorities and criteria do you use when you edit the plays, for example, when you write introductions or notes?

I use the same criteria as any experienced theatre-goer or intellectual might use, and I also ask the women themselves to contribute, so that their work and their voices are represented, in their own words, as well as in the plays themselves.

Do you feel strongly either for or against collaborating with other women in the theatre?

I collaborate with men and with women. Most of my assistant directors have been women, because I wanted to enable women who passionately wanted to direct. My great collaborations have been with Sue McLennan, Annabel Arden (we are about to do *The Women of Troy* at the National Theatre together). But I have also had assistant directors who were men, and sometimes I prefer to work with a male collaborator: I am currently enjoying my collaboration with Simon McBerney.

In what circumstances would you prefer male to female collaborators ?

It depends upon the nature of the work, and collaborators are chosen specifically because of the nature of the work. It's an evolutionary process as opposed to a positive discriminatory process. My collaboration with Biyi Bandele Thomas, a black writer who is now becoming very prominent, was a great joy to me. He chose me and asked me to direct his play *Marching for Fansa*. My collaboration with Stephen Daldry on bringing the Fleisser[1] plays to production was based on a shared passion for those plays.

How would you define 'feminism'?

I would define feminism as being highly conscious that women's role in society is very undernourished, continuously under threat, that the feminine principle is not understood and is very often feared, and that, on the whole, women's perceptions and views are not encouraged or respected. I would describe my own feminism as trying to make sure that that does not happen whenever I am concerned, or have the power to affect a piece of work.

Do you see yourself as a feminist director in any way?

Of course I am a feminist director, although the label is inadequate. I am what I am, so I carry all those thoughts and philosophies into every piece of work that I do.

Do you think that feminism has had an effect upon the theatre?

Yes, I think it has had an impact on the theatre in the sense that it has had an impact on certain theatre workers — writers, directors, actors — male and female. So you get Gillian Hanna, or Liz Mansfield, or male practitioners too, like Stephen Daldry, Neil Bartlett, who are conscious of feminism, and the fact that they are conscious informs every bit of work that they do.

Do you think that theatre can affect social change?

I believe theatre can and should affect social change; otherwise I don't think I'd be involved in it. Very powerful pieces of theatre always affect

---

[1] *Pioneers in Ingolstadt* and *Purgatory in Ingolstadt*, The Gate Theatre, London, 1991.

the individuals' attitude towards the world they live in and towards their fellow human beings — more compassion and understanding are developed, and a decision not to subscribe to certain beliefs can carry through into individual lives. I don't necessarily think theatre affects world movements on a huge scale, but I certainly think it affects world movements on a domestic scale.

What do you think the future is for women in the theatre in the UK?

Theatre has to be very carefully nurtured: it is a very delicate form of art and it is under threat. People want reassuring theatre, which is why Shakespeare and physical theatre are very successful. On the other hand I have also seen responsible, conscience-stricken theatre having an intense effect upon the public. That intensity is required in the theatre of the future. We need theatre which engages not only the intellect but also the emotions, and which is superbly done. Skills have to be highly nurtured and honed for theatre to be an exhilarating experience.

Do you think that the present climate can nurture theatre?

If you are talking about government policy, then of course it's not nurturing it. But theatre is happening despite government policy. Often when an art form is under seige it tends to rise to the surface with huge flamboyance and that is what is happening now.

Finally, looking back over your career, do you see any through-lines which are feminist, or perhaps female or feminine?

The through-line in my career is the fact that I am always trying to experiment with form and in how to reach an audience. There is nothing specifically female about that: Robert Lepage, Peter Stein, Simon McBerney and Theatre de Complicité are doing that too.

But, I should think that I have chosen many many more plays by women to direct than anybody else living in the theatre world. Is that just an accident?

Jane de Gay
Interview recorded on audiotape, London, November 1994.

TASHA FAIRBANKS

Performer and writer Tasha Fairbanks has been involved in theatre for 20 years. She worked with Sidewalk Theatre and Gay Sweatshop before co-founding the lesbian feminist Siren Theatre Company in 1979. She has been a freelance playwright since 1987 and worked with Sphinx and Monstrous Regiment and Graeae (Theatre of and for the Disabled and Differently Abled). She has also written screenplays for television. While her work continues into the 1980s and 1990s, her interview is included in this section because the issue of funding for lesbian theatre which Fairbanks describes is informative to many of the other interviews which follow.

Does gender matter in the theatre?

Yes, of course. It's a huge subject. Where do I start? I feel discriminated against and this affects my position to bring about change. Men are in control in the theatre and it is the male experience which is mythologized in plays. As a woman one is set in the periphery or in opposition. Theatre is my way of trying to effect change, of examining my gender position—not that I entered theatre because of this, but the work clarifies and focuses my views on gender. I began working in community theatre and mixed groups. I discovered that women were struggling with certain issues even in the socialist groups: it was OK to discuss equal pay but not sexuality. Making theatre was an enormous struggle, but essential to the process of investigating new ways of perceiving things, of fighting the mechanisms of power.

It was crucial for me to look at my position as a lesbian in theatre. Theatre was a focus for radicalization. It gave me a lot of strength. I could make statements — even though theatre is often a frustrating arena in which to fight.

Are you aware that the position of women in the theatre has changed in any way over the years?

For a while I thought so. In the seventies and early eighties — especially in political theatre, as it's called, I thought there was progress being made. Women were strong and vocal. There were many forums and joint actions could often be taken. Now all this has gone and the position of women has suffered. The funding has gone from the places where women had power in theatre, partly as a result of negative criticism or a *lack* of criticism of women's work. In the mainstream theatre, the few women playwrights there are carrying the hopes and dreams of all women. There are fewer and fewer arenas for women. Most actresses I know are unemployed, and there is so much ageism and racism in the theatre. There is very little money for lesbian theatre, and new writing is not supported. Currently most plays produced (and subsidized or sponsored) are 'classics' or new versions of 'classics' or adaptations of novels.

Siren was a grass roots theatre. We hardly had any funding, so we lived mainly on income support. The wages were terrible but we survived for well over ten years on adrenalin and love and the guarantee-against-loss funding for our regional tours. Now we don't keep going, because in this climate, on such little money, you can't.

Are you conscious of writing and performing as a woman?

I'm white and lesbian and these positions inform everything I write and do, and the things I want changed. In Siren everything we did mattered. We exerted control over every aspect of the process. We did everything ourselves. Very often the male technicians were amazed that we had our own female technicians. We set up our own sound and played the instruments ourselves. That gave us both a lot of power and a lot of vulnerability. We were once attacked (physically) after a show. As women, especially as lesbian women, we could and did incense others by our aim of taking control. We operated on so many levels; to many women we were a real support, we gave courage and strength. We created real debate. Very often the heterosexual couples in our audiences would be arguing after a show!

Could you give an example of a show and the reaction it received?

Mama's Gone a-Hunting, our first full-length show, posited the idea that women should leave Planet Earth until men decided to change. The show would often start very heated debates in the bar afterwards. At that time, in 1980–82, the idea that women could choose to be without men was a 'hot' topic, which was framed in the compulsory heterosexuality debate in, for instance, papers by Adrienne Rich and others.

Do you feel strongly either for or against working collaboratively with other women in the theatre?

Obviously I'm for. The best work for me is with other women, showing what it is to be a woman and a lesbian woman (or able and disabled women, as in my work with Graeae). My experiences in mixed groups have been different. The dynamics are different — women are usually so much stronger emotionally. I think women are more able to deal with a group process. They're more mature. Often the women end up mothering the men. The clarity is more evident in women's groups. The private space is strong and more can be explored. In Siren we were able to delve deeply into issues like class and sexuality, for instance, to look at a lot of the personal pain around these issues, as well as treating them to a radical political analysis during the process of devising new material.

How would you define 'feminism'?

I'd define feminism as being something to do with the repositioning of those of us who are marginalized. Feminism challenges the universality of male experience.

It celebrates that difference. It says that this experience as a woman, a black woman, a lesbian woman, a disabled woman is just as valid. It shifts the male position from centre stage and fractures it.

According to your own definition, would you call yourself a feminist?

Yes. Everything I do tries to tackle that universality. The way I live. Everything.

Would you say that feminism has affected the theatre in any major way?

It's important to hang on to the fact that it has. Feminism may, at times, seem to be in shreds. But there has been change. In the mainstream theatre there's been some change but it gets diluted and then all but crushed by 'post-feminism'. Even what has been achieved is negligble. I myself am in a divided state about what has changed. We have lesbians on *Brookside* [a popular British soap opera] and I suppose this exposure is good. Ten years ago this wasn't possible. People are far more aware of women's issues. Male playwrights have to think before they plunge into a male world, as they used to, and call it 'universal'. Women playwrights have more assertiveness but no money. I'm trying hard not to be discouraged, but it's a real effort to remain positive. Feminism has made most people look at issues they wouldn't have looked at before. People have questioned their ways of being and behaving, but how much of that questioning is cosmetic? I suppose even if this kind of self-examination isn't from the heart, it still has its place in that it encourages the challenging of sexist, racist and homophobic conduct. I still feel that a lot of it's just lip-service. Where are the money and the access for women in theatre? The power must be wrested from men. It must still be fought for.

Do you believe that the theatre can affect social change?

Certain kinds of theatre can affect social change. The closer you are to the experience and aspirations of your audiences, the more likely you are to affect change. I see theatre as a meeting-point, a coming together. Siren toured outside London throughout the 1980s to places where women really fought to get us a forum for our shows. You could see that our visits were very important, a source of strength and encouragement. In small towns many woman find it difficult to talk about their sexuality or to be heard, so we started debates after the performances. Many women came up to us after our shows and told us they were lesbians, but that they had never been able to say so to anyone before. Our public expression encouraged other expression. Siren looked very deeply at issues. We were very radical in that we talked of lesbianism as a political choice. For instance, in our play *Curfew*, we named and located male violence and women's revolt and created a new theatrical context for it. In our show *Pulp*, we explored 'male' and 'female' roles, masculine and feminine characteristics and character types.

What's the future for women in the theatre in the UK?

Where do you start? We have to take control out of men's hands and get the big money. The big problem for women is always poverty. Women's new writing has no money at all. We need money, expertise and stages. So many women have written plays and don't know what to do with them. You can't progress as a playwright until you get dramaturgical input, workshops and small productions. When are the generation of David Hares going to die?! He and his like have all the resources tied up. Theatre is producing stipends for old people. We need strategies. We probably need death squads!! Theatre is poor and getting poorer and women are at the bottom end of the economy. There are no places to send plays anymore. I'm saying goodbye to theatre as it's not possible for me to continue. My bereavement is enormous as is my anger and frustration. My hope is frustrated: hope for my career and for any kind of real change. I've been fighting for twenty years and I'm retiring reluctantly — kicking and shouting — but I'm going for the sake of my sanity. My creative energies are going towards working with people in a different way.

We need the energy of people starting up in the theatre, new to the theatre. The more positive and uppity they are, the better. After ten years of Thatcherism, many of my contemporaries have left the theatre as well. I have to channel my energies now. What kept me going was a sense of solidarity. I hope new writers will confront political agendas with ferocity and depth and commitment to instigate change. I hope they don't forget that we (those of us

5.   Jude Winter in *Pulp* by Tasha Fairbanks for Siren (1985). The Drill Hall, London; photographer: Anita Corbin.

who started working in British theatre in the 1970s) were there, have been through a lot, and have a lot to say to younger people — that they can learn from us. Sometimes I feel there's a tide coming in and it's obliterating everything we've written in the sand. It's so important that the new generation doesn't buy that. Let's not reinvent that wheel.

Mary Luckhurst and Lizbeth Goodman
Interview by Mary Luckhurst June 1994; revised and expanded by Tasha Fairbanks with
Lizbeth Goodman, January 1995.

GENISTA McINTOSH

Genista McIntosh has been Executive Director of the Royal National Theatre since 1990. Previously, she was at the Royal Shakespeare Company, as Casting Director then Planning Controller, and — after a short period as the director of a theatrical agency — as senior Administrator, and then as Associate Producer.

Does gender matter in the theatre?

The short answer is yes, gender matters everywhere. It doesn't matter any less in the theatre than it matters in any other organization. The longer answer is that it matters in a different way: the theatre is generally a more tolerant and flexible environment than, for example, banking or accountancy. So the extent to which discrimination about people in relation to their gender is visible is probably much less obvious than it is elsewhere.

Does the fact that it is less obvious make it more difficult to do anything about it?

Yes. It has been more difficult certainly until very recently and certainly within some organizations. It's more difficult to get people to accept that there is a problem because the broad culture of theatre is liberal and therefore people don't see themselves, in the main, as behaving in discriminatory ways.

In *this* organization [the Royal National Theatre], because we have a very strong emphasis upon management training, we *do* deal with equal opportunities, we *do* deal with fair selection procedures, we *do* deal with the proper way of managing people and dealing with difficult situations. Although I don't think that training is all there is about it, it does go a long way to helping people to understand their own and other people's behaviour and therefore to deal with things in a structured and rational way.

Is there a lingering sexism (however implicit or unconscious) at work in the major theatres of Britain, such as the Royal National Theatre and the Royal Shakespeare Company?

Yes, but as I have already said (or implied), it's quite subtle and consequently hard to confront.

Has the position of women in theatre changed in any way over the years ?

Oh *hugely! Hugely!* I came in to the theatre properly when I joined the RSC in 1972. At that time, there actually was a woman directing plays —

Buzz Goodbody — but the whole organization was completely dominated by men. Buzz was pretty much at the outer edge of pioneering at that time and, unfortunately, she died two years later by her own hand.

What has happened since then is partly generational. It's not that theatre has changed — though it has — but it's changed in response to a big change in the world. The generation of women who are ten or fifteen years younger than me have had much higher levels of expectation: they have pushed themselves forward and there have been many more of them. So gradually there has been a distinct change in the profile of the National Theatre and of the RSC and probably a number of other major theatres too. There are many many more women directing, designing, producing, though still far fewer than there are men.

What would it take to bring in more women, especially into the upper echelons of those theatre organizations?

More of them achieving positions and experience which make their suitability unarguable — it is finally about numbers. Compare and contrast this with the drive to get more women into Parliament....

Are you conscious being a woman working in the theatre?

It's very hard not to be conscious of that. For most of my working life I have frequently been the only woman in a room full of men where I've been dealing at my own level. It must affect my behaviour but I can't tell how. I try not to behave as a woman in a manipulative way, but of course I can't avoid recognizing that in some ways being the only woman is very helpful.

In what ways? Conversely, how can being the only women be unhelpful?

It's helpful because at least you get noticed, even if it's for the wrong reasons. It's *un*helpful in the obvious way: you feel isolated, you *are* isolated and you have to fight your corner much harder.

How would you define 'feminism'?

To me, feminism has meant that I didn't have to live my life the way my mother lived hers. It has meant that I have been able to make choices and haven't felt judged. Of course, not everybody experiences it in that way: I've been fortunate.

Would you call yourself a feminist?

I never have called myself a feminist because I think it makes one a bit of a hostage to fortune. But certainly I have a very strong drive to see established certain principles which will make it impossible for women to be relegated again to a position of subservience or unimportance. That battle is largely won. We are now at a stage where we are finding hidden rather than overt obstacles, of which there are many.

What kinds of hidden obstacles do you mean?

Well, by definition if they are hidden, they're a bit difficult to describe. I would imagine most women are conscious of the daily (but unchallengeable) prejudice that expresses itself most clearly in surprise that you're there (as a woman) at all.

Has feminism affected the theatre significantly?

Feminism has affected the theatre because it has been and intermittently still is a strong political force. And theatre has always been partly a means of expressing political ideas. It's also quite clear that women writers, directors and designers are all expressing themselves and many of them want to make their points specifically from a feminine perspective. Its influence has also meant that we no longer regard it as unusual to listen with equal care to what women say.

Do you think that the theatre can affect social change?

Oh yes, I think it does, but not directly. The theatre is inevitably partly a reflection of what is going on around us, but because it deals with ideas, it can feed ideas into an audience quite insidiously in a way which can eventually effect a change cumulatively. I don't believe that there have been great theatre productions which have changed the world, but I think that the theatre is very important as a means of locating the spirit of an age, at a point of change.

How do you see the future of theatre and women's theatre in the UK?

I don't see the future of theatre in Britain for anybody as particularly bright. Therefore, I don't see it as particularly bright for women. The theatre is in a very difficult position at the moment. It can't any longer attract mass audiences, except in certain very narrow fields, and it's becoming more and more difficult to keep a continuous flow of work coming. There isn't the political will to keep on resourcing it. Fewer and fewer people will be able to make a decent living out of working in the theatre, and so fewer and fewer women will be able to do so. I don't feel terribly optimistic, but on the other hand I don't think that theatre will ever die.

What do you see as the biggest problem facing women in the theatre ?

The thing that preoccupies me now is not how women can rise and pursue positions of influence but how they can get to be genuinely in charge.

I don't run this organization: the man sitting in the next-door office [Richard Eyre] is director of the theatre and although he and I work together he's the one everybody thinks about. Nearly all the major arts institutions in the UK are run by men. Women may get promoted to quite senior levels, but that last step is very hard to take. I think it has a lot to do with the constitution of boards and a general political belief that women can be jolly jolly good, but that the chaps are still the bosses — that's going to be much harder to shift.

Do you believe that this attitude could shift in years to come?

Yes, I believe it can and I believe it will, but it will take more time than it should and there will be hand-to-hand fighting along the way. Just look at some of the 'backlash' evidence from the USA, and consider how easily it could start emerging here.

Jane de Gay
Interview recorded on audiotape London, July 1994, revised by post February 1995.

MICHELENE WANDOR

Michelene Wandor is a playwright, poet and critic. Her plays include The Wandering Jew *(National Theatre 1987), as well as 'alternative' work with early women's theatre groups including Gay Sweatshop, Women's Theatre Group and Monstrous Regiment. For Sweatshop, Wandor scripted the landmark play* Care and Control *(1977). Her work for radio includes dramatizations of* The Brothers Karamazov, Jane Eyre *and* The Jungle Book; *and her adaptation of* The Belle of Amhurst *for Thames TV won an international Emmy Award. Her books on theatre and sexual politics include* Carry On, Understudies *and* Look Back in Gender *(Routledge).*

Does gender matter in the theatre?

Yes. People think they can understand the question about *women* because they immediately think about discrimination or whether there are good parts for women, but if you ask the question about *gender*, it means people have to think about the working relationship between men and women and how that operates, which means they actually do have to have some kind of overview.

In terms of theatre, it matters on two levels. First, it matters in the sense that there is something to think about, and a comment to be made on the gender distribution in the workforce, and then the different reasons why. Second, gender matters aesthetically in two senses: one is the material of theatre (drama, plays, shows) — how maleness and femaleness are represented within those works of art. The other is how that contributes to what a play is about and what it says. That is as true of performance art, music and opera, as of text-based drama.

Are you aware that the position of women has changed in the last few years?

I think it has changed marginally, in small ways, but not fundamentally, not in the structure of the way theatre works. The content of drama has changed to a degree: there are a lot more women playwrights whose work is published, so that's good, but they still form a relative minority. There are a few more women directors working than before, but again they are still a minority. Drama schools still turn out almost an equal ratio of men to women graduates, but on the whole, as far as I can tell, there is still more varied work for male performers. Actresses in their forties and over still very often find that there aren't enough good parts for women of their age.

Why do you think that is so?

The social institutions that produce art are absolutely part and parcel of the fabric of society as a whole. Looking across the board, the status of women in a very general sense has 'improved' in that women working at all levels are an accepted part of the fabric. But when it comes to basic power decisions, the important decisions are still made by men. The institutions that produce art are *industries* — the entertainment industries, the cultural industries — and they are very similar to other industries; they have their own power balances. The market operates in similar ways wherever you are.

Are you conscious of writing and working as a woman, and if so, in what way?

It comes and goes, there are good and bad things. I do more radio writing at the moment than other kinds of drama and that is very mixed. On the whole it works very well, but every so often there is somebody who assumes that I am only interested in 'women's subjects', in women writers, and that's not true. The awareness of the input of gender is fantastically exciting but it can be a limitation. Each of us comes to what we do probably without thinking about whether we are male or female: we go for what interests us. Gender is one of a whole number of factors — social, economic, individual and cultural, racial and linguistic — which inform our world-view.

Do you feel strongly for or against working collaboratively with other women in the theatre?

I try not to make assumptions, because gender is only one factor in our world-view. For example, I don't assume that I only want to work with women directors, because that is where professional skill and other bits of the world-view come into play. The people you work well with are people with whom you can have a rapport, based on a number of things, not simply gender. You may strike up an immediate rapport with another woman when you are working together, and then, if there are class differences, or racial differences, problems with ambition or power, or political differences, you can suddenly find that there's a block. Looking back, the strand of radical feminism that was very influential, very important at the beginning of the seventies quite rightly asserted that the important thing for women was to work together, and bond and find ways to collaborate, but that often covered over the differences that made working together difficult.

I have had working experiences with men which have been awful; I have had some which have been very very good. I have had working experiences with women which have been dreadful, as exploitative as with men; I have had some that have worked very well.

How would you define 'feminism'?

I think it is particularly risky at the moment to try and define feminism, because the sense of any feminist movement has very much dissipated.

But it may be true to say there are very strong feminist impulses in all sorts of women, whether they see themselves as political or not. One is the desire for self-determination. You do not want to be blocked off, discriminated against, confined, just because you are a woman: you want the same range of options as the men around you. Being seen to be equally valid is a very strong impulse, but it doesn't exist as a political force unless women themselves organize together, with or without the support or involvement of men.

But as long as there are societies in which the relative positions of men and women are different within their particular classes and social groupings, there are always going to be feminist impulses and there is always going to be a need for feminism and feminist argument to change things. And there will be power struggles between men and women.

According to your own definition would you call yourself a feminist?

Yes, obviously, but I worry about what that means to other people. Perhaps it would be a threat for some people if I said I considered myself a feminist. I just don't know how people respond to it, particularly since there isn't anything you can identify as a feminist movement.

But of course I am a feminist because, like lots of other women, I still need to be feminist because we still need to ask questions of gender and the position of women. Not every second of the day, but where it counts, and it's there in our work in different ways.

Would you say that feminism has affected the theatre in any major way?

No, I don't think it has in any major way, but it has affected it in lots of important minor ways. The major way would be (and this is utopian) if all theatres had a policy which was strategically planned ahead to make sure that any new work they did had a parity between male and female playwrights. The same applies to directors: that where possible they try to cast equally. Now, it's easy to say that because most theatres have to survive on a diet of work that is traditional and accepted, and the traditional canon of theatre employs on the whole more men than women.

What are the 'minor' ways in which feminism has affected the theatre ?

A handful of women directors and playwrights are known and highly respected. There is a large-ish group of actresses now in their middle years who are still working — although they are very much aware of the relatively few roles available to them. But it is not enough. It is not 50%.

Do you believe that the theatre can affect social change?

Yes and no. Theatre does appear to move people very powerfully — it can provoke you, it can challenge you, it can upset you, it can make you think. But theatre is not a political organization — it can ally itself with politics, it can have politics as part of its staff, it can be politically very self-conscious, but it's not where political decisions are made. So it impinges on social change, it can affect social change, but it's not executive in it.

Feminists made a lot of noise during the seventies, and believed that if only they could convince enough people, then things would change. But it has become very obvious that while art is a very important part of the social fabric, it's not the political decider.

What is the future for women in the theatre in England or the UK?

During the 1970s there were some active groupings of women — theatre groups, conferences, etc. This generated a whole range of work, and boosted women's confidence. The fact that these organizations no longer exist means that there has been some progress — some awareness and change. But there is a long way to go.

It depends on women. It has got to be a bit easier than it was, but I would be very cautious about saying it's going to be alright in ten years. We may find that we will be equally represented and there won't be any need for books like this, but I can envisage quite easily that in ten years' time we may need another book of interviews. That's not pessimism, it may be a recognition that gender differences are part of the fundamental social structure and it still will take a while to rock those. It's a very delicate thing, a very difficult thing to do.

Gabriella Giannachi and Lizbeth Goodman
Telephone interview by Gabriella Giannachi, September 1994; transcribed and edited by Jane de Gay,
revised by Michelene Wandor with Lizbeth Goodman, January 1995.

PART II

FEMINIST STAGES

OF THE 1980s

INTRODUCTION

In the 1980s, a new generation of women playwrights took up their pens (or word processors): Sarah Daniels, Heidi Thomas, Clare McIntyre, Sharman MacDonald, Jackie Kay, Winsome Pinnock, Charlotte Keatley and Deborah Levy began to write different kinds of 'feminist theatre'. Plays by women which included parts for men began to be replaced with all-women's plays, or with forms of theatre work which focused on women's relationships to each other, rather than to men or family. As the decade wore on, more women's plays reached audiences through two different routes: a few plays by women were produced by most of the 'mainstream theatres' — in seasons of work including mainly the work of male playwrights and the 'classics' — while a great deal of women's work was taken up and produced by women's collectives, female directors, and specifically feminist theatre groups and organisations. Women's Theatre Group and Monstrous Regiment remained strong and Siren (a small-scale lesbian collective) became known, as did Scarlet Harlets, Red Ladder and many other companies — mostly small scale and largely unfunded or project funded only, so that individual productions could not be developed and followed through in terms of a developing company profile.

Some new plays were written, though not all benefited from a working knowledge of the legacy of previous generations. Charlotte Keatley's play *My Mother Said I Never Should* used a title very similar to one of the first plays of the Women's Theatre Group; the similarity is interesting in its reliance on oral story-telling culture (a childhood rhyme often repeated by young girls in Britain), yet also indicative of the relative dearth of writing about women's work.

Methuen launched the *Plays by Women* series, with the first volumes edited by Michelene Wandor and later volumes edited by Mary Remnant. The first major studies of women's work in theatre also began to be published in this period (see list of suggested further reading p. 13). In addition, the second half of the decade witnessed an ingenious publishing strategy which benefited women enormously: The Royal Court Theatre began to sell programmes including the texts of the plays produced. It was this initiative which first made plays by Sarah Daniels, Clare McIntyre and Timberlake Wertenbaker familiar to a wide audience.

The many important developments in the networking of women's theatre in the period include the establishment of The Women's Playhouse Trust by Jules Wright, and founding of The Magdalena Project by Jill Greenhalgh. A short-lived Women's Project within the Royal Shakespeare Company also developed, culminating in the production of Deborah Levy's play *Heresies*, directed by Lily Susan Todd, while many smaller and less well-publicized women's and feminist companies also developed. Women's Theatre Group's organization of The Glass Ceiling Events — a series of talks and conferences with women in theatre — was important, bringing together theorists and academics and journalists with playwrights, directors, actors, critics and people interested in women's roles in theatre.

Devolution of funding to the regions had a major impact on the development of all theatre work, including women's work, particularly in the last few years of the decade. Apart from the inevitable reduction of numbers of active members in theatre companies and the closing of many companies and venues altogether, a shift of some performers to the 'screen' from the stage and thankfully, back again began in earnest in this period. Juliet Stevenson, Fiona Shaw and Harriet Walter are, for example, known for their 'on camera' performances, as well as for their continuing commitment to the stage.

In addition, a range of cultural/political events had an impact on the theatre. Notably, the passing of Clause 28, restricting the 'promotion of homosexuality' in theatre and arts within educational and other establishments, affected the representation of lesbian and gay issues in the theatre — especially touring theatre and TIE (Theatre in Education).

Lizbeth Goodman

SARAH DANIELS

One of Britain's leading women playwrights, Sarah Daniels' work includes Masterpieces, Byrthrite, The Devil's Gateway, Neaptide, Beside Herself, The Gut Girls *and* The Madness of Esme and Shaz, *produced at the Royal Court Theatre Upstairs in 1994. Daniels was the first woman to have a lesbian play,* Neaptide, *staged at the Royal National Theatre (in 1986), while her play* Masterpieces *is one of the most frequently performed feminist plays in many cultures. All her plays are published by Methuen.*

Does gender matter in the theatre? That is, are you aware (as a playwright) that your gender matters either in the way that you're treated by critics, or by directors or actors or audiences?

I don't think that gender matters as much as having the label 'feminist', or being known as someone who writes 'feminist plays' matters. This label of 'feminist playwright' matters because it feeds into the way people see you: it gives them an expectation which is often prejudiced, of yourself or your work. I have mainly worked with women directors, and in all my plays, there are more women actors than there are men, so I've never worked in an environment that's been mostly male.

How would you define 'feminism'?

I suppose feminism is the awareness that we live in a patriarchal society, with a desire to challenge and hopefully change it.

By your own definition, would you define yourself as feminist?

Yes.

There's no question that your work is respected and studied by many women and men who admire its feminist politics, as well as its theatrical values. But you've written quite amusingly about the flexibility of the term 'feminism'...

I said that feminism, like 'panty-girdle', seems to be thought of as a very embarrassing word these days. Today it seems to be connected to restrictive, confining ideas and images and stereotypes. And those associations, unfortunately, do carry over into theatre reviewing.

Have you had particular critical reactions to your plays about the representation of the male characters?

Oh yes. It would probably fill a large volume of books now. Largely, the criticism is either that I can't write for men, or that I don't write enough for men. One of the criticisms of *Beside Herself* (which has the theme of sexual abuse) is that I hadn't taken on board the fact that boys are sexually abused as well. Of course they are, and of course that's quite horrible too. But it's not the point of my play. This kind of criticism of what isn't included, rather than on the obvious focus of a play, is quite common, unfortunately. It comes from people with a point of view that to be a white middle-class educated man is the norm and anything else is 'other'. Women's issues, or a focus on female characters, gets translated into a 'minority issue'. If you don't deal with what the critics see as the majority you are indeed — sorry to use that cliché — marginalized.

In your experience of working in British theatre over the past ten years, has the position of women begun to change, perhaps to improve?

I don't have the statistics, but I think there are more women working in the theatre, and there seem to be more and younger women playwrights coming through than there were ten years ago. I don't quite know how far into the mainstream they're getting, though. Against that, there does seem to be a feeling that we're now living in a 'post-feminist' society, and therefore to bang on about these boring old things is not necessary any more. My view of that is that we can't have post-feminism, because we didn't really get full-blown feminism! There's a postcard which sums it all up (one I sent you a few years ago) — 'Post-feminism: Keep your Bra, Burn your Brain'! [printed on page 12 of this book].

There's another postcard which conveys a similar message: 'I'll be a post-feminist in post-patriarchy.' In these two postcards, as in many of your plays, comedy makes very serious points. And of course, there's the old joke about feminists supposedly lacking a sense of humour. But the serious side of the joke comes into play when we try to work collaboratively in the theatre, especially in producing plays with serious, 'feminist' points. Your plays often deal with serious issues — pornography, reproductive rights, lesbian rights, the exploitation of working class women, incest, madness — and yet they all somehow balance these real issues with a powerful and refreshing humour; a use of language and characterization which makes the work enjoyable as well as thought-provoking. Having sympathetic directors and actors must make a very big difference in the process of getting your work on the stage. Do you feel strongly either for or against working with women directors or working collaboratively?

I've always tried to work with women directors. I feel quite strongly about that, although I have worked with men in circumstances where I haven't had any choice. Having said that, to be fair to the men I've worked with, I have had very good productions and good working experiences.

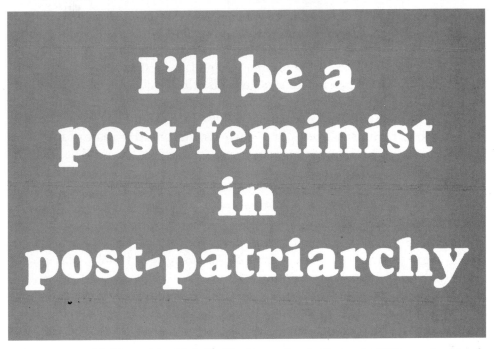

6. Post-Patriarchy postcard by Christine Hankinson (Leeds Postcards, 1991); courtesy Leeds Postcards.

What sets the theatre apart from other art forms?

It's the fact that it's live, performed in front of an audience. Theatre is a collective process in so much as that without each person in their own individual role there wouldn't be a play or a piece of theatre. So for a piece of theatre to work, everybody has to invest their own talent in it — the actor, the director, the designer, the writer and everybody else. When a play or a theatre experience works, it's not because of any one of those individual people or jobs, but because everybody works really well together, making the process work, allowing the play to take off. And when theatre doesn't work (I'm bound to say this because I'm biased) I always think people blame the writer, because with new plays they can't see the difference between directing, writing, designing and acting.

Do you think, in any political or personal sense, that the theatre can actually affect people's lives?

I am a little bit too old to think that the theatre can change lives but I do think it can change or at least affect the way we think, or make us rethink. A play can certainly challenge assumptions, and encourage audiences to examine the way they think or feel about certain issues, and indeed about other people. In terms of 'women's theatre' or 'feminist theatre', you know that I have trouble with these terms, just as I have trouble with the term 'post-feminist'. It seems to me that feminist theatre is out there, it means something, but we only find out what it means when we make it, and watch it. As I've written in my Introduction to *Plays: One* (Methuen, 1991): 'I didn't set out to be a feminist playwright... however I'm proud if some of my plays have added to its influence.'

Lizbeth Goodman
Interview recorded for a BBC-OU audio cassette; updated for publication in December 1995.

POLLY TEALE

Polly Teale is currently Associate Director of Shared Experience Theatre, with Nancy Meckler. Among the plays she has directed are: Babies, Uganda, Mill on the Floss, *(co-directed with Nancy Meckler),* A Taste of Honey, Somewhere, Waiting at the Water's Edge, Manpower, The Stairwell, Flying, Other Voices Other Rooms, What is Seized, Ladies in the Lift *and* Now You See Me. *She has also worked in television, directing* A Better Life Than Mine, *and her own screenplay* Afters. *Among her other written work is* Fallen *(1987), which is published by The Women's Press.*

Your career has spanned a wide range of work, from fringe productions about single women, double-handers, and large-scale work with Shared Experience Theatre. You're also one of the youngest directors, let alone female directors, to have done so much work on the country's main stages. And yet your work is not in any typical sense 'mainstream'. To mention only the productions I've seen over the years: Now You See Me, Fallen, Ladies in the Lift, What is Seized *and now* Babies... *there seems to be a through-line of a 'female focus' running through much of the work. Would you agree?*

Yes, not in all the work, but in a lot of it. Although *Babies* is written by a man, I think the writer is most drawn to the woman in the piece: it is her energy which powers the play. *Mill on the Floss* is an example of a well-known novel adapted for the stage in a way which shows the significance and relevance of that story today: a story of a woman who is supposed to be silent or 'feminine', according to her era and culture, and who has to find ways to express herself within that. So yes, I enjoy exploring female themes in theatre work. That enjoyment has been nurtured in working for the past few years with Nancy Meckler at Shared Experience. Our way of working with actors is very physical, very body-centred and focused on bringing life to performance from within the actors, working with the hidden, the inner life of emotion and imagination which might not be expressed in more naturalistic theatre. That way of working may seem alien to a 'classic' like *Mill on the Floss*, but actually it works quite well when you consider that the story is about a silenced woman.

One of the aims of much feminist work in the theatre, and indeed in feminist theory, is of course to do with giving voice to the silenced among us. So it sounds to me like much of your work is feminist in method, if not necessarily in aim or intent. Now I know how difficult it is to define the term 'feminist', but however you define it for yourself, I wonder whether you believe that there is such a thing as 'feminist theatre'?

I think that all theatre that's female is in some sense feminist; the word came about because there wasn't enough that was female, so if you do something female, with a purpose, it is feminist, whether it's overtly political or not.

Often, the points of conflict in your life are the source of creativity. You become creative when something doesn't work, doesn't make sense, or puzzles you, blocks you... That's the spur to explore, to investigate. With *Babies*, for example, the difficulty that a gay man has in existing in a straight world may not be so different from some of the conflicts we might feel as women trying to express ourselves. I mean, I feel very lucky to be a woman working in the theatre, because it opens up whole areas of work which might be harder to get to if I were a man. Theatre is about intimacy, about the things we hide in everyday life. Perhaps that's easier to get at as a woman.... Of course, everyone works in very particular ways, so this gender dimension may not be always be applicable.

Working as a woman, what kind of dynamic comes into directing work written by men (or performed by men)?

I remember when we started writing copy for *Babies*, what I saw as the centre of the story was the mother's crisis, in the death of her husband: the journey of grief and loss and reawakening as a sexual being which she experiences. But for Jonathan Harvey, the playwright, the centre of the story was the gay man. The play has lots of stories in it, and no one has to be the focus, but the writer had one overview and the director had another. This was healthy. It gave both the male and female stories equal importance.

Babies deals with a gay man, and with a fascinating mix of gay and straight, female and male characters. What attracted you most to the play?

The National Theatre Studio gave the script to me after a workshop. So it chose me in a sense, or it was chosen for me. But it does reflect many of my interests. The play begins with the death of the father, the husband, the man at the centre of the old social order. It was a play about change. About loss but also huge possibilities.

The first piece of work directed by you which I had a chance to see was Fallen, *in 1987.* Fallen *is a play which centres on the case of a missing baby and her mother, accused of murder; a play which deals in politics (the role of women in Irish culture) and feminist politics (reproductive rights, women's rights) to some extent, but which* is basically, first and foremost, a gripping story, based on a 'real life' case. Is the central concern for female politics similar to that in Babies?

Yes and no. I am still drawn to the female in work, but I have grown tired of making that my main focus all the time. When I was younger I used to think a lot more about women's issues. After a while, I felt I was getting repetitive in my discussions with friends, having the same arguments, which I may still believe, but don't need to articulate anymore.

Does that imply that you no longer experience any kind of 'gender pressure' in your work?

What I mean when I say that I don't like to talk about women's issues so much anymore is that I recognize their effect, and my problems with certain kinds of male power. And I know very well that I respond to theatre, and everything, as a woman, but I don't need to focus on it so much. I take it for granted in a way. Interestingly, gay men have written some of the best work about women: Tennessee Williams, Truman Capote, Jean Genet.... In a way, being an 'outsider' can be a powerful position, it lets you look into the world through a different window.

What's the view like from your window? And where is the window situated? Do you see yourself as an outsider or an insider?

Both. The roles always shift, perspectives shift. I'm still young to be working in large, 'main stage' theatres, and I'm a woman. So those factors make me an outsider looking in at the 'big' theatre. But in England there's always the problem of class. It's a commonplace to say that most theatre is still made by white middle-class Oxbridge-educated men. But the commonplace is based on a truth, and that truth is visible from both the inside and the outside.

Perhaps that's why I prefer theatre work which explores inner emotions, rather than external events. I'm interested in what it feels to be a person or character, positioned in some way within a larger scenario or culture. My way of working is about everyone contacting their own emotional life. And that way of working with emotions is a 'leveller'; it brings women and men together. In that environment, the traditional notion that women are more expressive than men ceases to be the case, just as the traditional male assumption of more space and power for themselves doesn't work.

What if either of those traditionally gendered situations was to emerge in one of your workshops?

I would try to explore that difference.

Do you prefer working in the theatre to other media: film, television, for instance?

Definitely. There's a roughness, a rawness, in the theatre. You're in the same space with the performers, and it's all about the effect and the physical presence of people in the same space with each other. It's intimate, human.

Do you think theatre, or live stage work, can be successfully transferred to video or TV?

Well, rarely. It usually goes a bit flat. But there are brilliant exceptions.

Have you got a particular view from your 'window' on whether things are getting any easier for women working in the theatre?

I've had some opportunities which women a few years ago probably wouldn't have had. Does that make me lucky? I believe that if you have confidence you can do anything. Being a woman needn't be a problem, if you focus on your own way of making work, and let that speak for itself. I am lucky to have reaped the benefits of feminism.

There is a general feeling that women directors do well for a while and then don't get promoted, don't move along the career ladder as men do. I know that many women have experienced that, but I haven't yet been frustrated in my own work.

Lizbeth Goodman
Interview recorded on audiotape, London, September 1994.

JULES WRIGHT

Originally from Australia, Jules Wright has worked in British theatre since 1978. She is Artistic Director of the Women's Playhouse Trust (WPT) and also works as a freelance director. She started her theatre career at Stratford East, the home of Joan Littlewood, and has been the Deputy Artistic Director of the Royal Court Theatre and Artistic Director of Liverpool Playhouse. She holds a PhD in Psychology.

What was the idea behind setting up the Women's Playhouse Trust?

It was to redress the balance between men and women working in British mainstream theatre by ensuring that the principal artists — writers, directors, choreographers, composers — employed by the WPT were women, and that resources available to them were equal to those available in the mainstream subsidized sector. The overarching objective was to acquire a theatre base. It was intended to provide opportunities for women in all aspects of theatre, including administration, general management and technical work, too.

A survey of projects in 1994 demonstrates the breadth of work which now gives expression to the original objectives. February: *Shiny Nylon*, commissioned from Anya Gallaccio (visual artist), Deborah Levy (text and direction) and Kristina Page (choreographer) was produced in S-Shed, Royal Docks (a riverside area in South East London). It was shortlisted for the Northern Telecom Arts Europe Award 1994. March/April: *Warning for Life*, a series of education workshops for teachers and pupils led by major British actors. June: *Answers from the Ocean* was commissioned from Shobana Jeyasingh (choreographer), who created the work with pupils from Mulberry School in Tower Hamlets (an inner London borough). August: *Low Level Panic* by Clare McIntyre, originally the subject of a development commission and production by WPT at the Royal Court (1988) and at the Lyric Theatre (1989), was filmed by the BBC. October/November: *The Rover* by Aphra Behn was staged at Jacob Street Film Studios in a collaboration with the BBC and Open University, for screening in 1995. October: WPT commissioned three key British composers to make a song cycle with young people in Tower Hamlets. December: *Leave Taking* by Winsome Pinnock, produced by WPT in 1989 at the Lyric Theatre, was mounted by the National Theatre. It confirmed Winsome as the first black British woman playwright to be produced at the National Theatre.

During 1994, WPT commissioned a song cycle from Deborah Levy, Jackie Kay, Jo Shapcott and Katie Campbell (poets), and Ilona Sekacz, Errollyn Wallen, Ruth Byrchmore, Jane Gardner, Priti Paintal, Roxana Panufnik and Nitin Sawhney (composers), for performance in 1995. They also commissioned Krishna Sobti, one of India's leading novelists, to translate sections of *Mother Courage* into Punjabi.

Our building, a nineteenth-century warehouse in Islington, is currently being restored and we will move there in mid-1995. It will provide several studios and an office which we will share with a number of similarly-sized companies.

And what are the plays you've produced?

We began with Aphra Behn's *The Lucky Chance* at the Royal Court, which I consider was the recovery of Behn's work in performance: the first production of the work for two hundred and fifty years. We then went on to commission a series of writers: those who have become household names include Winsome Pinnock, Sarah Daniels and Clare McIntyre. WPT sometimes mounts classics, some of which have been written by men, but the company always commissions a new translation from a woman writer. For example, Ibsen's *The Lady From the Sea*, in a new version by Heidi Thomas, was seen at the National Theatre of Norway, as well as in London.

Since 1992, WPT has diversified. I became acutely aware that female visual artists and contemporary composers have an equally tough time. This led to WPT commissioning a new opera from an increasingly important composer — Nicola LeFanu, who has just become the first Professor of Music in the UK. It was her first full-scale opera. We continue to work with Anya Gallaccio, and also commission a range of new dance pieces.

This is exciting work because it informs WPT's work with text. My own work with choreographer Kristina Page elaborated the physical life of Nicola's opera, while Maya Krishna Rao's input as a choreographer and Kathakali dancer distinguished her performance as the Courtesan in *The Rover*. The physical life of her performance conveyed a world larger and more profound than the text alone could do.

This extension of WPT's focus is the most important development in the company's artistic policy since 1990.

Your work with the WPT in the 1990s has pioneered site-specific performances, and multi-media performances. Do you find the use of unusual spaces and working methods particularly liberating for women?

I believe that women construct stories in a way which is fundamentally different from the way in which men tell stories. The structure

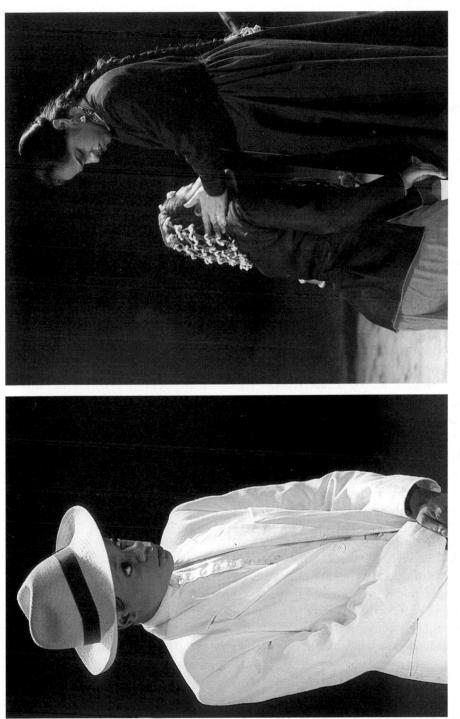

7. Two images from *The Rover* by Aphra Behn, directed by Jules Wright for the Women's Playhouse Trust (Open University/BBC video, 1995 — produced by Tony Coe); photographer: Trevor White

is less linear. I believe that it often demands spaces which are less constricting than conventional proscenium arch spaces. Therefore I do find such spaces more apposite for work by women, especially when the work involves a number of artists from different disciplines. In any event, unconventional spaces demand different ways of telling stories and liberate the creators from straight narrative forms. Importantly, the commonplace conviction that women write or create for small spaces is wholly untrue.

In 1994, you produced Aphra Behn's The Rover, *another important contribution to 'women's theatre' in Behn's day and ours. What were your aims with that production?*

Behn writes about violence towards women, female oppression and women's drive to evade the constraints of a patriarchal world. The historical distance created by mounting *The Rover* allows us to look objectively at the degree to which we have internalized our cultural conditioning. On a more positive note, it shows how urgent and long-standing is the female desire for emancipation. I wanted to place the violence which Behn represents, directly, even confrontationally on stage. I hoped that the production would disclose how integral to our behaviour such ways of thinking are, and in recognizing it to know what must be confronted. The cast was multi-racial, making a link I hope between male violence in all its manifestations, including colonization. There is a whisper of recurrent themes in the way our behaviours replicate the past which must be understood in order to alter them.

Now for the broad overview question: does gender matter in the theatre?

Absolutely. Gender is fundamental, and alters the way stories are told. For example, Lady Percy has one very small scene in *Henry the Fourth: Part One*. Percy is going to fight: he subsequently dies. Its an extraordinary scene — Lady Percy wants him to decide *not* to go. She refers to herself, her love for him, their children and his responsibilities. Lady Percy is traditionally played as a woman using her 'feminine wiles'.

I remember vividly the night I first understood it. Harriet Walter was playing Lady Percy. She brought a maturity and a depth of understanding of Lady Percy's position in the scene which made the audience grapple with the politics of the couple's relationship. Harriet's grip of gender politics enabled the scene to be created with a sense of reality — of course Lady Percy has every right to demand that he should not go, to argue that his responsibilities to his family outweigh those to his king. Harriet made everyone in the house sit up, listen to the scene, confront its meaning directly and make a judgement. The audience was challenged and engaged. I believe the scene was played as Shakespeare intended. That event, however slight, explains the essence of taking gender seriously in the theatre.

Do you believe that theatre can affect social change?

It's why I do the job. It's why I was drawn to the theatre through the works of Brecht. It's why I went to Stratford East, because of Joan Littlewood and Clare Venables who gave me my first break. There's no question in my mind: people can walk out of the theatre as different people from those who entered it.

Is it getting any easier today to work as a woman director in the theatre?

No. It has become more complex. While the perception of the men I work with in a rehearsal room has altered, become more 'liberated', this is expressed in the use of the language of feminism which sometimes feels appropriated. Other feelings remain more elusive and unexpressed and these are difficult to address. By contrast, while women have got braver in the rehearsal room, they do not seem to be more equal. This, I think, is because they feel their political views have been usurped. In other words, basic behaviours and the construction of power have not altered meaningfully. However, I remain optimistic.

I am in the happy position of having a female board. Boards are still predominantly male, and while they appoint women (perhaps to earn brownie points?), they don't authorize their female Chief Executives in the same way as they do men. I find it depressing to see how many women still leave these posts. Theatre is not unique in this respect.

Do you think that you approach material in a different way from male directors ?

Yes, but that is because I have a particularly political perspective. There are differences in the way that I look at a piece of material because of the sum of my distinctive personal experiences as a woman, but the real differences are because I am politicized. In Britain there is a prevailing view that there is broadly a single or 'correct' vision of a work, reinforced by the critical culture: the majority of critics are male. I like to read Kate Kellaway in *The Observer* — her views almost always run against the dominant analysis of a work and I find that I am often in agreement with her. Take the plays of Caryl Churchill or Sarah Daniels — I don't believe that their work is valued as highly as their male contemporaries, largely because in form, style and content their work differs significantly from their male peers[1]. Their work is not viewed as equally valid descriptions of how the world operates. Critics do not understand the politics of gender and are not equipped to see the world from the other side of the fence.

---

[1] Sarah Daniels discusses critical receptions of her work on pages 99–100.

So you'd say that there's a difference in the way that some women see things, perhaps different ways of writing and directing for women and men? Would you approach a play such as Caryl Churchill's Top Girls, *for instance, in a different way than you've seen it produced before?*

Yes, but that is not because of the differences between maleness and femaleness but rather because of my political grip on the world. As Clare McIntyre said, 'How can you fight an enemy who has outposts in your mind?' Being a woman does not mean that you don't have a male perspective of the world.

As far as *Top Girls* is concerned, it is now a modern classic and has to be examined in the light of the political context in which Caryl was writing. I have not looked at it recently. I found it provocative and disturbing at the time. I suspect paradoxically, I would be both more sympathetic and more shocked by the characters' attitudes.

Let's reverse the question: do you think that any man could direct a play such as Sarah Daniels' Masterpieces *in a way which was true to the play which Sarah wrote?*

I don't think so. It is a life-changing play and has impacted as potently on those people who have performed it as it has on the audiences who have witnessed it. I imagine that a male director would construct its meanings quite differently. It is a politically confrontational work, there are such clear feminist perceptions at its root that I believe it would be difficult for a man or a non-politicized woman to draw out the writer's intentions accurately. *Masterpieces* was created over a long period of time, involved many re-writes which continued well beyond its initial performances. There are many things in the play which are not necessarily explicit or expressed directly in the dialogue. A simple example is the scene set in a tube station at night. The woman's experience of that situation is quite different from that of either of the two men — she feels threatened while they do not. Indeed, the moral questions which arise from this scene are at the centre of the play and always divide the audience — usually along male and female lines. My understanding of that experience wholly informed the way in which we chose to play it. The key debate in the play therefore centres around the way in which the scene is represented to the play's audience — lose the scene, lose the play. To use Brecht's term, the *gestalt* of the scene is one thing, and one thing only. As a director, if you cannot represent that scene as Sarah wished it to be represented, the ideas in the play are completely subverted. This principle applies to the whole play, in my opinion.

How would you define 'feminism'?

Feminism is a philosophical construction which provides ways of describing and understanding the way the world operates. It facilitates ways of thinking about how the relationship between men and women might be different, and how the balance of power between them might be altered to enable women and men to function fully in our society.

Would you consider yourself a feminist director?

　　　　Yes. As a feminist, it is difficult not to be a feminist director. My feminism therefore influences all the choices I make in staging a piece of work. It is the philosophical perspective I bring to bear, and it is not a 'popular' position to hold in the UK. Being Australian, however, feminism has a philosophical validity for me. It has, too, at some level, altered the course of everyone's life since 1968. Many British women (and men) find the word itself frightening. There are lots of closet feminists in Britain! I don't actually understand why.

Is 'feminist theatre' defined differently, in your experience, in Australia, from the way it is defined in Britain?

　　　　Yes. In Australia feminism is a valid view of the world to hold. It is considered to define a crucial arena for argument and debate about how to change society. It is to do with hope for a better future. Feminism has impinged, especially through government legislation, on the lives of women and men. Gender is therefore consistently addressed on stage. Many more women hold key artistic posts in Australia. They are in my experience women who operate from a feminist perspective. Through theatre, film, television, print and radio, their views have become integral to the way Australian society is described.

How has British feminist theatre changed over the past few decades, in terms of themes, styles, ways of working?

　　　　It has moved from an agit-prop form, to narrative/realistic forms of story-telling, to more elusive, less direct performance-based work. Its focus has shifted from an examination of the practical conditions of women's lives to raising existential questions about who women are, what they want and where they are heading. The process which initially emphasized collective approaches has become more individualized.

What is the future for feminist theatre in Britain?

　　　　I am not optimistic but I am hopeful, which is a different thing. At present I don't see a future for feminist theatre in Britain. I believe, however, that if there is a change of government, the issues and views which exercised feminists may be addressed again on our stages in ways which may point to a more uplifting, more equal, healthier Britain. Good and important art is about content, not style. Things have to be said from our stages for theatre to be valuable. I look forward to hearing those voices again expressing a vision of a future which will challenge us and which we may embrace with optimism.

Lizbeth Goodman

Based on an interview recorded for a BBC-OU radio programme in spring 1994; updated for publication December 1994.

JILL GREENHALGH AND SUSAN BASSNETT ON THE MAGDALENA PROJECT

The Magdalena Project is an international women's theatre organization which is based in Cardiff, Wales, and which has attracted participants from many parts of the world, including Latin America, Eastern Europe, Scandinavia and New Zealand. Jill Greenhalgh is the founding Artistic Director of Magdalena; Susan Bassnett, who has been involved in the project from the start, is the author of Magdalena: International Women's Experimental Theatre *(Berg, 1989).*

How did the Magdalena come about?

Jill: The subtitle of the Magdalena Project is the 'International Network of Women in Contemporary Theatre'. My roots come out of the kind of theatre which was generated from such theatre practitioners as Jerzy Grotowski and Eugenio Barba. As an actress for ten years. I was involved in exploring the work that these particular practitioners had instituted. This theatre was not coming from a text base, from plays, in the way that we know it in traditional theatre in this country, but from devised work, coming from the work of the actors and the directors. Using much more visual and musical inputs and using the actor's voice was fundamental.

The Magdalena was born during a festival in Rome in 1984, when ten or fifteen theatre groups doing a similar type of work had come together for two weeks of different special events, performances, and concerts. Many of these groups were at a turning point in their work, wondering which way to go next. I was looking at the work that was on show, enjoying it, but feeling that something new was needed. And I observed that, in all the groups and pieces of work I was seeing there would be a central female actress, and it was her words, her energy, her presence, which seemed to carry the whole thing. When I came away from it, what I remembered was her and her energy, not the message of the play, or the design or the directing: and her voice: not necessarily what she was saying. Around a table, with various other women from these different groups from many different countries, we took this idea that 'wouldn't it be wonderful to pluck all these women out of these various groups, away from their male directors, and put them together in a time and place for a period of collaboration and exchange and see what happened with all this very strong, female, talented energy?' That idea was the beginning of the Magdalena Project. The Magdalena Project was initiated with a festival in 1986 in Cardiff, when we invited women from seventeen different countries, from all these different groups, to come to Cardiff for three weeks to see what would happen.

In what ways were these groups developing an alternative theatre for women?

Susan: A lot of the theatre in Britain until fairly recently has been text-based. That is, the play and the playwright have been important and most of the playwrights have been men. The directors have been very important and again, until recently, most of the directors have been men. So what we've had in Britain or certainly in England, has been a very patriarchal, very male-dominated, very academic, text-dominated theatre. For me, for many years, the exciting work has been overseas. It's been looking at what some of the 'itinerant groups', as Jill calls them, could do with their bodies, and often with texts, but deconstructing texts, not playing texts according to any criterion of faithfulness, but actually performing texts and doing exciting things with them.

Do you consider the Magdalena Project to have feminist objectives (however you might define that term)?

Susan: In the beginning, there were strong feelings expressed that Magdalena should not be seen as 'feminist'. I think this was due to the sense that feminism was predominantly issue-based and had fairly rigid parameters, whereas the women coming to work on Magdalena wanted a looser, more flexible structure within which to work and didn't want to be tied to any particular ideology. There was also the fact that so many of the practitioners had close links with male guru figures like Barba and Brook, and again the idea of being labelled 'feminist' was off-putting to some of them. But over the years I think that attitude has changed, because concepts of feminism have also shifted. There is more pluralism in feminist thinking now, there are different positions across a large spectrum, and I have heard the word 'feminist' returning to the floor in Magdalena. Also, feminism in Britain has a very different history from feminism in other countries, where it has tended to be less issue-based and dogmatic, and the internationalism of Magdalena is a powerful factor here.

The question of language in the theatre has featured prominently in many Magdalena meetings. Can you give an example of how the Magdalena Project has explored this issue of language, and of any 'answers' the project may have found?

Jill: After the 1986 Festival, we organized a three-day meeting to which we invited various people from different countries to come and address the question, 'Is there a women's language in the theatre?' They addressed this, not in a conference or discussion, but in actually leading workshops, bringing their own methods of work, and asking that question of themselves as teachers. I wouldn't say that we came up with any answers. All we did was re-define more questions.

Susan: The big thing for me that came out of 1986 — out of the festival — was the desperate need that women had for voice-work. Lots of women could create terrific physical images but they didn't have a voice, and there was need not only for voice exercises but also for ways of telling their stories, of actually making visible, I suppose, whole areas that had been invisible — of breaking a silence.

Has the Magdalena found the larger women's language in theatre they've been looking for?

Jill: I think we start to step onto very dangerous ground if we try to over-define something, and say 'this is women's language'. That was our mistake at the beginning to think, 'We can look for a woman's language in theatre: we'll have it next year'. The more you explore, the more you realize how naïve and idiotic that is. There isn't a women's language. There is a need for women to voice their work: there is a need for women to have space to make their work, and that's a need which must be addressed.

For me, what the Magdalena Project aims to do is actually to make space so that women can come together and work, without saying, 'We're looking for this, we're looking for that, we're looking for the other', because every woman artist is as distinct from the next woman artist as a male artist is from the next male artist. What has been lacking in our culture is space for women to actually work, to explore.

Susan: There's also a need for women to share their experiences cross-culturally, and also cross-generationally: because that's been another aspect to the Magdalena. The women involved have gone from women in their fifties through to undergraduates and to women in their mid-teens. The importance of a network like Magdalena is that it puts women in touch with one another and it provides a basis for continuity. It brings together women who often have not got a common language: their common language is the physical. We're crossing cultures: we're crossing generations, and also crossing boundaries between the academic and the practical: between the professional and the amateur theatre. The point about this alternative way of theatre-making is that the performers have an enormous amount of power and authority in controlling what they do with their roles. They're not handed a part by a writer: nor are they handed a specific role and a specific task by the director, so that it actually involves quite a long period of study.

Jill: Susan's point about the power of the actor in this kind of theatre is very important. As I direct now, I find it very difficult to get it across to actors, that they have much more power than they actually realize, particularly women actors. The director can ask you, the actor, for something, but they can only use what you give them, so as an actor you have an enormous power. It's not a question of trying to give the directors what they want. You give the directors what you want, and that's the material which they must use to build the work. I wish more actresses had the opportunity to understand that they have that power and then wield it.

You were speaking about the cross-generational nature of Magdalena. How would you divide the generations, and what do you perceive as the main political and artistic differences between them?

Susan: The difference was put to me in one way at a Magdalena meeting in 1993, when a woman in her late twenties told me that she admired my generation for what we had done, but felt unsympathetic towards us because we had been motivated by rage, which was pretty unconstructive. I think she was right; we were so angry, at the state of the world, at the Vietnam war and the proliferation of nuclear weapons, at being treated as sex objects, at being *relegated* all the time, and we must have been in a state of permanent anger at someone or something, which did come out in the work. Now there is less rage, but there is also a much stronger sense of having rights, of being entitled to those rights rather than having to fight for them. There is also a lot more professionalism. Where you can see this is in the structure of companies and their choice of performance material. There is also more concern now for aesthetic criteria; it isn't enough just to make a piece about an issue such as abortion. What also matters is how it's made, how it works and where it is going in terms of theatre and its development.

How was the development of women's images in theatre explored as a theme at 'Raw Visions', the Magdalena gathering for young performers?

Jill: During the life of the Magdalena we have given many women artists the opportunity to extend their skills through training workshops. The purpose behind 'Raw Visions' was to take this a step further, by bringing together young women artists who were starting to create their own performances and wanted professional support and advice on both their artistic ambitions and the practicalities of allowing these visions to survive.

Over three days, the participants were able to tap into a wealth of artistic experience. An international forum of successful and independent women theatre artists and administrators led 'Raw Visions': their sole function was to respond to the artistic and practical needs and concerns brought by these young practitioners.

Another Magdalena festival was held in Cardiff in 1994. What important changes have you noticed between this festival and the first festival?

Susan: In my opening lecture in the 1994 festival I tried to summarize differences between 1986 and 1994. The biggest difference, of course, is that in 1994 Magdalena had a history, whereas in 1986 it was, for all we knew, a one-off event. What came out of the 1986 festival was the desire to continue meeting, to share experiences and in particular to work on developing a female voice, literally to break the silence.

Now in the mid-1990s I sense that there is an increasing desire to work on material — not only the how, but also the what. At 'Raw Visions' in 1993, I gave a talk on biography/autobiography and theatre-making and have been amazed at the response that came back to me, and is still coming back after all this time.

Feminist thinking has become more pluralistic. There are many voices claiming to be feminist, and of course since 1986 the whole map of the world has changed. The collapse of communism has given us a different perspective, and the sinister rise of fascism, anti-semitism, ethnic violence and plain old nationalistic war-mongering remind us that the beliefs some of us held in the 1960s and 1970s about changing the world were absurdly naïve. I also see this as a moment when, far from being the end of history, as some have suggested, we are desperately in need of history. We need to understand our past, to see where we are coming from and to see whether abusive patterns can ever be broken. I think this is why we have seen so much work on archetypes and on female figures from the past in Magdalena Project events and gatherings. After all, think of the basic law of human dynamics — to leap forward you first have to crouch or bend your body backwards and prepare to move.

Jill: When the Magdalena Project was initiated it sprung from a personal need that can be summarized in my wanting to break the silence within which I felt much of women's theatre was trapped: my own was trapped in that way, certainly, I wrote of 'a deep feeling and fear of never being heard. Of feeling you've been silenced. That somehow the work that you can feel lining your stomach wall, that you can't quite see because it's in shadow, has got no place. There isn't a language invented to cover or search for it... it's as though the feeling doesn't exist. That's frightening when you know it's not true... when you know that there is something new and vital and female that is lying latent and untapped, trapped under thousands of years of patriarchal art'.

Today, eight years on, I feel very different. I sense the presence of many women artists as autonomous from their groups or group directors; I have seen many women take up the challenge of hosting international events and confronting the administrative and financial responsibilities that go hand-in-hand with the challenge to organize. There are so many who are confidently defining their own work, more actresses becoming directors, and making their own strong performances. I have seen women artists stop hiding behind the excuse of 'not being able to write' and expressing themselves very powerfully in articles that are being published more and more widely. Many have started to pass on their knowledge through workshops and have become fine teachers as well as makers of theatre. I have seen many taking advantage, in countless ways, of the network. The silence and the isolation have been broken.

The strength of the 1994 Festival lay in its diversity — in the gathering of 150 women from across the globe, with all their unique experience and different voices, communicating through theatre, what is important to them[1]. The 1994 Festival was a pivotal point, providing both a chance to evaluate and celebrate the achievement of women theatre practitioners internationally and a platform from which to launch new challenges.

Lizbeth Goodman, revised and updated by Jane de Gay
This interview was adapted, revised and updated, in February 1995, from the transcript of a BBC
'Artworks' radio interview.

---

[1] See Goodman and de Gay, eds. *Voices of Women/Languages of Theatre: Magdalena '94*, a theme issue of *Contemporary Theatre Review* (1996). Susan Bassnett's book gives background to the project as a whole: *Magdalena: International Women's Experimental Theatre* (Oxford: Berg Publishers, 1989).

YVONNE BREWSTER

Yvonne Brewster is the Artistic Director of Talawa Theatre, which was founded by four women in 1985. Talawa aims 'to use the ancient African ritual and Black political experience of our forebears to inform, enrich and enlighten British theatre.' Brewster has been active in the theatres of Jamaica, Africa and America and has worked as a drama teacher, television production assistant, presenter and director, and film director. She is the editor of Methuen's three volumes of Black Plays *(1987, 1989, and 1995).*

What does 'Talawa' mean?

It is a Jamaican word which refers to powerful women, and it means strong, female and dynamic. There is a saying: 'she lickle but she Talawa': she is small in size, but you best not mess with her. It's a great compliment.

Is Talawa a feminist theatre company in some sense, and if so, in what sense?

This feminist labelling is always a little bit problematic for me, to be quite honest. You see, I was born in Jamaica and only came to England, in the first instance, to be what was called 'finished' in a girls' school: they finished me for true!

Coming from a West Indian background, the word 'feminism' had a really hollow ring. Simply, it's a matriarchal society. There, the women *rule* the roost without actually wearing the trousers. So, entering a European or British situation, one found the feminist hang-up a bit difficult to grasp. It was hard to understand what all the fuss was about.

I suppose that in a way, however, Talawa is exceedingly feminist, if to be feminist means to look at things from a woman's perspective.

Does Talawa work from a female perspective then?

Oh yes. That has been the point of the company's existence from the very beginning.

Would you describe the formation of Talawa?

I had been freelancing in the theatre and in Arts administration in this country for some years. When the demise of the GLC [Greater London Council] was imminent — in 1985/1986 — I founded Talawa. The GLC had a lot of money to give to Arts groups in those days, just before it died away. I was asked if there was a project I passionately wanted to do. I said there were

8. Yvonne Brewster, Artistic Director, Talawa Theatre Company; photographer: Amrando Atkinson.

lots of projects I wanted to do, but they were all very large-scale and would require an enormous amount of money and why were they asking me this silly question... I didn't think they would take me seriously. But they told me to write up one of my ideas as a proposal. Quick as a flash, my six pages of wonderful huge ideas were in the post.

The major idea I 'proposed' later became Talawa's first production: *The Black Jacobins*. This is the story of the first Haitian revolution. It needed twenty-five people in the cast and several weeks of rehearsal: it was going to cost — oh, I don't know — eighty five or ninety thousand pounds — and I wanted a long, funded rehearsal period and a three-week run at the Riverside Studios. I went overboard: I proposed the ultimate, assuming that it would all remain a proposal. Then they phoned up and told me I'd got everything I had asked for. Amazing. It wouldn't happen today.

It was clear I could only take the money if I formed a company, so I phoned up three of my really close female friends in the business, and we formed Talawa Theatre Company: Carmen Munroe (a really leading lady, who has been acting in this country for more than thirty years). Mona Hammond (extremely talented: she went on to the National Theatre, *East Enders* — a UK television soap opera — and elsewhere) and Inigo Espejel (a German woman who was our Production Manager).

Are all four of you still working together in Talawa?

We all worked together for the first few productions. Then Inigo went to Wales, Carmen went on to work on *Desmonds* — a UK television show concerned with the lives of Black characters — although she remained on the Board until fairly recently. Mona has appeared regularly with the company, her last outing being the Fool in *King Lear*. I seem to be the constant so far.

As things have turned out, however, it was some time before Talawa produced a play written by a woman.

To ask the obvious question: why not?

Not for lack of enthusiasm. We have always wanted to produce plays by women, but during the first few years we had difficulty in finding appropriate plays by a woman which we felt suited our working style.

What is it about your working style which excluded plays written by women at that time?

In the first years I simply didn't find any that appealed to me. It's pointless to try and find excuses. We did what appealed to me, OK? More specifically, it's the scope, I think. We do epic theatre. We needed epic plays.

Epic in the Brechtian sense. or epic in the more general sense of theatre which emphasizes largeness of scope, breadth and powerful images?

We use big, bold, powerful images. I don't suppose I am the subtlest person you'll ever meet. I like theatre which takes on the world. Even if it's domestic in the specific sense, my theatre must have a vision which goes beyond the domestic. I know this is contentious but I will say it anyway: I think women are better at looking at things in the small scale prism. This may be partly because women have children. They tend to see the future writ large, to think of future generations. But for some reason, this vision has not come through, until very recently, in much of Black women's writing for the theatre. As women we are doing this in our lives, but perhaps not so much in our theatre.

Talawa does not do the kind of work similar to other Black theatre companies in Britain. There is not a homogenous style of Black theatre, you know. It's therefore quite important that the plays we choose combine a personal introspective element that we as women in the company can relate to, appreciate, explore and then present in the larger scale.

The classical plays from the international canon which we have produced so far have all been re-viewed in order to highlight modern parallels of significance to Black people in the first instance — for example, a Nigerian *Oedipus* given from Jocasta's perspective, *Antony and Cleopatra* with a funky Egyptian Queen, Edmund in *King Lear* showing all the signs of a streetwise Brixtonian [someone who lives in the South East London area called Brixton].

I have to say I find classical women playwrights difficult to decipher. The Aphra Behns of this world are beyond my ken. I don't understand what the bloody hell she's on about.

And contemporary women playwrights? There are excellent women's plays — some of quite 'epic' proportions — being written by women these days.

Of course there are many very talented women writing for theatre these days. But there are far fewer *Black* British women writing for the stage...

What about Jackie Kay? Winsome Pinnock...?

They have wonderful things to offer. And also Maria Oshodi. I admire Winsome's *A Rock in Water*, it's her biggest play, and my favourite. It's about Claudia Jones, a larger-than-life woman. The poetic nature of Winsome's writing in this play has a deep richness. And I do admire Jackie Kay's poetry, though I do not know her plays so well. From what I know of her work, she does transcend the 'standard' and certainly goes beyond the domestic. Her poetry is always questioning the presumed.

And it brings in past and present, real and surreal, large and small together…

Yes, I would like to see Jackie Kay working with Talawa on a project someday.

In 1992/3, you produced Ntozake Shange's The Love Space Demands — *a new play by a well-known African-American woman writer. How did you choose that piece, and what response did it receive?*

The text by Ntozake Shange's was the first work by a woman which we produced. The play was sent to me to read and write a report on! A few months later, we were producing it. It's a case of knowing what you like! *The Love Space Demands* is a thoroughly modern performance piece. We had a Black woman installation artist design the set/environment. Jean Binta Breeze, the well-known performance poet, played the main and only speaking role, supported by two live musicians and two dancers — a choreo-poem. The response from the audience was encouraging. In fact, many of our most faithful women patrons were introduced to us during this show.

Would you say that the current economic climate, which encourages playwrights to write for four actors or less in order to save money, is shaping the writing which does emerge these days?

Other Black companies have defined themselves as producers of Black plays. But at Talawa we have very little money for commissioning, so our policy is to search out the classical Black plays, present the historical and the ritualistic. My experience with regard to new Black plays is therefore somewhat limited. However, I have to plead not guilty to limiting playwrights to numbers. I think they should be allowed to write freely first. We try to put as much money as possible into the part of the budget covering the actors on stage — their number rarely drops below ten.

Because I was very conscious of the need to give Black women a bigger bit of the cake, Talawa wrote up a proposal for a scheme called the Black Women Writers Project which has been funded by London Arts Board for three years now. During this time some nine Black and Asian women have been allowed to formulate individual programmes which have had no pressure of performance and which have led to some really exciting results. For example: novelists and TV script-writers writing their first plays; established writers ironing out the kinks in a play through workshopping; a young writer working with an internationally celebrated dramaturg, and so on. We live in hope that the project will be renewed for a further three years, as it has proved really stimulating and might provide us with a script for production — who knows?

This scheme is the sort of thing that a company like Talawa can administer. We can bring up plays like babies. And that's the kind of theatre work I understand. That's my kind of feminism. In a sense, I don't understand the term in any other way: certainly not in its most strident forms. I suppose I feel that I'm a bit too old to take on the more radical aspects of feminism. But then that's not only because of my age, but also because of my origins, my background. And of course, I'm from a different generation than you young feminists today. We share a sense of the richness of women's contributions, but as far as I'm concerned, men don't have to be excluded from that. In fact, I think men can and often do (in my experience) help and encourage women's accomplishments, just as women encourage men and other women.

You have been resident in the Cochrane Theatre since 1992. What difference has having this building-base made to Talawa?

It's been challenging and rewarding. We are a more solid team now that we have had the luxury of knowing where the shows would be performed and being able to work with practitioners on a more regular basis. Our three years here have proved, if proof was necessary, that a Black company is perfectly able to take responsibility for the smooth running of a building base. I must make it quite clear that Talawa was renting space in the theatre and therefore had very little say in the overall programming or the aesthetic of the place. That is one reason why after producing eleven middle-scale productions in the Cochrane over a three-year period, we have not renewed the lease. Watch this space!

Can or should a play which employs lots of actresses, but is written and directed by men, be called 'women's theatre'?

We *do* have to ask that question, even though we know the answer, which is *NO*; that is *not* women's theatre. It's difficult to draw the black and white line (Ooh: that's a bad pun). But when we come down to it — you have to say yes or no sometimes. An actor is an entity and to be an entity who joins with another entity — not to be amoeba-like and split — and to still maintain your own full sense of self-sufficiency and your own 'entity' status, even in that union, you need some objectivity, a third eye, which is the role of the director. Like it or not, we are all caught up in the same state of affairs: the director plays an important part in shaping the theatre as we know it. That sounds funny coming from me (a director): it sounds as if I'm trying to protect my job. But I think it's true.

Let's try to get to the bottom line: what defines a play as a 'black woman's play'?

A Black woman's play is a play written by a Black woman. The director shapes the play. And much will depend upon the direction: what is stressed and not stressed, which characters are made Big and which are deflated or maybe ignored. So if the director is not a woman, then the play produced has less chance of being 100% a woman's play in production. And if the director is not black then the play produced stands even less chance of being a 'Black play' in production. I suppose the best definition of Black women's theatre is theatre written by and directed by Black women.

Failing that…?

Plays written by women are also simply good theatre, but you are asking for definitions.

I think the writer does the most important job in creating, imagining and shaping any play. Her work comes first, and cannot be underestimated. And performers make the play work on stage, and designers make the play fit an overall vision. But if we are talking about the final shaping of a play to reflect the Black woman's perspective, then the direction is crucial.

So if the director is not a black woman, then the play produced is not a black woman's play?

No. Black women's plays, directed by Black women are 100% Black. That's the bottom line.

Lizbeth Goodman

A longer version of this interview was published in New Theatre Quarterly, *vol. VII, no. 28, November 1991, pp. 361–368. Edited and updated in 1995.*

PENNY CASDAGLI OF NETI-NETI

Neti-Neti Theatre Company was founded in 1987 by Penny Casdagli (alias Maro Green), playwright, and Caroline Griffin, teacher and poet. The company produces theatre for young people which incorporates English, Bengali and Sign Language. Neti-Neti's work is widely recognized for its challenging approach to multi-lingual, multi-cultural theatre work. In early 1995, they produced Philip Osment's play Who's Breaking?, *about coming to terms with AIDS (for women and men, homosexual and heterosexual); the play was performed in English and Sign Language, with dance and comedy (The Lyric, Hammersmith).*

What was your first play for Neti-Neti?

The first play we did for Neti-Neti was *Aesop's Fabulous Fables.* It was performed twice a day, seven days a week, for five months, in London Zoo. It was, from the zoo's point of view, meant to make the zoo a more exciting environment.

The next full-scale production which Neti-Neti mounted was *The Beggar in the Palace* (1988). It was a re-writing from a feminist point of view of *The Odyssey.* It was all researched very thoroughly. For instance, Penelope was obliged to marry Odysseus; and so our play is about home, dispossession and women being dispossessed and obliged to marry (a topic which has special resonance for Asian girls and women, who make up a large section of our audience).

The important thing is that in the work the issue of language is crucial, essential. That is true for many feminists. It's important to look at the language of power, and to look at what is enshrined in certain terms that we use, because a lot of the basic notions of our patriarchal society are enshrined in language. That's why language has been an issue for so many feminists.

We apply that in our work by looking at the concept of who uses what language where, and why. So in Odysseus's patriarchy in Ithaca, English is the dominant language, his language, and Sign Language was something that he did as a compromise because his wife, Penelope, happened to be deaf. And Bengali was used as a subversive language, the language of an oppressed section of the community there in Ithaca.

The inter-relation between language and power seems to be a theme, or link, between all Neti-Neti's work. Is that true?

Language and power are very relevant to all our work. Our next large-scale play for Neti-Neti was *Only Playing, Miss,* about bullying in schools.

Now to answer the question of the relationship between content and company style, it is important to remember that we are a multi-lingual company, and are also integrated in terms of race and physical ability of the performers. The *armoury* of bullying is very often racist, or about physical difference, or about disability of some kind. Because we were using three languages, and because we work with an integrated company — both in terms of race and ability — the way the play was performed was *innately* anti-racist. The way we performed the play gave a tension to the content. You'll notice that there's nothing abilist about the play; even the insults used by the children are not racist or abilist, but of a more general kind. The play, while 'about' bullying, raised consciousness around language.

The three languages are needed in order to reach as wide an audience as possible. The imperative is to try to communicate. The relationship of the language to the text, or content, or theme changes with every play, and sometimes from performance to performance as well, depending on the audience.

For us, multi-lingual work is a challenge because it is still such a new area. The thing is to get at the relationship between action and meaning. It is not enough to add sign language as a second way of narrating the action of a spoken English play. That is superficial. We use Sign Language as a conceptual part of the play's structure, asking what can and cannot be said, in English, and in Sign Language, and what is best said in both. The same goes for the Bengali. The conceptual way we think as hearing people can't be easily translated, and the way we think as English speakers cannot express most accurately the experience of all cultures. We must respect the fact that language and culture are inextricably mixed.

The juxtaposition of Sign Language and Bengali with English emphasizes the rich depths of Sign Language in its own right. Implicit in the context, we use other languages to challenge and interrogate English.

Is Neti-Neti an explicitly feminist company?

Neti-Neti is an integrated company, rather than a feminist company, but the foundation is in feminism. There's no question about that. I am feminist, and so is Caroline. All our work is explicitly feminist. And we're tackling issues of racism as well as sexism, communication problems as well as gender issues, ability and disability as well as sexuality.

Neti-Neti's work is based in feminist ideas, because the two women who founded the company did so as feminists. Men can't be feminists. They can like and admire feminist work, and perhaps change their own perspectives and be influenced by feminist ideas, but I don't think that men can be feminists.

Our feminism is developing, and has been qualified by our experience. I can't answer for new definitions of feminism these days. I am not sure how other women working in the theatre are defining their feminism. But I haven't stopped being a feminist.

One possible definition of feminist theatre would include that theatre which puts girls' and women's experience first. We have to make a distinction between our way of working and the plays themselves. We certainly prioritize the experience of girls and women in all our work practice, but the female characters' experience is not always put first in our plays.

Your show, Grief, *received considerable attention and acclaim. What was* Grief?

In *Grief*, the three languages are used again and again, in a different relation to each other. The play is about bereavement and loss in young people. It is based on some very moving pieces of writing from young people who have been involved in our workshops. In *Grief*, six people who all loved a boy (who died) express their feelings about the death. They all need to break the taboo silence around the issue of death. So for this very sensitive topic, the research we did was very thorough. We worked with Childline and other agencies and in careful consultation with one particular educational psychologist whom we have worked with several times before. We have published the playscript, including the wonderful writings by the kids themselves. Young people defining loss and grief is not something you normally read about, especially not first hand. *Grief* will also come out as a book and a video for sale to schools.

If listening and learning and recognition of difference and the importance of young people's consciousness and concerns — if all that is feminist, then we are a feminist company. We always think of our audience, and they are the centre of our work.

What kind of funding does Neti-Neti have?

Any kind of funding we can get. Project funding as you know isn't automatic from the Arts Council of Great Britain. For each project, we do an awful lot of preparation, and then submit it to the Arts Council and hope to be awarded project funding. But it's important to say that project funding doesn't give any continuity in the work, and continuity to *our* work is absolutely crucial. We try and raise whatever we can from wherever we can: that might include such sources as regional arts associations, local boroughs, educational charities…. In 1991, British Gas gave us one of their four awards for small theatre companies. It is very difficult to operate when you don't know if, or how much, money you'll have to work with. But we're very optimistic. We always plan as if our work is funded and then try to make sure it is. We imagine that the ground is firm, and so far it has been.

What does the name Neti-Neti mean?

Neti-Neti is a Zen term meaning not this and not that: in Sanskrit, it means both things, neither one nor the other. Some of us are women, some men, some are black and some are white, some are hearing and some non-hearing, and so on. The idea of 'neti-neti' is of perfect balance, not something we always achieve but an idea we strive for.

What is the structure of Neti-Neti as a company?

Of the five core members of Neti-Neti in 1991, for instance, each 'comes from somewhere different': Caroline Griffin (co-Artistic Director, poet, playwright and teacher), myself (co-artistic Director, playwright and director), Francis Gobey (our Education Officer), Ian Lucas (our assistant director) and Karen Smith (our administrator) .

It is important to say that Caroline Griffin's contribution to the company is immeasurable. Because Caroline job-shares being a teacher and working for Neti-Neti she keeps us up to date with changes in education. She's a classroom teacher so she does know what's going on. She couldn't believe that theatre was so ephemeral, and it's due to that perception that we started to print all our work, to publish it and leave permanent educational resources in our wake after we do each project.

There shouldn't be a contradiction between the process and the content of theatre work. That is (I think) a feminist idea.

What is the most important thing to say about Neti-Neti's work?

The way in which we are each viewed and valued in society has profound effects on the ways we see ourselves, and on what we can achieve. Changing those social views is the aim our work, and part of our equal opportunities policy.

Lizbeth Goodman
Interviews conducted April–June 1991; Neti-Neti did not feel it necessary to update this version.

BERNARDINE EVARISTO ON THEATRE OF BLACK WOMEN

Theatre of Black Women was formed in 1982 by three women who had all trained as actresses at the Rose Bruford College of Speech and Drama. The founder members are all playwrights and creative workers: Bernardine Evaristo is the author of Island of Abraham *(Peepal Tree Books, 1994), a collection of poetry. Her writing is widely published in anthologies and magazines, and she teaches creative writing. Patricia St. Hilaire has written and directed children's opera for the English National Opera, is a published poet and lectures in both drama and arts administration. Paulette Randall left the company early on to train as a theatre director. She has directed many plays including* Leave Taking *at the Royal National Theatre. She is also a television producer.*

Was Theatre of Black Women a feminist company?

The company came within the category of 'Black Feminist', a term introduced from America, which embraced both black and female concerns. We were very much part of the burgeoning black women's cultural movement of the eighties and often engaged in debates about the historical exclusion of Black women from the women's movement. 'Black Feminist' as a term seemed most appropriate at that time. However, as individual members, we defined ourselves separately, adopting or rejecting labels.

What was the history of Theatre of Black Women's funding?

We received funding from many sources, beginning with an award of £500 in 1982 and working our income up to around £80,000 a year. Our sources included the Arts Council and Regional Arts Boards, the Gulbenkian Foundation, Greater London Council, London Borough Grants Scheme and local borough councils. We received annual, project and capital funding, enough to survive but not really to thrive. Forward planning was especially difficult as we never knew from year to year whether our grant applications would be successful. Often we would be in the middle of rehearsals before we knew if the production was to be funded. We also raised our income through performance fees. We were an Equity company and employed up to fifteen people around production time.

Eventually we lost a key grant from Greater London Arts because of an argument we had with them about racism. They demanded an apology, none was forthcoming, so their grant to us and matching grants were withdrawn. The cut had nothing to do with the merit of our work, which was not in question. It had become clear eventually that the funding of black arts in the eighties was a fad, and we were the flavour of the month. When the fad passed, most groups were cut. In 1985 there were approximately 17 black theatre companies in London; ten years later there are less than a handful.

Would you consider revitalizing Theatre of Black Women, if funding could be found?

Theatre of Black Women played an important role in the alternative/ fringe theatre of the eighties. We were the first black women's theatre company in the United Kingdom, seating black women at the steering wheel of our own creativity. In our company, for the first time black women were involved in theatre from conception, management, production, performance, to audience. I am not interested, however, in revitalizing the company, even if funding were found, as I am now more interested in a broader canvas. Sometimes we need to separate in order to develop, and then a point is reached at which integration becomes possible again. The situation has also improved since the early eighties for black women in theatre generally. There are more and better opportunities, and the mainstream has become more accessible.

When the company was active, did it function as a focal point for black arts more generally?

Not really. We could never be a cultural centre in any broad sense because we didn't have the resources or space. We were a theatre company touring plays and running arts workshops. We rented an office but we did not have our own premises. In one sense, we were a focal point for black women's theatre, and we introduced many women from different media to working in theatre. Ten years ago, there were very few black women who worked as directors, stage managers, designers, playwrights, etc. We offered training and guidance in the theatre arts to redress the imbalance.

What was Theatre of Black Women's most important production?

It's quite difficult to pinpoint one play as the most important or successful, as each production represented a stage in the company's development. Certainly the first two plays, *Silhouette* (1983–4) and *Pyeyucca* (1984–5), which Patricia and I co-wrote, established the company's reputation and secured funding which we built upon over the years. Both plays also had extensive tours of up to ten months and were taken to Holland and Germany. These were among the first black women's plays to be performed in this country, and our style, which used poetic language, was experimental. We strove to find a form that evolved alongside the content of our work rather than using traditional European theatre styles. *Miss Quashie and the Tiger's Tail*

9. *The Cripple* by Ruth Harris for Theatre of Black Women; photographer: W. J. Herbert.

(1987) by Gabriela and Jean Pearse was our first Theatre-in-Education play and was very well received in schools. *The Cripple* (1987) by Ruth Harris was also popular. It was a one-woman play about a disabled woman with an indomitable spirit, and her journey through life. Based on the life of a real woman, coupled with the director being disabled herself, it had a quality of authenticity which moved people.

Were audiences for your plays mainly women? Mainly black?

Initially our audiences were mainly female, both black and white. Gradually this changed and our audiences were often a real mixture of society: male/female, black/white, young/old. We toured to a very wide range of venues and this influenced the composition of our audiences. We performed in theatres and arts centres as well as community centres, schools and universities. There was no tradition of black people going to the theatre in this country, so it was often hard to attract black audiences in large numbers. Our plays were quite serious and often people would tell us that because we were black women, they expected some lighthearted singing and dancing. Needless to say, we challenged people's assumptions.

Was there a particular political line to the work you produced?

Our remit was to produce theatre that explored the lives of black women in this country. If that's political, then we were political.

Were there ever men involved with your work?

We sometimes employed men as stage managers, photographers, designers, but not at management level.

Did you ever have non-black women in your plays, or involved in their production?

Yes, on production teams, and occasionally as actors.

What is the most significant thing to say about your work with Theatre of Black Women?

I think Theatre of Black Women was an innovative and challenging theatre company, the first of its kind. As such, it was a spearheading organization. In 1982, there were really very few opportunities for black women in theatre. Acting roles were few and far between, and often the parts were stereotyped or marginal or offensive. The existing black theatre companies were run by men with a male agenda and the other companies were white-run with perhaps a token black person.

It was very important to us that we created our own space because there was so little on offer to us in the theatre world. We considered the formation of the company to be a logical move but we were seen as radical. We were denied positive opportunities so we made our own, yet we faced open hostility from a lot of people who found our very name threatening. We were always being asked to justify our existence, which became very trying. We always felt that we were surviving against the odds although there were many people who wanted us to succeed. In six years we produced ten plays, employed many people and performed to thousands of people in this country and abroad. We enabled black women to take control of the creative process of making theatre, from start to finish. This was a new and much-needed initiative. Our commitment to the company was absolute, and that was the key to our success.

Lizbeth Goodman
Interview conducted in London, March 1991; updated in 1995.

CHARLOTTE KEATLEY

Charlotte Keatley was nominated Laurence Olivier Most Promising Newcomer to British Theatre in 1990 for her play, My Mother Said I Never Should. *The play premiered at Contact Theatre, Manchester, in 1987, won the George Devine Award in 1987 and the Manchester Evening News Best New Play Award, before an acclaimed run at the Royal Court Theatre, London, in 1989. The play has since been translated and produced in fifteen countries and is an A-level set text. It is the most widely performed play ever written by a British woman. Other work includes: setting up a performance art company in 1982–4, for which she co-devised and acted in* Dressing for Dinner. *In 1985–6, Keatley wrote, designed, directed and choreographed* The Legend of Padgate, *a musical community play for Warrington, including eighty actors and musicians;* Waiting for Martin *toured by the English Shakespeare company in Britain and Canada in 1987. She co-wrote* Fear and Misery in the Third Term *for Liverpool Playhouse in 1989;* The Singing Ringing Tree *for children (Contact Theatre, 1991–2); numerous radio plays for BBC, and a live broadcast on the fall of the Berlin Wall. For television, Keatley has written* Badger *for Granada, nominated for the Prix Danube in 1989; and the film* Falling Slowly *for Channel Four/European Co-production Association. She co-directed Heathcote Williams'* Autogeddon, *which won a 1991 Edinburgh Festival Fringe First Award. Two new plays,* Our Father *and* The Genius of Her Sex *will open in 1995. Keatley also teaches playwriting in schools and universities.*

Do you think of yourself as a 'women writer' or as a 'feminist writer'?

It depends what room I'm in.

You can't ignore the fact that you perceive your ideas, and therefore write, in a social and political context. You will inevitably be influenced by what is current; you might purposely write against the current, but it will still be an important factor. The inevitable shift of opinions and perspectives over time is what makes doing interviews for publication such a risky business. I think that when you talk about your own writing, you should do so with the working proviso that your opinions change, that you can write something today to completely contradict everything you said before. I think that's a playwright's job. Playwriting has been confused with political journalism in the past few decades; I think theatre is a place to access taboos, magic and the unconscious.

I tried devising, acting and directing in community theatre and performance arts for three years, while also working as a theatre critic for numerous papers. I saw about four hundred plays a year. I educated myself about theatre by watching it in 3-D, and sharpened my critical awareness of how and why a play works, or doesn't. I also know how arbitrary and personal a theatre critic's opinion is. I remember this whether a review I get as a playwright is good or bad. But most importantly, I educated myself in the context of theatre writing, and performance possibilities, European as well as English.

Do you think of your audience as gendered, either as female or male?

You could say that I write for women because even if I write a play to be performed entirely by men, my whole consciousness and way of enjoying life is so much caught up with watching and listening to how women find their way through the world. If I trace male characters, it's inevitably from a women's perspective. Male playwrights are not continually asked, as I am, if they can write for the opposite sex. In this way, male-devised theatre is considered the 'norm' and female writing an aberration.

How would you define 'feminism'?

The word 'feminism' is over a hundred years old — Virginia Woolf complained that it needs to be redefined... Our ways of assessing ourselves are greatly influenced by a culture mostly created by men. This opens up huge and complicated arguments which I can only enter into by writing plays because I find theatre the best medium for exploring contradictions. My 'feminism' was learned through living and talking with women in the North of England, in working-class areas, where the women are very strong but also entrenched in a family system of doing things. So my feminism is pragmatic. I haven't actually read the classic feminist texts of the past thirty years. But in my play, *My Mother Says I Never Should*, I wanted to acknowledge that, in those 'ordinary' women, there's a lot of strength and independence. They are in a compromised position but I admire them and consider them to be as revolutionary in changing society through this century, as women who call themselves 'feminist' with an intellectual awareness.

You are perhaps best known for your very successful play, My Mother Said I Never Should; *what does that play mean to you?*

My play *My Mother Said I Never Should* was my attempt to acknowledge the debt of university-educated middle class women to their working class or stay-at-home mothers and grandmothers. You and I are where we are today due to the efforts of women in the past who made progress for us bit by bit, through small changes in their daily lives. I also wanted to show that this kind of domestic life can be *creative* in its own way, it can be self-fulfilling. The characters are strong and assertive in a variety of ways, but not in *male* ways. To generalize, men seem to need to be aggressive in order to assert themselves. I'm not necessarily referring to physical violence, but to status games. Women have an extraordinary ability to assert themselves through compromise: a resource of the oppressed.

In the play, I wanted to capture that way in which women, whatever class, are much more likely than men to be working, to be *doing* something all the time. All the way through this play, the characters are doing: folding sheets, providing food, packing or unpacking, dusting and polishing, often when they desperately need to talk to each other. Ominously, this suggests that women *themselves* have come to believe that their ideas and emotions aren't enough in themselves, aren't worth giving time to. For example: I recently went to a conference on feminism at the ICA. One woman there was knitting, another was doing a tapestry…. These women had brought things to do while they were talking, as if talking, even talking about feminism, is not in itself a sufficiently productive use of time.

What is the significance of time, and the passing of time, in this play about women's experience?

I think women have a different sense of time: this urgent need to get something valuable out of each hour is often to do with continually doing tasks for other people. It is as if we have to justify our existence by always thinking of and providing for others. I think this is critical. It is the biggest factor which has held women back from being inventors: scientists or artists. It is incredibly hard for women to be psychically singular, to be 'selfish'. And if a woman does think of herself first, it still tends to preclude her from family life in a way which being 'selfish' never does for men.

What was the process of writing My Mother Said I Never Should?

I wrote the first draft very quickly in 1985 and then spent three years working on it, off and on. I wrote the play because I didn't know any plays about mothers and daughters; it was not a commission. From the first draft, I structured it in a non-chronological form, juxtaposing long-ago past next to the present, in order to enact how past expectations for women jostle inside us and affect our daily choices. The child scenes are the oldest version of these voices inside us. And trying to make all time simultaneous was my device to give the play to all four women, not letting it belong to any one of them, so as not to suggest any one woman or her generation is more 'right' or 'wrong'. And I think actors enjoy the experience of working in this ensemble way. I wanted to create audience debate, not pontificate. People who come to see this play tend to attach themselves very strongly to one character or another. They'll say: 'Oh but it's Jackie's play', or 'I love Doris', or 'Margaret is my mother', or 'I am Rosie'. The reactions to the play reflect the spectator;

mine change as I grow older. It is *not* an autobiographical play, by the way. I am between Jackie and Rosie in age. If I identified strongly with one woman, I couldn't write a play balanced between all four.

I also wanted to expose our preconceptions about mothers and about women. So you see on stage four actresses of very different ages who play themselves at many different moments in their lives. It's unexpected to watch an old woman being sexy or being a child.

Do you find comedy an effective dramatic or political tool in your writing?

Yes. I like to create situations in which we laugh at moments when we may actually feel the most angry or hurt or sad. There are many ways in which plays can release taboos in ourselves. The child scene in *My Mother Said*, played seriously by adults, work like this. I think comedy is better than a tragic form, if you're trying to get an audience to actually question what they're seeing on stage. Maybe it's just that it's a better medium for this twentieth century.

Was the context of your work — experience of visual theatre in the decade of the 1980s — influential in the development of your voice as a playwright?

I'd say so. I was working with people to whom both 'narrative' and 'writer' were dirty words. Those performance companies challenged me to think about why we need a playwright at all. I think the playwright's job is to structure images and ideas; I tried this out by making pieces of non-verbal theatre. One of the worst pieces of theatre I've ever seen was devised by me — I was acting onstage when I realized this: a great way to learn.

No male characters appear on stage in My Mother Said. *Was that a deliberate (feminist, political) choice?*

The decision not to present the men in *My Mother Said* came very early on in the writing process. I wanted the women to be onstage and the men offstage, for once — to show how different our language, humour, sexiness and violence are, when women are alone together — not because women are 'better' in some quaint moral way.

What do you make of the general assumption that women playwrights don't write 'good' parts for men?

My two latest plays, *Our Father* and *The Genius of Her Sex*, have as many parts for men as for women. Nobody asks — for example — David Hare or Howard Brenton whether they can write for women. We have an art form that has 2,000 years of recorded texts, and we've got so used to having all the imagery, language and structure made by men that it seems odd when it's done in a different way by a woman: it seems abnormal because it's not yet a convention. We are told: 'You can't do it that way'. It appears that many people still don't think about the fact that we've only seen one side of the story, one way of making theatre.

Do you prefer to work with female or male directors?

I want to work with a director who has intuitive and intellectual understanding of the play I am writing.

What is your starting point, your entry into the process of writing plays?

My starting point, always, is feeling my way into a territory of images, emotions, fears and later character and story. It's usually images which I begin with, and only if I have a real passionate attachment to an image or a story will I decide to write a play.... My political consciousness, my feminist consciousness are both strong, but these aren't my starting points for writing. I'm basically trying to work out how to live. I think if a play costs me this much to write, then it will affect other people too.

Are things changing for women writing for the theatre?

Yes, in the sense that women now may start from a different place. I think the kind of starting point I describe for myself is very different from the starting point of women ten or twenty years ago. If I were writing then, I expect that I would have been more urgent or didactic about being a *woman* making a play. That was a necessary stage of women making their voices heard. Even since I spoke to you five years ago, today we have more and more women writing plays, all kinds of plays. I think today we're into the second wave: women now use theatre as an art form, not a platform.

Lizbeth Goodman

An earlier version of this interview was begun when Keatley was Judith E. Wilson Visiting Fellow in English at Cambridge University in 1988–89. The discussions which led to the publication of that interview/article were conducted over a period of many months in 1988–90, and the piece was published in New Theatre Quarterly, *vol. VI, no. 22, May 1990, pp. 128–140. That interview was the starting point for this one, which extends the issues addressed and updates them considerably.*

FIONA SHAW

Fiona Shaw has performed many key stage roles, including Celia to Juliet Stevenson's Rosalind in the RSC production in Stratford of As You Like It *(1986), and Rosalind in Tim Albery's production of the same play at the Old Vic Theatre (1989). Her extensive credits include work with director Deborah Warner in* Elektra *(stage and film versions) and the controversial production of Beckett's* Footfalls *in 1994. She won Laurence Olivier Award for Best Actress for her role in Sophie Treadwell's* Machinal, *produced at the Royal National Theatre in 1993/4. She played the eponymous king in Deborah Warner's production of* Richard II, *at the National Theatre in 1995. She has also worked extensively in TV and film, including roles in* My Left Foot, Mountains of the Moon, *and the 1995 BBC television production of Jane Austen's* Persuasion. *She is also a theatre director, and has recently toured in Ireland with her version of* Hamlet. *In 1994/5, she directed workshops and production extracts from* As You Like It *for the Open University BBC (see photo).*

You're known for playing particularly strong women characters: and also for cross-dressing roles, say in As You Like It *and in* Good Person of Sezchuan. *When you play such roles, do you think of yourself as playing a strong woman? What's your conceptualization of gender?*

I'm not sure I *do* play strong women. I sometimes play weak women who may appear strong in so far as they're the focus of the plays. Hedda Gabler is a particularly weak, vulnerable woman who is defined by having no courage. Elektra has no strength except in the area of argument — she has no life strengths, no physical strengths, no sexual hopes, no emotional hope. *Machinal* is about somebody who has no access to emotional or intellectual power at all. Shen Te is defined by poverty and a soft heart in *The Good Person* and Rosalind is silenced in *As You Like It* until she reaches Arden, and Katherine is not silent but is unloved and abandoned in *The Taming of the Shrew.*

What all these characters share is the attempt to become whole. They refuse to live in death whilst alive. They are all engaged in self-realization, which is what makes them theatrically viable, talismans of knowledge for the audience.

If the memory of them is strong, it is because they surmount the catastrophes of their life with panache, which is often unconscious. Fundamentally, the lesson I have learned is that vulnerability releases identity.

10. Fiona Shaw on the set of *As You Like It* workshop scenes, St Pancras Hotel (Open University/BBC video, 1995 — produced by Amanda Willett); photographer: Trevor White.

Do you approach cross-dressing roles in the same way — looking for identity through exploration of a character's strength or vulnerability?

Well, in relation to cross-dressing, the argument is doubled. The crisis and suppression of characters has to be very desperate for female characters to cross-over in terms of the representation of gender. *Deuteronomy* warns against cross-dressing as an abomination to God. I suppose it is to protect the eye of the beholder, rather than the cross-dresser, from sexual confusion. Gender is a seeming absolute that can be broken by the magic of suggestion. For me, gender is. But I enjoy the area of 'if'. As Touchstone says in *As You Like It* [V, iv, 102]: there is 'much virtue in If'.

If Portia in *The Merchant of Venice* dresses as a boy, her area of activity is expanded as she is empowered. The same can be applied to other Shakespeare heroines who ultimately tire of the disguise and want to return to their integrated selves. I think gender cross-casting is an exciting aid to releasing received notions of personality. People are not defined by gender but by the role of that gender. To have the opportunity of viewing the world from a different power base inevitably produces surprises. For the actress, this poses an enormous challenge, as she cannot hide behind the mannerisms of her received gender role. By changing gender one is exposed and hidden in an exciting way. Gender by its seeming absolutism demands the assuming of play. An audience vicariously enjoys the opportunity of travelling the uncharted waters with the crossed character.

I think this is terribly complicated, if only because at the moment we seem to be pushing towards exploring cross-dressing in a new way. By the early twentieth century, you find that cross-dressing is sentimentalized, so you have a principal boy, or men dressing as women, as dames; and they're just funny characters. They're partly funny, because there's a status drop of a man dressing as a woman. And it's partly to do with anger: the male has a chance to be angry at the female in the form of the mother-in-law or the wicked witch or the ugly sisters. The new wave of cross-dressing is present in the trend towards looking again at Shakespeare. Suddenly, people are not cross-dressing in a sentimental way. Of course there are productions like Declan Donnellan's *As You Like It* where all the men play women.

Did you have one vision of how Hamlet *should be directed or played when you decided to produce that play in Irdend?*

No, I had merely to respond to the conditions in which we worked: we were given a very tiny budget. I was given ten very inexperienced Shakespearian actors (some of them remarkably good actors in their own right but inexperienced in terms of Shakespeare), and we were given no theatre. It was an experience of people discovering text with rhythm and through games, so that their imaginations would be exposed to the chaos of the imagery while their discipline with language was sharpened. As it happens, the production was very dark, which I did not intend it necessarily to be. My intention was merely to release what they decided the play to be, not to direct a concept. I wanted to find out how the Irish consciousness met a seventeenth-century text freed of the barnacles of tradition.

Do you think there's any basis to the idea that women may work more successfully than men in collaborative situations (as in the process you described in your production of Hamlet)?

It's hard to say because the history of direction up to the last ten years has in this country been mainly male. In Germany which off-hand would appear to be more advanced in that way, it was also male-dominated until practically five years ago. So I think it's a bit early to make a generalization except to say that I suppose women by their natures tend to be more compliant to the ideas of others because of their cultural training.

I regularly work with Deborah Warner who's massively collaborative but in no way weak, in that finally she's also by far the most directorial of directors. Her ability to wait until every avenue has been explored indicates a sort of unparalleled patience. That patience may be female or it may not: maybe a lot of men feel a need to see something completed in the first week. She doesn't; she waits and waits, but then is very very precise in defining the moment.

Sophie Treadwell's play Machinal *has only recently been 're-discovered'. Do you think that the discovery or re-discovery of women playwrights has had a major impact on the theatre?*

No, because I don't see that doing *Machinal* at the National Theatre necessarily encourages the National to do any more women playwrights. It may do, at some level, and maybe in time we'll find that it did, after all. But I don't see it yet.

I don't think the National's intention in staging *Machinal* was tokenism. I think it just literally was a play that became present. It's very odd how these things come about: rights get released or somebody gets interested in doing it, somebody mentions it. In this case, I think an American wanted to play it here, so the play got sent here. The American wasn't allowed play it here, so the play got left here and and finally somebody began to read it and see its potential.

What I think is very important is that women in writing (and performing and directing) do not need to follow a form which — for some reason, at some cultural level — has been largely defined within a male frame.

Lizbeth Goodman
Interview recorded for an OU/BBC programme; updated 1995.

JULIET STEVENSON

Juliet Stevenson is known for her acclaimed acting work on stage, film and television. Notable television roles include Nora in the 1993 BBC production of A Doll's House, *directed by David Thacker, and the title role in the BBC production of* Antigone. *Film credits include the role of Nina in the internationally successful* Truly, Madly, Deeply, *directed by Anthony Minghella,* Drowning by Numbers, *directed by Peter Greenaway, and* The Secret Rapture *by David Hare, directed for film by Howard Davies. But Juliet Stevenson is still known primarily for her stage work. She has won three Laurence Olivier Awards for Best Actress for her roles in* Measure for Measure, Troilus and Cressida, *and* Yerma. *She won a Time Out Award for Best Actress for her role in* Death and the Maiden, *and an Emmy Award. She also wrote and presented a BBC programme on the* Great Journeys of Isabella Eberhardt. *In 1994/5, she participated in a workshop scene from* As You Like It, *with Fiona Shaw, for an Open University/BBC video (see photo).*

Does gender matter in the theatre; and more specifically, are you aware that the position of women in the theatre has changed in any way over the years?

Gender does matter. When I first came into the profession, about 16 years ago, there were very few women directors working in the theatre other than on the fringe. Now there are more women directors working in the big institutions and in regional theatre, partly as a result of the long campaign to make it a public debate. With more women directors working, different kinds of perspectives are being brought to bear upon the plays those companies do, particularly the classics. There are more women writers, and certainly more of them working for television now, than when I first came into the profession. People like Linda La Plante and Carla Lane have led the way — the commercial success of their work has encouraged people to start trusting women writers more.

All this is good, but one must always be vigilant about the situation, because women's fortunes in the theatre, as in so many things, are precarious. It may be fashionable to listen to the arguments and consciously encourage women to come into those places for a while, and then it may become unfashionable. They can get dropped again.

There is an enormously long way to go: if you are a conscious woman and you are working hard to bring a perspective to your work it can still be very difficult. I don't have the sense that I am working within a large community of women who are concerned about altering the images of women on our stages. The times are quite reactionary again now and some of

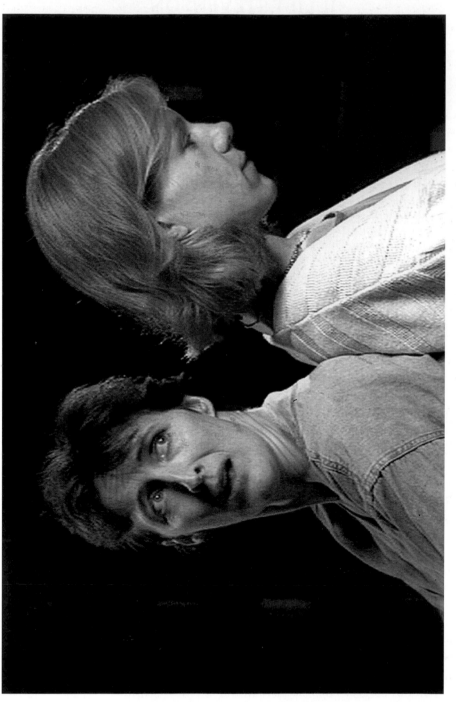

11. Fiona Shaw and Juliet Stevenson and reading a scene from *As You Like It* (Open University/BBC video, 1995 — produced by Amanda Willett); photographer: Trevor White.

the images of women on stages have reverted to something more traditional and externalized.

In what ways have you noticed this reactionary trend developing during your career?

When I started work, at the very end of the seventies, I joined the Royal Shakespeare Company, which was then in some ways committed to progress, change and self-examination. The commitment did not necessarily come from the top so much as from the body of the company: there was a ground-swell of feeling that things should be looked at and changed and challenged. I don't get a sense of that now, perhaps because the nature of company has altered. Actors used to keep coming back to the company during their lives, and as they matured, they brought that maturity to bear. Now, where the casting of the company is concerned, there is less sense of continuity. And in an era of individualism, and economic hardship for theatres, the notion of 'company' has, I think, declined and with it the grass-roots debate.

Also in the seventies, change and radicalism was reasonably respected, and there was a sense that change still had to happen. Now, many people have become more self-protective, scared even. Unemployment is running extremely high; everybody has to watch their backs and their pockets. Companies, theatres are struggling to survive. Those conditions tend to propel artistic directors back to more conservative choices, in terms of the material they put on, and actors, fearful for their future employment, may feel less inclined to challenge and ask questions. None of this is conducive to changing the status quo, or to attempting to shift the primary culture. But it's a microcosm of what is going on everywhere.

Are you conscious of 'acting as a woman', and if so, in what way?

I'm conscious that in any play there is always a different story to be told, because on the whole you tend to be dealing with material written by men, working with male directors, and in the company of people (whether it's a film or play) in which the cast is dominated by men. So, it's very difficult not to look at the situation other than from a kind of sub-culture.

I think female characters are judged more severely than their male counterparts. Therefore they are more concealed: there are constructs around women which are harder to break down than those around men. Part of the job when playing a character is to explore peculiarities, contradictions, complexity, and in doing so to shift the construct or the pre-conception that tends to encrust women's roles. This has been my great passion with the Shakespeare heroines: to scrub them down and start again and say 'let's have a fresh look at this woman'. To see what shape she is underneath the legacy of dramatic tradition and convention.

I have no interest in polemics, feminist or otherwise, but I have great interest in bringing my experience of life on the planet as a woman very much to bear when interpreting the women's stories, the women that I'm playing. I like iconoclasm in many of its forms, and it's great fun to debunk preconception and to try to reveal something more complex and self-contradictory. That's the great joy of the work, and that joy deepens as I get older and become more conscious of my own contradictions and complexities.

Do you feel strongly either for or against working collaboratively with other women in the theatre?

In theory, I am very much for it; but in practice and to be honest, it has not always been a very good experience. I think this is where we need to look really hard at ourselves. The great danger for women who are identified with the women's movement, is that there can be a wide breach between that self-description and what they do in reality. I have had some bad experiences working collaboratively with women for this reason. In the workplace, fear or ambition, or the need or desire for power, or a feeling of powerlessness have sometimes undermined collaborativeness and made life competitive, manipulative and difficult.

I think this is partly because there is a great pressure on women to be collaborators and to connect with one another, while that may not be what they actually want or need. We've got to be very self-knowing and realistic about these things. Real collaboration can only come from a desire genuinely to pool your strengths, and from openness, not through any self-conscious sense of what you ought to be doing, or from a potentially irrelevant focus on gender.

How would you define 'feminism'?

Who was it who said: 'The struggle for women is to be perceived as human, in a world which sees them as merely female'? I think it was Virginia Woolf. Anyway, it's a definition which I think is hard to better.

According to your definition would you call yourself a feminist?

If a feminist is a woman who is conscious of what being a woman means in this culture now, then yes of course I am a feminist. The notion of 'post-feminism' I find laughable — it's a bit premature, isn't it, to be relegating the feminist movement to history? The word 'feminism' has been much maligned, and I suppose we ought to change it, but that's the word which I find myself using — in defiance. I find it difficult to go along with received patterns of thought about what feminism means: each woman has to find out for herself.

Would you say that feminism has affected the theatre in any major way, and if so, in what way?

Our mainstream women writers now are successful partly because they were fostered and nurtured by feminist theatre companies back in the seventies. Caryl Churchill, for example, did much of her groundwork with Monstrous Regiment. Many women who are now writing for theatre and television have their origins in companies set up by the women's movement.

It would be difficult to point at any single development in the theatre and attribute it unequivocally to feminism. Rather, I think, the influence of the women's movement has bled into the fabric of the theatre by degrees, patchily. But for the real answer to your question, look around at what theatres are producing — at the *product*. As a member of the audience, whose stories are you hearing? How much of women's experience and perception are you invited to share, and in what ways? What is the *range* of images of women on our stages at the moment? It is only here that feminism can claim its influence, if any.

I am often struck by the innate conservatism of the theatre. It is a place which enshrines and cherishes many of its traditions, and is arguably more resistant to change than any of the other arts. I have ambivalent feelings about this conservatism — l love the theatre's rituals and repetitions in so far as they strengthen and protect it, but I am often exasperated by its self-perception, as of some tired old court jester churning out the same tried jokes, the same familiar anecdotes, always anxious to please, and therefore fearful of changing its act to incorporate new thinking, to take up new challenges, to mount fresh and freshly vigorous debate.

Do you believe that theatre can affect social change?

I think its chances of doing so are small because it's not taken seriously, and it refuses to take itself seriously on a lot of occasions. Theatre is widely perceived as an entertainment machine, and not as a means through which we can examine ourselves. I've always thought of it as a place where people can go and gather together in the dark and look collectively at human nature in all its silliness and ridiculousness and tragedy and triumph and then go away with a degree more understanding of who we are, a degree more compassion, and a greater confusion if necessary. Its job is not to provide answers but to ask questions. At the moment one of its potential functions is to throw chaos back into the community.

But the theatre is starved and undermined and shoved to one side. It's still dependent upon the marketplace to survive, and therefore becomes exclusive because most people can't afford to go. Most theatres now have to survive on box office rather than by subsidy, so they tend to play to a tiny minority from a particular class. The main reason for subsidy is to keep theatre classless: to subsidize ticket prices so that everybody can afford to go and everybody can be affected by it. Until this is the case, its impact as an agent of change must remain limp and relatively ineffective.

What do you think is the future for women in the theatre in England and the UK?

I don't know. There isn't the same culture or the same consciousness around at the moment as there was 10 or 15 years ago. In a sense this is partly because things have been absorbed into the mainstream: they do not have to be conscious any longer. Any movement has its cutting edge but doesn't need it any longer once it has carved into the mainstream.

I suspect that the younger generation of women now working in the theatre are much more conscious than they are given credit for. Perhaps more of the legacy of the movers and shakers remains than often seems to be the case. I don't think that many young women these days would take the flak that women who are now in their fifties took when they were beginning their careers. In other words, I think that a lot has been absorbed, but it is a situation which we should *never* take for granted.

We have to keep vigilant, keep asking questions, and also *change* the questions. We should never have any polemic or identity which stays fixed, although there are some questions which we keep having to ask. Self-examination, I think, is the key: we have to look in as searchingly as we look out.

Gabriella Giannachi
Telephone interview August 1994; transcribed and edited by Jane de Gay; revised for publication in
March 1995.

DIANA QUICK

Diana Quick's professional career in the theatre began as an undergraduate at Oxford, where she became the first female president of the Oxford University Dramatic Society. She has acted in a many plays, including Bond's Lear *and* The Sea *at the Royal Court; the British premiere of Jean Genet's* The Screens *(translated by Howard Brenton); the West End musicals* Threepenny Opera *and* Billy!; Plunder, Phaedra Brittanica, Troilus and Cressida, Tamburlaine, *David Hare's* Map of the World; The Changeling *(RSC); Doug Lucies's* Progress; *W. Humble's* Fly Away Home; *T. Frisby's* Rough Justice. *She translated and performed Simone de Beauvoir's* A Woman Destroyed *in 1994. Her many film and TV credits include* Brideshead Revisited *and* The Orchid House. *Her recent projects include the film* Nostradamus; September Song *for TV; and* If We Are Women *by Joanna McClelland Glass at Greenwich Theatre (March 1995).*

For a long time, it was generally true that actresses were mainly offered stereotypical characters to play. Is this still the case, or has the position of women in the theatre — and film — changed during the past few years?

I think the position of women is starting to change. Parts for women are getting better, and that is a direct function of the fact that there are far more women in commissioning positions now, as writers or producers or directors. And of course the work that they want to do is going to reflect their experience.

I've been working as an actress for over twenty-five years, and for the first fifteen of those I don't think I worked for a female director and I would only very occasionally work on material written by a female writer. In more recent years that's become a commonplace. I'm now in my mid-forties and the received wisdom when I was a young actress was that over forty you were dead as a performer, that you had to be young and nubile. Or, you had to be an old crone, and there was nothing in between. I'm happy to report that that seems to be changing. In the last seven or eight months I've played *Boadicea*, Madam Arcadina in *The Seagull*, and Diane de Poitier (who was the mistress of the King of France, who had been his wet nurse and later became the power behind the throne). I played a lecturer in classical archaeology who re-meets her holiday romance thirty years later: she falls in love all over again, and her lover becomes her house-husband, effectively, since she is the one with the career and he is the one without. I'm currently playing a prosecuting QC at the Old Bailey. I played a nice widow from Eastbourne. I have also been performing my own translation of Simone de Beauvoir's monologue 'The Woman Destroyed'. I feel myself to be very lucky at the moment: there is this richness and variety available to me and I hope that is the case for other performers as well. It may just be a lucky streak, I don't really know.

I had felt for some years that I was fighting a sort of rear-guard action and that there were many parts around which were for stereotypes or for secretaries or understanding listeners or whatever — characters who had no real action and were not protagonists. That's definitely changing, but not very quickly.

Fiona Shaw recently told me that, in order to do *Richard II* at the National Theatre, she had virtually to package it herself and do a trade-off, agreeing to do another play in order to do this one. My (female) agent, whom I consulted, said that in film and TV, the situation for actresses is 'diabolical' and 'desperate'. She pointed out that even Emma Thompson, who must be the hottest actress in the UK at present, has had to write her own script (for *Sense and Sensibility*) in order to play a part which is ten years younger than her actual age.

What is women's status in the performing arts more generally?

There's no getting away from it that the mechanical media — television and films — are still very dominated by the male sex, from technicians up through all the different departments. Even the cast tend to be more male than female and there are still far more male characters in the average script than there are female. What would make the most crucial difference would be for women to become producers, so that they can start to actively legislate in whatever medium they're working, so that our lives are more accurately reflected. Certainly our lives are very interesting and full of ambiguities and full of humour because of those ambiguities, and full of conflict, and therefore full of dramatic possibilities.

How would you define 'feminist theatre' in Britain?

Still marginalized — although female directors are starting to make serious inroads into subsidized theatre, both regionally and in the capital. I'm looking forward to a time when gender will cease to be an issue.

How do you contextualize feminist theatre at the moment, is there work which has similar anger to the plays of the 1960s, or has the anger changed into something else now?

I think there is still anger but there is much more humour now, and that's a sign of health, a sign that we have moved on and that we're starting to be able to hold ourselves up for a more humorous analysis. Humour is a great way of making a point too.

Do you think feminist theatre, or political theatre, can make a real difference?

It's a moot point whether theatre ever makes a difference: it's probably much better to see it as a mirror, reflecting the times rather than leading change. Of course there is the occasional play, which seems to encapsulate the spirit of the times — the obvious example is *Look Back in Anger*[1] in the mid-fifties or the plays of Edward Bond in the late 1960s and early 1970s, but I can't think of a feminist writer who has had that radical an effect.

It is a sad truth that it is still very difficult to bring women's writing to a mainstream audience — it still tends to be marginalized. Fiona Shaw is very interesting on the subject of performing in *Machinal*[2]; she points out that this is one of the only plays by a female writer to be performed at the National Theatre. The first one was by that 'well-known feminist' Lillian Hellman. And then, Sarah Daniels' *genuinely* feminist play *Neaptide* was performed there in the 1980s, and Caryl Churchill's *The Skriker* in 1994. But there's a terrifically long journey still to be made in terms of making theatre even reflect what women's lives are, to portray their lives in all their ambiguity and variety, let alone transform them. It's starting to happen but it's a slow process.

What about reception of theatre: are there more female critics now than there were or do male critics still decide what is good?

Well, senior theatre critics and movie critics tend to be predominantly male. I don't really know why that should be, there are lots of very good female literary critics indeed, perhaps they just haven't made the transition yet.

Amanda Willett
This interview was recorded for an Open University/BBC audio cassette, updated for publication in 1995.

---

[1] Ann Jellicoe comments on the impact of *Look Back in Anger*, page 21.
[2] See page 145 for Fiona Shaw's comments on *Machinal*.

HARRIET WALTER

Harriet Walter is best known as a classical actress in the UK, famous for her work in Shakespeare, Chekhov and 'modern classics' such as the National Theatre's recent production of Tom Stoppard's Arcadia *and Lillian Hellman's* The Children's Hour. *Her film work has included* The Good Father *and Louis Malle's* Milou in May. *Her television work includes Ian McEwan's* The Imitation Game, The Price *and (perhaps her best-known role) the adaptation of Ann Oakley's* The Men's Room.

I know that the representation of women has been an issue of importance to you, in your TV work and in your work for the theatre, both with political theatre companies such as 7:84 and with the RSC. How far were you able to make political points about the representation of women through the parts you played in the theatre?

Your politics as an actor cannot be directly expressed through a character. You have got to find someone who wants to say exactly what you have to say, and that's very rare. Your politics operate in the choice of parts you play, the 'editorial' choices you make in playing those parts, the things that interest you about the story which you tend to bring out. Or, you might understand how a character behaves, in the light of feminism. Politics also come into the way you behave in the work situation: my socialism means that I like to place the emphasis on company work and interaction, rather than playing the star hierarchy game. At the same time there is a balance to be found, one mustn't shirk grabbing the 'lead player's' baton when it is required on stage.

In the 1970s, I worked on the fringe in political theatre, in companies like 7:84. I found that my political convictions could be very unambiguously expressed, but that the actual acting skills required of me mostly had to do with the mimicry of class stereotypes, and this eventually made me feel limited. Also the socialist theatre in general was notoriously guilty of marginalizing women as much as the establishment theatres.

In the 1980s, when I joined the Royal Shakespeare Company, I found the situation was reversed. Direct political expression was compromised, and had to be subverted into subtler forms — through the interpretation of character, for instance. But on the other hand, the acting challenge was far greater. The sheer scale of Shakespeare's language demanded that I dig deep into myself, and that I use and expand that self as my chief imaginative and physical resource. At the RSC I found myself mixing and evolving with a generation of classical actresses, newly empowered by the women's movement to question the structures and systems they worked under, and the role of the female both on and off stage.

How much impact did feminism have on your work?

I discovered feminism in the same year as I went to drama school: 1970. So, thanks to the women's movement, I have had access to some forum of debate and analysis all my working life. The feminist movement has done much to release the perception of women from the stranglehold of male interpreters. For a short period during the seventies, we were held in a different stranglehold by the new feminists themselves, whose perfectionism required us to embody an ideal role model which never wavered from the positive. Now, I like to think we have come through to a maturity that allows us to be human — that, is imperfect — even if still reaching for perfection, and I want the right to reflect this on stage. The trouble is that feminist consciousness has not percolated through to the whole of society. I may have given myself the licence to be honest, confused, flawed and human, but the general public does not always want it so. Too many of them still want their women portrayed as heroines or harpies. So that became the challenge: to find the human being in the heroines and the harpies.

That was the theme of your paper, 'The Heroine, the Harpie and the Human Being[1], which you've given at academic conferences in Italy and in the UK. Is it still relatively unusual for actresses or performers to be asked to speak and write for academic contexts?

It was not so common until recently. I don't know if that's because we were too busy or because people didn't take us seriously. In the last five or six years my fellow female actors and I have been asked to contribute to books and to the debate. So there are signs that we are being taken seriously, because we are involved very immediately in the way in which women are perceived and accepted. I called it 'The Heroine, the Harpie and the Human Being', because I wanted to address the difference between the objectifying of women in which male writers often participate — either in a fantasy image of the heroine (how he would like women to be) or the harpie (which is the biggest threat, the sort of woman he is most frightened of). Whereas when you are a performer, and you are female, you are only addressing yourself to the human being. You perceive yourself, you feel yourself, you experience yourself as a human being, not as a judged, categorized female type.

The sad thing is that, while you accept the limitations of, say, a repertoire based on the seventeenth-century playwrights' view of the world,

---

[1] *New Theatre Quarterly*, vol. IX, no. 34, May 1993, pp. 110–120.

such as exists in the RSC, it's harder to come to terms with the limitations in twentieth-century modern writing.

What are the limitations of stage roles for women?

I am disappointed that so few male and female writers have responded to the emergence of women in all walks of life, their struggle to balance the new demands in their public and private lives and the fresh perspective that their new position brings with it. There are still infinitely more roles for men, the male ethic dominates most films, and such female roles as exist are too often created out of male fantasy.

In Shakespeare, and in the work of other (mostly male) 'great writers' of the canon, do you get frustrated with the range of roles available to you and other women?

Shakespeare's plays offer a rather mixed blessing to the feminist actress. On the negative side, Shakespeare was a man of the establishment and, for all his genius, couldn't be expected completely to transcend the patriarchal and hierarchical ethics of his time. So, in the history plays, the women are mostly peripheral onlookers, if they are present at all; in the tragedies, with a few exceptions, the women are either victims or monsters; and it is only really in the comedies that the female characters are allowed to dominate the stage.

On the positive side, when his women do speak, the language he gives them is as wise and witty, as profound and rich in imagination as any actor could hope for. When speaking such lines, one sees that Shakespeare had no less insight into the female mind than the male, and the technical, imaginative and emotional challenge of acting his works is no less for the female actor than the male.

How do you deal with stereotypically negative characters, or 'harpies', such as Lady Macbeth?

When I did Lady Macbeth on the radio, it became clear to me that Macbeth doesn't have the same horrific reputation as she does. I simply had to tell myself that I was not going to take any heed of that great bulk of reputation; I would try and just apply the reason that I apply to any character: Why do they do it? What do they want? What is the situation they're in? What options have they got? And the hugely important factor of your inter-reaction with the other actor, which I found very interesting. I also found it interesting that, as a woman, she speaks the words 'unsex me'; that is 'make me unnatural'. The assumption is that a 'natural' woman has 'the milk of human kindness' and that an abhorrent changing of character is required to do anything cruel or ambitious. You can set that firmly in the context of the time. The reactions to her are pretty strong because there are fewer women on the stage, so each one becomes an example of something; either of wonderful goodness or of terrible evil. In the male repertoire, you've got all the gradations in between.

In looking for the human being in characters, you're actually empowering the female characters and also yourself as the actress on stage — allowing yourself the power to interpret. But when you begin to empower female characters, does someone else (ie — the central male character, if there is one) necessarily lose power in the process?

The struggle is often there, yes, but it needn't be. I've experienced people being frightened that they're going to lose, and so getting defensive, but I feel philosophically, both in the theatre and in the larger world, that my liberation does not result in confinement for someone else. You have to tiptoe through that. You do get some defensive reactions from fellow actors when you're playing Rosalind, or Portia or the Duchess of Malfi: the opposite number can sometimes be thought to be a weaker role. I think it depends on the attitude of the male actor.

Women constantly have been in that position of being dependent on the male role to feed them and define their character. We've had to learn to work 'round that problem. In work, as in life, strong women don't want weak men, but equals. When both actors are good, the scene comes to life and it's great and you both feed one another.

What do you do with words such as 'chastity' and 'virtue' if you want to bring them to life, or make them mean something to women today?

This is a fascinating subject. Certainly for most young Shakespearian heroines, virtue and chastity are synonymous and at the centre of the character. I found that I had to substitute a word like 'integrity' or some such word meaning being true to oneself, in order to approach that idea. It is interesting to ask oneself whether there is such an idea as 'honour' in a modern context. What would I die for? What bit of my self could I never sacrifice, if I wanted to continue to be able to live with myself? That is what chastity meant to those women, I suppose.

One of your most famous modern-day roles has been that of character Charity in The Men's Room. *Were you surprised by the reactions you had to this programme?*

I was and it slightly knocked me back. There were two grades of reaction. There was very silly press hype about the steamy sexual nature of it, but people would have been very disappointed, if that's what they were tuning in for. The more important areas, which made it really talked about, are the contentious issues of love within a sexual domestic relationship between a man and a woman in the late twentieth century, the power tussles between men and women in this evolving society where some of the more restrictive rules (like 'women should stay at home' or 'people should be monogamous') have broken down and where we are the products of those generations that have been living through that kind of 'freedom'. Most viewers have a very strong reaction to that story, either of rejection or identification.

I was pleasantly surprised that it seemed to matter enough to provoke people to talk about it, because that's almost the greatest achievement for a TV drama to aim at in a way. Unfortunately the message went through so many bends and hiccoughs and funnels of prejudice in press coverage and people's own defences that I doubt whether what I feel and care about really transmitted out there as much as I'd hoped.

Now that you've got considerable status, and you've performed most of the Shakespearean roles — ingenues and the heroines and some of the 'harpies' as well — do you find that you're moving up the career ladder — and, what comes next?

This is the point where the road peters out: it's unknown territory from here on. I'm hoping that I can make it into something exciting, because I'm not alone. There's a whole huge barrage of very good, strong, articulate actresses alongside me, arm-in-arm, and we're not going to disappear and retire. Somebody out there has got to reflect the world we live in and the energies and talents that are in the theatre at the moment. On the whole, the roles are created by men and their interest in women is reflected on the stage: they're interested in young (nubile, marriageable) women, and mothers and grandmothers and landladies or whatever. They don't know how to handle actual, active, sexual, individual complicated human beings who are female, in the middle of that age bracket. They don't know how to write them, so we don't have the roles.

We've just got to either create them ourselves or encourage women to do so. One of the many reasons why women don't write as much as men is lack of confidence. They say: 'I don't know about the big bad world; I can only write about my kitchen'. You've got to encourage them that they do know about the world and they can write and that anyway the kitchen is interesting. They are held back because we don't have an economically fertile arts industry at the moment but I'm hoping and praying that we might.

Do you think that acting as a job is something that can make any difference — that your performance can make any difference in real life as well as the theatre?

It's one of the few areas in the theatre where a female can arrive at a prominent position and, from that platform, can exercise a kind of influence.

I get letters from people which suggest I've made a connection with them which I don't even know about. But I don't want it all to be on our shoulders: I wish it would proliferate into all the other areas of work in the theatre — the writers, the directors, the administrators, the producers.

Lizbeth Goodman

Transcribed and edited from an interview recorded and broadcast as part of the Open University BBC Art Works Radio Programme, 1991/2 season. Revised and updated in 1995 by Jane de Gay.

SUE POMEROY

Sue Pomeroy has worked extensively as a director in regional subsidized theatre, as well as in the mainstream commercial theatre. She has worked at the Royal National Theatre, spent three years as director of the Waterhouse Theatre, Croydon, and won an Arts Council bursary to work in Berlin with the Berliner Ensemble. Her company, Good Company, teaches through theatre: in particular, they use a combination of drama and workshops. Their production of I Bertolt Brecht, *toured the UK and was performed in the newly united Germany — at the Theater am Schiffbauerdamm, home of the Berliner Ensemble — by special invitation in November 1991, and throughout India in Autumn 1992 at the invitation of the Prithvi Theatre International Festival in Bombay. The play is performed each summer at the Open University summer school for the course* Literature in the Modern World.

What was your entry into British theatre in the 1980s?

When I went into theatre as a professional director, I was twenty-two. I don't know how that compares with other women in theatre. But funnily enough, in my year, the IBA [Independent Broadcasting Authority] Awards Panel seemed keen to try to redress the balance. Of the three awards recipients in that year, two were women (and I was one of those two women).

What was your involvement in the Conference of Women Theatre Directors and Administrators?

I first got involved when a number of my colleagues were setting up a meeting and invited me along. I was in at the beginning, the most exciting stage of the project. What was so liberating was the fact that we were able to talk collectively about our experiences. Directing is such a solitary business. I think the fact that directors now talk more frequently to each other about all sorts of practical logistic everyday events which are common in the job of directing was one of the results of those early women's meetings with the Conference of Women Theatre Directors and Administrators [CWTDA]. There certainly hadn't been a forum for that kind of positive exchange before CWTDA's initial meeting. Now, both women and men are far more open about directing as a work process.

Yet when we first discussed some of these issues at CWTDA, open discussion about directing as a job was quite rare. It felt like the lifting of a huge burden off our shoulders: the 'oh, you mean that happens to you, I thought it was just me...' syndrome. In particular, we began to discuss some problems which primarily affect women directors. In the late 1970s and early

1980s it was unusual for a large show to be directed by a woman. I did encounter some resistance from certain people. And the Conference revealed that this was not a problem individual to me: many women shared that experience.

Did you encounter problems of authority as a woman director in the male-dominated theatre world of the time?

Yes. Particularly at the beginning. But at some point, relatively early on, I came to a very important realization: that if people were uncomfortable with women directing — with women in positions of creative authority — then I had to make sure that this discomfort did not become *my* problem. I had a job to do, and I wasn't doing anybody any good if I let other people's negative attitudes affect my work. Once I realized that, life became much easier and I was able to concentrate on getting on with my job, and doing it properly.

In your opinion — based on your knowledge of the theatre in general as well as your own career development — is the issue of authority in directing exacerbated for women directors?

Absolutely, though of course, problems of authority are not unique to women directors. All directors must grapple with these issues at some point. But women directors have particular problems in finding a balance of power in the theatre space which often involves (primarily) male actors. The same is often true for young directors where the balance of power may be determined according to age and experience, rather than by gender. For young women directors, all these factors come into play, and authority can, therefore, be a very problematic area.

For instance, quite a few women at the first CWTDA meeting said that the way they handled this problem was to do the motherly bit: to go in and mother people, which was somehow more acceptable and provided a 'legitimate' place to begin asserting themselves in a workable relationship. Others relied on a 'sophisticate' dynamic: they went into rehearsals looking a million dollars so that the actors would be impressed with their appearance and think: 'Wow, I bet she's sharp'. Of course, others of us said, 'Well, hang on! Surely we shouldn't have to play these kinds of games.' It was quite interesting to compare the different people's techniques for commanding the respect they needed in order to get on and do the job of the director. It was something we really needed to share. Everyone, I think, benefited from that sharing.

After those early meetings, there was a sort of change: the problem at the time was that women in the theatre were still seen in a tokenistic way. If you had one woman in your organization, that was fine, that was enough. Therefore, women directors were used to being competitors. What was brought out in those meetings of women directors was a certain group spirit: the idea that we could try to support each other rather than compete with each other. Now, at least we could begin to aim for a relationship which was more open and healthy.

Out of that effort you wrote and published a paper for the Conference of Women Theatre Directors; what was the aim of making that paper public?

That paper was written when I returned to Britain from my trip to Berlin in 1981. It grew out of concrete questions which arose from my experience of working as a director, and from the discussions in the conference meetings. I took on the job of researching the training of women directors, and of finding out what happens to women once they've got into the profession (a subject in which I was very interested). My early research showed that there was a 'weeding-out' process operating in regard to women. So I wrote a paper about the training of women directors in relation to the career opportunities which training opened up. Interestingly, the findings supported a view which differed from my original hypothesis. I began by thinking that training opportunities were limited, which was why (in part) there were so few women directors. But in fact, it became evident that at training level, there was a relatively open attitude toward women. It was at a higher level that women were closed out: once women had advanced in their careers and were due to take on more senior positions where they might have prestige and power. And that's the stage at which many women want to take time out to have children: another good excuse to keep women from advancing up the career ladder. So I found a number of significant pressures on women, either to get out completely, or to keep directing at a certain level, without expecting further promotion.

The glass ceiling effect.... Did these problems of what we might call 'unequal opportunities' affect your own career development?

The 'state of the Arts' has changed so dramatically in the past decade that it's very difficult to talk about my career without talking about the larger situation as well. When I first started directing there was everything to play for. I do believe that had theatre and the Arts not been threatened financially to such a large extent over the past decade, the gap between women and men working in the Arts might not have developed in the same way. As funds are harder to come by, the boards governing the hiring of directors at theatres begin to look more and more carefully at who they are hiring to control their dwindling resources. They must be very careful. They are looking all the time for safer and safer people. Often, as we all know, women are not regarded as 'safe'. Safe directors are usually male, middle-aged and so on, primarily because those are the people who were given the opportunity to take chances years ago, and who have benefited from their mistakes and failures as well as their successes.

My own career progressed rapidly through the early 1980s, including my work at the Croydon Warehouse (with my excellent administrator, Madeline Hutchins). I also worked extensively in larger subsidized theatres across the country. Then, I went to work at the Royal National Theatre as an Associate Staff Director, and after that working experience, I was ready to move on, to climb a rung higher. But years later, that chance to take a step up still hasn't been offered. Of course, several women in this country *have* taken that next step. But there are still very few women in pivotal or powerful positions in British theatre. In fact, I was at a meeting at the Arts Council at which many of the women present said that they shared my experience of reaching a certain level — of being the first woman to do this and the first to do that, of breaking barriers up to a certain point and then not being able to move any further.

The bastions of power have not yet been stormed! Yet, set against that, there is no doubt that much of the most vital and dynamic work — both writing and directing, in theatre and television — is produced by women and that the female perspective is proving progressive, challenging and visionary. Much of the most exciting work at the moment is done by women.

To what extent do you think that your advancement and career development in the coming years may be affected by the (white, middle-class, male) monopoly of theatre directors?

That stranglehold of power has been shifted to some extent, but it is still a real issue. I'm one of only a few women at the helm of a company that is working at a regional level, producing touring shows which reach people across the country. If we look at the people in positions of authority with big venues, big tour schedules, big money — they are mostly men, of a certain class and background. Of course, it's difficult to make sweeping statements. We have to keep the overall context in mind. There are very few working-class male directors in positions of power and also very few black people directing in the mainstream. If you do not fit the profile in any of these ways, it is difficult to rise above a certain level. But the reasons for this are complex: words such as racism, sexism, class consciousness don't go far enough. The real situation is much more complicated, and therefore more difficult to tackle.

The logistics which you mention raise a question of representation. I'm thinking of the cross-disciplinary dilemma of the successful woman finding herself viewed as 'representative' of all kinds of other women...

This was once a significant issue, but may be less so today, because many young women now beginning their careers are assuming that it's their right to do as they like. They are finding it possible to advance relatively quickly and freely within the business. Similarly, women are now working more frequently in television and radio drama. Despite these advances, though, there is still a way to go. Consequently, I feel a continuing responsibility towards other women. If I have an opportunity to talk about the place of women directors, and to encourage people to look more positively and openly at the issue, then I will do that, even though many people may not appreciate it. Speaking out for women, as a feminist director, will not necessarily win you any friends.

Which may account for the fact that many women who are successful do not speak out for other women...?

Exactly. Mrs. Thatcher is an obvious example. She got to the top and succeeded in a man's world, but what did she do for women? (Answer: very little). In a way, that's one of the most important things we can do: taking responsibility for and speaking out about the positions of other women. If we as women abdicate responsibility for the opportunities of other women, then we will be tacitly contributing to the self-perpetuating negative situation which has always existed. But if we continue to stand up and support other women in a loyal way, then whatever commercial or competitive pressures there are on us to do otherwise, we may begin to advance the position of women. Mutual support is the way to solve the problem in the long term.

Do you think there may be a 'women's direction' in the theatre, or a feminist influence on directing techniques, for instance?

Yes. I think that's very important. I am convinced that theatre could be much more exciting than it is, if women had more real influence; to come in with a real depth of spirit and vision and fundamentally change the shape of the theatre.

I must say that I think there is a real dearth of vision in contemporary British theatre. This negative attitude has got to be changed somehow, or that theatre will dwindle away. It's all very well to keep walking the safe line, with a safety net. But live exciting theatre won't grow out of that philosophy of safety.

If more women were given the scope to use their talents and abilities — if more women were in key positions in the theatre, and if those women cared about promoting other women's work — we might well see a major shift in the theatre. In the sort of work that's done, in the values that are promoted and supported, and in the shape and development of the Arts. And since the Arts are so important to the fabric of society and the quality of life, this change would necessarily have far-reaching effects.

Good Company isn't a 'women's theatre' company as such. What is the relationship between your work with Good Company and 'feminist theatre' (however you might define it)?

Good Company isn't a feminist company in the most common sense of that term. There are particular companies which have devoted themselves to one kind of feminist theatre, in as much as they produce work by women and employ women exclusively. They are overtly political, and are known for political feminist theatre work. I'm thinking — in terms of this country's theatre — of groups such as Monstrous Regiment, The Sphinx (formerly Women's Theatre Group), etc. In a sense, those companies have been carrying the feminist theatre banner for some time. They have done some very important work, and I support that kind of theatre.

I think, though, that there is a lot of theatre in this country which is feminist in a wider sense. Many women have made feminist theatre, some of them taking feminist ideas into mainstream theatre, taking a slightly less overtly political stance, but perhaps reaching wider audiences. I would position myself in that second group. I think there is room for both.

In fact, both may be needed: each may rely to some extent on the other?

Yes, I think both are needed. Theatre must take on the perspectives of many different women: it can't just assume that there is one female perspective. Nor can it assume that women just want to get in on 'men's territory'. Feminist theatre can cover a very broad area. The system can change because of feminist input. One thing which is happening, slowly but surely, is that opportunities are expanding for women: for black and Asian women as well as for white, middle-class women. Though of course, there is still the problem we were talking about earlier: it is important that doors be opened to women, but also that they be kept open and that promotion and development be made possible — or at least not deliberately impeded — once women are working in the theatre.

Good Company exists in order to make people see everyday events and things in a new light. As in our show *I Bertolt Brecht*, we're interested in exploring and utilizing Brecht's concept of the 'Alienation Effect': we 'make things strange' or try to highlight and emphasize ideas and images in order to make them stand out, to help people to see in a different way. With my work on gender issues within the theatre as well, the aim is to inform and to amuse, and to instruct and to entertain. Yes, that's a useful way of looking at our work. Of course, the German phrase *Verfremdungseffekt* would be more accurate: it loses something in the translation. But crucially, we as Good Company are always aiming to get through to people: many different people, and audiences of all kinds.

Lizbeth Goodman
Compiled from interviews and discussion 1991–92; updated and edited in March 1995.

CLARE VENABLES

Clare Venables is a freelance director, working in theatre and opera. She has held directorships at Lincoln Theatre Royal, Manchester Library and Forum Theatres, The Theatre Royal, Stratford East, The Crucible Theatre Sheffield and Monstrous Regiment.

Does gender matter in the theatre?

If the play is about relations between the sexes, and an awful lot of plays are about this, then of course the gender and sexual identity of the characters will be enormously important.

I've directed Mozart's *Don Giovanni*, and that was the first time it was difficult for me to grapple with my main character. My internal dialogue with him was interrupted by the fact that, for him, I was the wrong sex to have a conversation with — he would just want to screw me or not. But the problem is not solved by calling Don Giovanni a shit — you can't plonk your global anger about women being the second sex onto an individual manifestation. You have to be androgynous when dealing with a script.

How has the position of women in the theatre changed?

Women aren't as isolated from each other as they were. There is now a language for dealing with psychological issues and gender issues which wasn't available to me when I started. Thirty years ago we would have assumed that any problems we had were our own neurotic reactions.

Actresses seem freer with their own bodies, freer to be their own type of person. There seems to be more of a celebration of different kinds of femaleness, not so much stereotyping.

Are you conscious of directing as a woman?

I am very aware of it because I still often work with actors or actresses who have never worked with a woman director before. It's a new experience for them, so each time it's a new experience for me in a way. I have worked a lot with male assistants and associates, and I have been aware of the different ways in which we relate to people, but I've never come to a conclusion about whether that's because I'm female or because I'm me.

The specific problems for women directors are to do with authority: the difficulty of women coping with themselves as authority figures and of others coping with them as authority figures. All the words that are associated with authoritative women are still negative: 'she's hard' or 'she's a bitch'. Whereas for men it's rather sexy for their self-image if they are considered hard and ruthless.

How would you define 'feminism'?

A feminist to me is someone who assumes, believes in, wants and works for the equality of the sexes.

According to your own definition, would you call yourself a feminist?

I am absolutely a feminist. It doesn't mean I'm a 'feminist artist' because I'm not very keen on -ist artists of any kind, but it's not something that you can leave behind at the rehearsal room door. It does permeate your responses, but my primary response when I direct is towards the work of art.

Would you say that feminism has affected the theatre in any major way?

In terms of its structure, yes: it's a much more user-friendly place for women in the profession. But you've still got all the problems that you've got in society generally which are to do with the glass ceiling. That's endlessly frustrating.

Do you believe that theatre can affect social change?

I do, but I don't practise that sort of theatre. There is a place for campaigning theatre — and I support it, particularly in education. I have used theatre as an educational tool in the past, but not on issues of feminism.

Even when I was at the Monstrous Regiment, when I did pieces where I wanted to express exactly what it felt like being female in the 1990s, I still leaned towards the attitude of 'this is the experience — make of it what you will', rather than feeling comfortable with 'instruction'.

What's the future for women in the theatre in the UK?

My fantasy is that eventually we will not talk about 'women in the theatre' — it'll just be people in the theatre. I rather dread the time when the first woman gets one of the big companies because that's all they'll talk about — the fact that she's a woman and not whether she's any good or not.

Women have just got to keep pushing themselves and pushing each other and grappling for what they want to get. They shouldn't hang around waiting for the blokes to give it to them.

What special tensions and problems still face women working in the theatre?

Something which is quite central to issues of gender and theatre is to do with eroticism and hiding. The relationship between the stage and the audience is an erotic and animal relationship as well as an intellectual and emotional one. And our experience of ourselves as women has been that we are eroticized in proportion to how far our selves are hidden. But the theatre demands exposure, which makes it very difficult for an actress to be physically and emotionally 'in harmony' onstage. Some actresses vault over the problem and quickly become celebrated as they are so rare... Sybil Thorndike and Fiona Shaw spring to mind. Others — like Mrs Patrick Campbell or Juliet Stevenson, become celebrated for living on that boundary between the hidden and the overt.

Another thing worth mentioning is combining children with the theatre. It's a bloody nightmare. Bad for directors, worse for actresses. At the root of it is the assumption that children are brought up 'elsewhere'. And that 'elsewhere' is the female domain. One of the biggest changes that we could try in this country would be to make some shift towards actually liking children. Then our working practices might change. Then equality might peep over the horizon.

Jane de Gay
Recorded on audiotape, London, July 1994; updated for publication January 1995.

CLAIRE MacDONALD

Claire MacDonald is a writer, performer and teacher. With Pete Brooks, she co-founded Impact Theatre, which pioneered visual theatre in Britain. She has served as Artistic Director of the Cambridge Darkroom, and is currently Senior Lecturer in Theatre Studies at DeMontfort University and co-editor of Performance Research.

Does gender matter in the theatre?
> Yes.

Are you aware that the position of women in the theatre has changed in any way over the years?
> It isn't so much that the position of women has changed in relation to theatre but that what we think of as theatre has also changed. We now have a constellation of performance practices, and of critical and curatorial practices, which cross the visual and performing arts. That change has come about in part through the challenges which women have brought to the field of performance — not only as artists but also as administrators, curators, writers, and as venue and festival directors. It is very significant, and too little acknowledged, that many of the people running the innovative arts programmes in this country are women, and that these women have created networks and practices which have favoured innovation, openness and change. For instance, the Magdalena project, the LIFT festival, the National Review of Live Art, the live arts programme at the ICA, the long-term support given to new work by the Oval House and the support for artists given by administrators like Arts Admin are all run by women. The fact that these innovations come from outside the mainstream and are self-created and managed is very significant. The other important issue is that the concerns of performance have changed in response to feminism and gender politics. In the light of these changes, the position of women has changed a great deal.

Are you conscious of writing, performing or teaching as a woman?
> Very much. My gender continues to inform who I am and what I do. I find myself drawn to the work of other women artists, whether or not that work is to do with gender issues. The sense of other women out there has always been very important to me and more and more I feel a need to acknowledge that, especially as I get older. That sense of acting as a woman

is one which is always developing and changing — in response to one's own life changes, and the culture around.

I was very involved, from say 1976 until around 1986, in feminist politics, especially in Women's Aid but at the same time I was deeply involved with Impact Theatre which was mostly men. For me it was the most liberating and formative theatrical experience of my life, immensely exhilarating because of our concern to explore what it meant to be a man or a woman and to take that exploration into fantasy and to extremes. I was able to do that in many of our shows: in *Certain Scenes* (1980), which was a fantasy about a post-holocaust woman-hating society; in *No Weapons for Mourning* (1983) where Nikki Johnson and I were ironic parodies of those hieratic *film noir* women to Richard Hawley's archetypal, confused male private dick; and then in *Place in Europe* (1983) where we put on stage fantasies of sex which had men being suckled like babies and lots of death and suffering fantasies.

Recently, other preoccupations have surfaced, also very much to do with being a woman in the world. My mother died quite horrifically when I was 22 and my sister was 14. All my adult life I have felt very conscious of irredeemable loss and that obsession with love and loss deeply influenced Impact's works, and has now begun to surface much more clearly in my own recent theatre work. *Beulah Land* (1994) explores the fantasies of an adolescent girl and her sister, who happen to have the same names as my mother and her sister: Vera and Eva. In a sense, theatre is a way of stepping into fictional situations and, unknown to anyone else, answering very deep personal questions. With time, that fantasy world continues to be enriched by dialogue with other people, some men, some women, but always about what it means to be a woman or a man. It is a central part of the long-term creative relationship I have with Pete Brooks.

Questions of gender have always been complex ones for me and have operated on many levels — for instance, I have also always been interested in extreme violence. That interest, and the interest in the genres of horror, science-fiction, comics and pulp fiction was, until recently, deeply unfashionable with feminists. I have kept two lines working in parallel really, a commitment to feminist politics and a need to explore with others very dark areas in myself.

Do you feel strongly either for or against working collaboratively with other women in the theatre?
Increasingly, I work with people with whom I share a sense of history and a theatrical vocabulary, although I also enjoy taking on new challenges — like working with Lucy Bailey, who directed *Beulah Land* and whose

attention and dynamism I admire very much. I often write critical work collaboratively, at the moment with Susan Croft, and I work on and off with a composer, Jocelyn Pook.

I feel it's also important to widen the notion of collaboration to include the stimulus repartee, and exchange of ideas which feeds into the work from conversations with other women, and the work they do. Recently, discussion with Holly Hughes and Peggy Phelan has been important, and the wit of Deborah Levy and the work of Rose English and Sally Potter have meant a lot to me, as has inventive discussion with academics and critics.

How would you define 'feminism'?

I'm not sure if I can define feminism any more. It's like a long close relationship, sometimes abrasive and difficult, sometimes comforting and welcoming. Feminism is both the pursuit of justice and equality for women within the structure of the legal and political systems we have and a threatening and serious challenge to patriarchal authority. I now see feminism as a practice, as a body of ideas and principles, and as including the earlier women's liberation movement which formed part of who I am and for which I feel immense nostalgia. Feminism, like most things, has become very plural, embracing diversity and difference, more questioning.

According to your own definition, would you call yourself a feminist?

Yes, I have a historical allegiance but I also understand the reluctance to keep the allegiance which many women, especially lesbians, now feel. In the last ten years it is lesbian and gay politics and art practice which have really challenged ideas about what can be said: lesbians who have had the courage to say the unsayable, to open debate about sex and fantasy and representation, to address the body, to be daring and to hell with feminist disapproval — that makes me slightly less happy to give an unequivocal 'yes' to the question.

Would you say that feminism has affected the theatre in any major way? If so, in what way?

Feminism changed what it was possible to bring into the art agenda and the means of expression that were available to be used, the whole vocabulary if you like, across the spectrum of the visual and performing arts. Feminism more or less introduced the personal and took the idea of 'agency' by the scruff of the neck. It also changed the whole framework of thinking and working in performance, introducing new ways of exploring the representation of the body, the construction of subjectivity and agency, and the relationship of the artist to her performance persona.

Do you believe that theatre can affect social change?

I think public performance, including theatre, is part of social change, bound up in it, one of its facets.

What's the future for women in the theatre in the UK?

Women have always had to live by their wits and nowhere more so than in the theatre. The most interesting innovations in performance have come from those who have stood outside the mainstream. I think that has deep significance for the future. The cultural shift we are undergoing in the west is away from full-time jobs and linear careers towards diverse, plural, perhaps fragmented ways of living, but that change seems to match the complex, multi-faceted structure of most women's lives more than it does men's. The greatest contribution to the theatre in Britain over the last thirty years has come from people living by their wits. The vibrant, multi-voiced performance culture we have bears witness to that, and everywhere within that part of the culture, women are prominent.

Jane de Gay
Written interview, edited June 1994.

SUE PARRISH AND THE SPHINX
(formerly Women's Theatre Group)

Sue Parrish trained as an actress at Guildhall, taught and then worked at the Cockpit Theatre TIE before returning to university, later moving into professional theatre as a director. She won an Arts Council Bursary to assist at the Half Moon Theatre (now defunct), and then became a freelance director in repertory, community and fringe theatres. Since 1979 she has been active in many arts organizations, including a long reign as Director of the Conference of Women Theatre Directors and Administrators. She served on the founding board of directors for the Women's Playhouse Trust, and left WPT in 1987. She was appointed Artistic Director of the Women's Theatre Group in 1990, just as the company was changing its name to its current title: The Sphinx.

Does gender matter in the theatre?

It is of fundamental and paramount importance to me personally, and obviously, because of its history and its mission, to the Sphinx as a company. Women remain a visible minority in their representation in the theatrical repertoire, and as artists working in the theatre. The Sphinx's feminist vision, however, is not confined to a narrowing of the gender-gap in theatre, but is primarily to make a significant feminist intervention in an art-form hide-bound by male tradition and deeply conservative and resistant to change.

Are you aware that the position of women in the theatre has changed in any way over the years?

In the last few years (five or so) there are definitely more high-profile women in the theatre, as directors and as high-flying executives and managers. But we have yet to see the emergence of a critical number of women writers, who face particular problems in getting their voices 'heard'. This is not just a matter of content, but very crucially of form. I sometimes think that play-writing is too crude a form for women, who know that life is more complex than the standard realist model of play allows. They are interested in telling stories, but also very interested in bringing their unconscious, and the collective unconscious, to bear upon the whole experience of witnessing a theatre event. The realist mode has so often shut women out, cast them as bystanders to their own lives, both onstage and as an audience. This alienation drives women to the necessity of creating their whole world when they write, and they can be presented by a critical establishment, dominated by the male tradition and repertoire, as incompetent. Women critics often feel compromised by their own response to radical woman's writing.

Are you conscious of 'directing as a woman'?

No I'm not. Although I have had actors — particularly male actors — say to me that they have felt that I've created an uncompetitive environment in which to work, I don't know whether that's to do with my being a woman. Coming from a marginalized position in the theatre, I may work very hard to break down barriers for others. But younger men (under forty) are probably also less imbued with authoritarian attitudes than older men. So it's difficult to talk about, partly because we never see each other directing. We really only hear about other directors' work through actors' comments.

Do you feel strongly either for or against working collaboratively with other women in the theatre?

Collaboration is the nature of theatre. So I believe strongly in collaboration, with no regard to gender. But of course gender enters into it. It took some time for male actors, and female actors, to get used to the idea of a female director. It's just not the norm in this country (maybe not anywhere). Many actors are more comfortable now that women directors are getting more common. But in working with women, five and certainly ten years ago, there were often unconscious pressures at play; they might try out other kinds of gendered relationships: flirt with you or treat you like a mother. And the same problem in a different form arose with women actors, who are often used to seducing, in some sense or other, their male directors. With the growing number of women directors, the dynamics of gender in theatre don't operate in quite the same way. Libido, sex, is a driving creative force in theatre — and this has had to shift when women directors become more common. For male actors this has tended to mean that over time, they have got used to the idea, flirted less and followed direction more, for instance. For women actors, this has meant re-negotiating the very idea of what a director does. In both cases, this eventually leads to the creation of a more equal open creative space for collaboration, for everyone.

Social realities are at last penetrating into the rehearsal space, but probably not fast enough to keep pace with cultural change. It's possible that because of the stress placed on collaboration between women in political theatre groups in the 1970s, dogma was attached to the notion of collaboration, in a very unhelpful way. Women have spent the past few years trying to establish themselves as artistic individuals — to stretch themselves and the work.

But maybe having done that, we can now collaborate as mature individuals rather than as in the past trying to evolve a group identity. That was very important in its day — the history of feminism shows that it's an extremely complex set of issues and perceptions that bring us together, as women in theatre. We have to allow for our own diversity and each others', and sometimes that's still lost. Sometimes an orthodoxy is established, and that can lead to a very boring self-righteousness in the work.

How would you define 'feminism'?

Feminism is the single most important set of perceptions and analyses that have emerged towards the end of the twentieth century. Fundamentally it seeks to liberate (an old-fashioned term) women from a life of subjection and secondariness, in a male-dominated world. My own aim within that has been to bring, or for the company the Sphinx to focus on bringing, women's subjectivity onto the theatrical agenda.

According to your own definition, would you call yourself a feminist? And would you call the Sphinx a feminist company?

Yes. I do. We are.

Would you say that feminism has affected the theatre in any major way?

Yes, in major ways, though progress sometimes seems quite slow. Theatre is often behind social change, trying to catch up with change taking place out there in the world (though of course, there have been important periods in political theatre when this was not so much the case). I think British theatre is particularly slow to change, very inward-looking, hung up on 'tradition'. The theatrical repertoire has women's secondariness absolutely embedded in it, and has done for the last 500 years. That is the challenge to overcome.

As much as I thought our last Glass Ceiling Conference[1] was wonderful, open, frank and focused, with a high degree of feminist consensus in its discussion between the panels and the audience of 300, still I'm aware that the diet of most theatres up and down the country is absolutely based on Alan Ayckbourn, Shakespeare and Agatha Christie. Theatre isn't responding fast enough to the huge changes taking place in society. That's desolating, frustrating, sad. I go to the theatre again and again, and see the same male concerns channelled though a male protagonist with satellite females around.

As we know, female authorship is no guarantee of a feminist consciousness. I've seen so many women — mainly academics and political

---

[1] Organized by the Sphinx, at the National Theatre, London, December 1994.

women — say that they don't go to the theatre anymore. I suspect the unarticulated reason is 'what's in it for me'? Theatre today, in Britain, does tend to be so rational, so male-centred, that women can only ask what's in it for them, or us, and must look elsewhere for work which resonates personally and politically, or must make it ourselves.

Do you believe that theatre can affect social change?

Yes, despite what I've said about progress being slow it's crucial to remember that there has been progress. I believe that people can experience epiphanies in the theatre. A play may empower someone who sees it, who may see for the first time that she can take charge of herself. And on a wider scale, theatre is the most powerful forum for debating the culture itself. At best, theatre is not a simple medium. It's complex, cumulative.

So, if theatre is cumulative and women don't go too often because there's not enough work to engage with women, then the connection between theatre and the female audience will differ significantly from that for men?

Precisely. Which is why women writers so often reinvent the wheel. Each new woman playwright seems to have things to say, which she can't find in most of the theatre around her. She starts again by stating the bottom line, which she needs to state. A more equal theatre environment would therefore lead to conditions in which women could write more interesting, sophisticated work, not always having to start from the bottom line.

What's the future for the Sphinx?

I hope the Sphinx will grow in influence, support and empower other women who are working in theatres up and down the country. Of course, we're limited in our resources and can only do, at the moment, two productions a year. That's not nearly as much as we'd like to do, but still we can accomplish a great deal within that frame.

How does your work feed into the project of the Sphinx?

A very important part of what I'm trying to do is help the theatre community to re-position the male-centredness of its work, to allow women centre-stage, and to encourage everyone in the audience to identify with these women on stage.

Do you believe that bringing women centre-stage might affect, however slowly, change in the world, regarding the status and treatment of women in 'real life'?

Yes. Certainly. We can see this in looking at film. In the film era of the 1930s and 1940s, women were protagonists, for women and men to identify

12. *Black Sail White Sail* by Hélène Cixous, produced by The Sphinx (1994), The Gate Theatre, London; photographer: Dee Conway.

with. Everyone followed the journey of the central woman in the film/story. And by and large that was an era of great change for women. Since then, I believe there has been such an increasing polarization between the sexes that protagonists in all media have been seen as definitely gendered.

A protagonist on stage which is centred in a woman's experience is not a universal experience, no more than a male protagonist centred in a male experience is in any sense 'universal'. We all have to step outside defined gender roles and gender-identified experiences in order to truly offer 'universal' protagonists. And these are hard to come by. Hélène Cixous has created some, in her new play *Black Sail White Sail*, which the Sphinx produced at the Gate Theatre in 1994. The play offers six female characters, all of whom are a-gendered to the extent that they seem universal. But this is a very unusual achievement, notably by a French woman and an accomplished theorist.

What's the difference between men's writing and women's writing, in a nutshell?

Well, to simplify, I think men's writing is backed up by tradition: history, myth, structure, ideas and a male-centred way of seeing things. Men who want to write begin with all that as a base and move on, develop new ideas from there. But women start from somewhere else entirely. Of course, we may be educated into the same sets of ideas and values, and these will affect the way we see things, but we have a different relationship to a male canon, and myths about male heroes and female victims, than men do. We start from a different place, and so we go in a different direction. Women writers have to establish the world of the play before they can write, each and every time they write.

What would be your advice to women, or men, wanting to 'help the theatre community to re-position the male-centredness of its work'?

Trying to see women, not stereotypes, with the full set of human qualities accorded to male characters as their right. Women are people; that's my subtitle. And of course, we could say the same about ethnic minorities, often considered a 'subset' to the main set of people, just as women are.

Women are people, on stage and in life.

Lizbeth Goodman
Telephone interview, December 1994.

BETTY CAPLAN

Betty Caplan (originally from Australia) is a playwright, freelance journalist and theatre critic. She is a part-time lecturer on the MA course in Theatre Arts at Goldsmiths College, London.

Does gender matter in the theatre?

Yes — at every level. If I go to see plays with few women in them or very stereotypical female characters I feel angry. Recently I saw *Beautiful Thing* by Jonathan Harvey — a simple boy meets boy story. Though it was sensitive and well-performed, the female parts fitted neatly into time-worn clichés. But because it was avowedly a gay male play, it was as if this didn't matter — as with Tony Kushner's *Angels in America*. Critics did not pick up on the disparity in the quality of the male and female roles.

What plays would you characterize as more positive towards women — more feminist?

Of course there are plenty of women writers confronting the dilemmas of our lives in their plays — Caryl Churchill, Timberlake Wertenbaker, Sarah Daniels, to name but a few. The problem has been more with men; Howard Barker has been writing major parts for women for a long time — parts which don't trap women into idealization or whoredom, but he is rather the exception. It is a difficult balance to strike, treating women's issues head-on without turning them into victims. Tony Kushner's *Slavs*, recently performed at the Hampstead Theatre, had several meaty parts for women.

Do you feel women playwrights are addressing gender issues?

Yes, most interestingly, Caryl Churchill in plays like *Top Girls*[1] and *Cloud Nine*, where she plays with the notion of gender by using cross-dressing. Charlotte Keatley's *My Mother Said I Never Should*[2] and Winsome Pinnock's early *Leave Taking* both examine mother-daughter relationships intimately. Because women have been so under-represented for so long, there is a backlog of issues to be addressed. But women must feel free to write about anything: I think this will increasingly be the case.

---

[1] Jules Wright discusses *Top Girls*, page 112.
[2] See Charlotte Keatley on this play, pages 138–140.

Are you aware that the position of women in the theatre has changed in any way over the years?

I've lived in Britain since 1967 and have been involved in theatre in a serious way since 1987. Certain things have definitely changed over time: women in the 1990s have a higher profile than they did in the 1980s, and far more than they did in the 1970s and 1960s. There is a consciousness of equality issues at most levels, even if it is sometimes only token. But there is a worry that with difficult economic circumstances, some of these concerns may well go to the wall.

Women playwrights have increased in number and in prominence, but it is very rare to see the work of British women on a main stage of the National Theatre (though Lillian Hellman's plays have had that privilege). The management still considers women too risky and prefers foreign successes to home-grown products, even though Caryl Churchill is a far more inventive and original playwright than Lillian Hellman. Under Max Stafford-Clark's direction, women's work received an excellent showing at the Royal Court, but with the change of management this is unlikely to continue. Women suffer disproportionately from a problem that afflicts new writers, that is, the lack of opportunities for second productions. Once a play has finished its run, it is generally confined to oblivion, which means that the writer has lost a vital chance to learn and grow from the mistakes that have been made.

In regional theatre[3], women have made some significant contributions — Pip Broughton and Ruth McKenzie at Nottingham Playhouse and Jude Kelly at the West Yorkshire Playhouse, helping to make these institutions among the finest in the country. But women are still not controlling the important purse strings at, for instance, the RSC, the Royal Court, the National Theatre. Somehow it seems that structural and attitudinal changes are the most difficult to achieve. The presence of powerful directors like Deborah Warner and Di Trevis doesn't alter the climate sufficiently to enable other women to participate.

Are you conscious of writing as a woman?

Very much so. My subject-matter is obsessively feminine/feminist/womanist — whatever! I spent years trying to get the theme of mothers and daughters out of my system, and it took four re-writings of a play about Demeter and Persephone to do so. At present I'm working on sisterhood. I find that re-writing myths gives me the distance and perspective I need, so I've turned to the story of Antigone and Ismene, and tried to focus on the latter, whose story is so often ignored.

---

[3] See Ann Jellicoe's comments on the importance of regional theatres, page 20.

Do you feel strongly either for or against working collaboratively with other women in the theatre?

I think it's vital that women support and encourage one another. I think that many of us, especially writers, suffer from a lack of self-esteem and from feelings of isolation. Conferences and meetings like the Sphinx's Glass Ceiling Events give us a chance to network and remind each other of our purpose. I was lucky to be able to work with Sarah le Brocq on my play, *Demeter's Daughter*, for a showing at the Riverside Studios as part of the Women Writers Festival in 1991. That was mutually beneficial, and taught me more than months of sitting at my desk could have done. It is not sufficiently recognized, by funding bodies in particular, that playwriting is fundamentally different from, say, novel writing in that it is by nature a social, collaborative exercise, and the playwright needs to hear and see her work fleshed out by actors if she is to progress at all.

How would you define 'feminism'?

Feminism is an ideology which sees gender as the most important determinant, over-riding issues of class and race. To me, this is often the most interesting and satisfying approach to a problem, as long as one does not get stuck in rigid and negative forms of categorization. I think we must seek to expand our understanding and consciousness and not to narrow it, but any ideology carries within it the dangers of abuse. I make no apology for being a feminist: it is my agenda and I'm open about it.

I think people who talk glibly of a post-feminist era forget the astonishing advances that have been made — take publishing, for instance. No publisher worth the name is now without a women's list. Feminism has grown and diversified, but people who resent it wish to see it as a simple man-hating philosophy.

According to your own definition, would you call yourself a feminist?

Absolutely. More and more so over the years. Having two daughters and getting divorced provided my baptism into the faith! I try very hard to live by these principles and enable other women wherever possible. I think the current climate has made it much harder though, as chronic job insecurity does not make for an atmosphere of trust and sharing.

Would you say that feminism has affected the theatre in any major way?

Progress has been perceptible, if slow. Practitioners like Caryl Churchill have made a huge difference. The degree and style of her bold experimentation have had a big impact. Having women's work on mainstages like the Royal Court also sets an example for younger writers who feel emboldened to try. Inroads have been made everywhere into the repertoire: Wendy Wasserstein's *The Sisters Rosensweig* has been doing excellent business for months at the Old Vic, and the Gate Theatre recently ran a season of neglected women's work. There are more women designers, like Iona McLeish, and lighting directors, like Paule Constable, penetrating a field which has always been male dominated.

Do you believe that the theatre can affect social change?

It did in Eastern Europe in the late eighties. The theatre was for many years a space where taboo ideas and ways of thinking could be aired — albeit in a coded form. The theatre has been very important in the struggle for gay liberation — witness the 'plague of pink plays' as Milton Shulman recently called the contemporary wave of gay plays and AIDS plays, in the *Evening Standard*. Consciousness only changes subtly and slowly because there is always a strong resistance. The very fact that a play like *Angels in America* was shown at the National Theatre is very significant; it couldn't have happened ten years ago. Augusto Boal has a helpful phrase — 'rehearsing the revolution'. The theatre gives us a chance to try things out, to play, to speak the unspoken. Therein lies its power. Just think how shocking Ibsen's *A Doll's House* was when it was first performed and how many people urged Ibsen to change the ending! And how many women (myself included) are empowered each and every time they hear that door slam!

Because we, women, are actually a majority in this country, women's equality continues to pose a great threat to the status quo, in the theatre as in society. Conservative 'flagship' institutions funded by public money are the last to change, but even they are beginning to shift.

What's it like writing as a feminist reviewer in the 1990s (and has it changed since the 1980s)?

It is virtually impossible to be a feminist journalist. There are no feminists at all writing in any national newspaper, as far as I know, or not on the arts pages. When I first began writing at the end of the 1980s, the market for freelancers was far more open and a wider variety of contributions was possible. With the recession, papers drew their horns in and began to rely far more on staff. This was a financial necessity in the first instance, with many repercussions. Now it appears that they all compete with each other to offer the same thing. I see it as part of the general move to the right which has taken place here and in the USA. The other change is the demise of feminist magazines like the *Women's Review* and *Spare Rib*.

I my own case, I began writing for the *Guardian* in 1987 when there was a pool of freelancers and a certain commitment to giving a voice to the un- and under-represented. By 1991, that had changed: the arts pages had shrunk to a few column inches and interest had swung to trying to capture the youth market. These days, rock gets about the same amount of coverage as theatre. Call me a snob if you like, but I maintain that this is simply unjustified.

There are now some women writing on national newspapers, but they are not feminists. We need a range of responses to our work from all sorts of people, including some who share our outlook and perspective. That is not so that we can be kind to each other — quite the contrary. A feminist looking at a colleague's work[4] may feel freer to be honest than a male critic afraid of charges of sexism. This was certainly the case in the early days of feminist and black theatre. A feminist critic is more likely to understand the framework and context of the work and to be able to assess the intention. Given that women are relatively new to theatre and trying to deal with new forms and subject matters, this is important. Similarly, it would help to have lesbian critics who would have a particular understanding of where a lesbian playwright might be coming from. I take issue with David Edgar's complaint that we are all in danger of preaching to each other inside our black, gay or female 'ghettoes': the success of recent gay male plays by Tony Kushner, Jonathan Harvey and Kevin Elyot shows that there is a real public out there hungry for such plays and that writers need to find their feet inside their own communities before they launch out into the wider world. Revolutions generally happen in stages.

What's the future for women in the theatre in the UK?

We have made inroads into the repertoires of theatres more than the structures of institutions and funding bodies, so this is where I think we must put our efforts. Unquestionably, women are on the agenda as never before, but we must work to see that this is not mere 'tokenism'. We now have exciting role models in various fields to prove that women can do it and increasingly women are finding their way into technical fields like lighting, which is encouraging. The boldest women do not seem to fit into the existing institutions: Deborah Warner, Phyllida Lloyd, Annie Castledine and Katie Mitchell have all found it preferable to work on a freelance basis rather than in one particular theatre, which says something about both, I think.

The key issues remain building confidence for woman at all levels and enabling them to see the progress they have made. I recently read about an idea which I think we need to adopt here: in Australia, the Performing

---

[4] Carole Woddis discusses the role of the (feminist) critic on pages 290–291.

Arts Committee of the Australian Council funds Playworks: a women playwrights' development centre which was set up by a woman director to give dramaturgical support to women in theatre, and which has now grown to become a national service. In the current economic climate, new writers are the most vulnerable of all and need the sustained support of their colleagues.

One issue which remains problematic for me is the question of value. When asked at a conference why he hadn't promoted plays by women, National Theatre director Richard Eyre replied, 'I'll do them if they're good'. But the question of what is 'good' remains complex: look at the disagreement about almost every play in the national papers, and those reviews have been written by a fairly homogenous body of white male middle-class reviewers! Good for whom? These are thorny questions. We need to devise more criteria for judging work—both for our own benefit and for our critics'.

The eighties saw both progress and frustration in equal measures: after the fertile period in the seventies when new funding enabled many women's groups to get off the ground, it was a bitter disappointment to see that that could not continue. Women have had to learn to swim with the tide and to comply with new demands. In the area of performing arts, however, there have been real advances, with women receiving a better proportion of the money from, for example, the Arts Council's New Collaborations Fund than from more traditional sources. Live Art, with its freedom from the strictures of text and the need to please large audiences, has seen women go from strength to strength — witness the collaboration between Siobhan Davies' Second Stride company and Caryl Churchill in *The Lives of the Great Poisoners*. And feminist publishers have grown apace and added significantly to the canon of work written by women, preventing it from being swallowed up by oblivion, as so often happened in the past.

So we can look back on the 1980s, and also forward to the second half of the 1990s, with a mixture of optimism and uncertainty. We need to remember to be there for each other, and to remind one another that we are not alone in this endeavour. A book such as this should be a great boost for us all.

Mary Luckhurst and Lizbeth Goodman
Initial interview by Mary Luckhurst, May 1994; revised and updated for publication by Betty Caplan
with Lizbeth Goodman, January 1995.

PART III

FEMINIST STAGES

OF THE 1990s

INTRODUCTION

Perhaps the most important development of the 1990s was a move away from 'drama' (scripted plays, often published) to more experimental, non-text-based and therefore more ephemeral forms of feminist work.

The academic establishment has recognized feminist theatre and interdisciplinary art forms as serious areas of investigation, witnessed by a burgeoning of conferences on the subject, and a growing number of BA and MA courses on offer on subjects ranging from the representation of women to Gender and Performance, often offered across disciplines: literature, visual arts, history, art history, performing arts, cultural studies, British studies. Meanwhile, the concept of 'interdisciplinarity' has become more common in practice as well as theory; a range of economic and social factors have contributed to the continuing movement of many women theatre makers into the production and performance of television and film. For instance, Morwenna Banks — once known as a stage comic from her days with the Cambridge Footlights — is now best known as a writer/performer of the popular television show *Absolutely!*

The Arts Council's establishment of more flexible categories for funding, including development funds for new companies and funds specifically designated for groups which work in inter-disciplinary ways, enabled some experimental work to be developed. A shift in the visibility of Live Arts, or Performance Art and Multi-Media Art, meant that dance, movement, mime, and multi-media work could be brought together with theatre work. So, the women interviewed in this section offer the greatest divergence, the most challenging cacophony of voices. Some of the work develops ideas of earlier generations in exciting ways, other work reinvents the wheel... For instance, the first Magdalena Newsletter of 1995 includes an advertisement for a new company called Mrs. Worthington's Daughters; a telephone conversation with company members revealed that they were unaware of the group by that name run by Anne Engel and Julie Holledge in the 1970s. More writing about women's theatre might make such information available, as a resource for younger women entering the field today.

The early 1990s saw the growing popularity of the Women's Writing Workshops at the Drill Hall and elsewhere, and the foundation of the Out of the Attic series of new plays by women. Some venues began to be identified as particularly supportive of new work by women, including: The Drill Hall, the Oval House, the Gate, the ICA, Riverside Studios, and the Place. At the same time, more women's work 'made it' onto the mainstages, including some notable collaborations at the National Theatre; Caryl Churchill's *The Skriker* premiered at the Cottesloe in 1994, as did the revival of Sophie Treadwell's *Machinal* (for which Fiona Shaw won the Laurence Olivier Award for Best Actress). That same year, the Gate Theatre featured a season of work by European women, including Hélène Cixous' play *Black Sail White Sail* (produced by the Sphinx, directed by Sue Parrish). In 1995 Deborah Warner's production of *Richard II* opened at the National Theatre, Cottesloe, featuring Fiona Shaw as the King...

The attention paid to the publication of plays by women — begun in the 1980s, largely with the Royal Court Theatre's initiative of co-publishing playtexts with Methuen — continued into the 1990s. The Methuen *Plays by Women* series was handed over to Annie Castledine as editor, and the collections began to shift focus, to include a range of work by women in Europe. Peggy Butcher continued to build up the list of women's work at Methuen until 1994, when she moved to Faber and Faber, to commission performance work (including new work by women) there. Meanwhile, Nick Hern Books made an important contribution by publishing the work of key women including Caryl Churchill, and also of companies such as Monstrous Regiment, and of 'new writers' including Kim Morrissey. Aurora Metro Press also came into its own, publishing collections of plays by women and advice about writing for women. At the same time, academic books such as those in the Routledge Gender and Performance series further enhanced the reputation of the subject within the academy.

Meanwhile, a concern for specific social issues emerged in new theatre work of the period: AIDS was a major concern, represented in work by women and men. Issue plays of the 1960s and 70s — such as Louise Page's *Tissue*, about breast cancer, and WTG/Wandor's *Care and Control*, about the rights of lesbian mothers — were reworked in a number of ways in the 1990s. For instance (to name only a few of many examples): Sarah Daniels dealt with the issue of women's incarceration and madness in a number of her new plays; while Black Mime Theatre Women's Troop company did a show about black mothers and domestic violence. Neti-Neti, a mixed gender company dedicated to feminist and access issues produced Philip Osment's musical comedy *Who's Breaking?* about AIDS-awareness using English and sign-language, while Peta Lily did a movement/live arts show about the female psyche and sexual imagination (*Beg!*), Anna O worked on the representation of feminist theory in theatre practice about cultural boundaries and communication, Deborah Levy collaborated with the Women's Playhouse Trust on a site-specific movement piece (*Shiny Nylon*), and Emilyn Claid worked with the Hairy Marys on an experimental interdisciplinary dance piece about representing the female body in and through performance. The Magdalena Project brought together practitioners from all areas of the UK — including Jill Greenhalgh, Susan Bassnett and Sharon Morgan — with many women from South America, Africa, Eastern and Western Europe and Canada to explore inter-relations in the working practices and images of women developing out of experimental performance work. All the boundaries continue to develop and shift as this book goes to press ...

Lizbeth Goodman

DENISE WONG

Director of the Black Mime Theatre Women's Troop, Denise Wong has been with the company since its beginning in 1984. She joined Black Mime Theatre as an actor and began directing in 1986, before becoming a founder member of the company's Women's Troop. Their productions include: Mothers *(November 1990),* Total Rethink *(June 1991) and* Drowning *(November 1991).*

When and why did you decide to form the Women's Troop?

I have always been interested in women's roles in the theatre — mainly because I am an actress myself — and I wanted try out the idea of a female group, to explore issues relevant to women. We needed to diversify and to recruit women in order to achieve a mixed ensemble. It needed to be a separate company at first, so the women could develop their own style and not be overshadowed by the men.

Would you tell me about the origins of Mothers?

Mothers was a devised piece. We have established a process of research, reading, talking to mothers' groups and looking at our own personal histories. We decide what we want to achieve, then start working, researching, devising, trying things out. Sometimes we achieve something very different from what we conceptualized. Once we have a pool of ideas, images, information, ways of approaching our subject, I give it an overview, structure it, shape it. I try to work out the throughline, the scenario. This sounds easy, but actually, the ground keeps shifting. The scenario changed in *Mothers:* it could have fractured off into many different shows — a different play could be based on each scene, which was a danger.

In what way was this a danger?

Our work is like a sketchbook. It isn't detailed, heavyweight theatre. I can live with that at the moment. In both the men's and women's troops of Black Mime Theatre, we are trying something new: looking for a way to change British culture by enriching it with real Black experience, Black talent. We don't have a British equivalent to Shange's choreopoem/dance/theatre work. We want to develop a theatre which is British and Black and related to our culture here and now (not American, not African, but Black British).

But our style, scene-by-scene like the drawings in a sketchbook, is sometimes very crude. Maybe even naïve, if you compare our work to that of a company like Theatre de Complicité. In some ways our naïveté has a certain warmth and joy, maybe more evocative and accessible to our audiences. So even as we develop, I hope we won't lose that.

Your response implies that you have a particular audience. Who is it? Do you have a hypothetical audience?

I always ask 'who is this play for?' *Mothers* was for women, young mothers, teenagers who might be becoming sexually active. We wanted people to be more aware of motherhood as a permanent role with lots of problems attached. We wanted to stage that. We did, and if we look at the kind of audiences we're reaching (and this is demonstrated by the questionnaire which we conducted)[1], we are challenging people's ideas, particularly women's ideas. Theatre can move people, maybe even change their lives. That sounds naïve. There is something to be said for naïveté. And it is also true.

How many women are involved in the Women's Troop, aside from yourself and the three performers in Mothers?

The Black Mime Theatre Women's Troop is the three women in the main troop, plus the training troop consisting of twelve more women. That's fifteen Black women, plus me, all working in mime, trying to learn from each other and to make a difference with our work.

What was the audition process like for Mothers?

Auditions were open and advertised. We had over a hundred applications, which was narrowed down to thirty for auditions. But I don't run auditions in the standard competitive 'testing' format. I set up a two-day workshop for all thirty women, and gave them time and space to learn from each other. Everyone took something away from the workshop, even if they weren't chosen. I saw in those two days who worked well together and also who stood out (three were then cast). And those who seemed talented and promising got cast in the training group (twelve more).

Who wrote the music for Mothers; *was it devised as well?*

A woman named Challe Charles wrote the music for 'Unconditional Love'. Otherwise, all the performers contributed to the musical element of *Mothers*.

---

[1] Analysed in *Contemporary Feminist Theatres* (Routledge, 1993), p. 46, and in 'Feminist Theatre: Survey and Analysis', *New Theatre Quarterly*, vol. IX, no. 33, Feb. 1993.

This proves that even in devised work, it is not always the director who leads the actresses, especially in devised work like ours, it sometimes works the other way as well. I learn from them, more often than they know. For instance, in devising *Mothers* we found — together, when the performers were improvising — that what is sung about in 'male' love songs and what we represent in our songs as love are very different. The dichotomy makes a point. We pushed that to the limits, and made it comic as well. That allowed us to break down theatre conventions, and to delve into other aspects of mime, like comedy.

The musical element of our work is where I learn the most from the performers. Of the three women in *Mothers*, one was a session singer, and all had some experiences of singing. So even when I had a certain kind of music imagined for the piece, I would find that my notion of what the music should be would change when I saw — or heard — what the performers could do, what they envisioned. Sometimes, they didn't believe that what they were offering was good enough. It took some time for them to acknowledge the strength of their own contributions. That's partially conditioning of course. As Black women performers in Britain, they haven't exactly been nurtured and trained to the point where they are full of self-confidence.

What were the motivating factors behind incorporating comedy into the emotional story of Mothers?

The choice of using comedy was partially due to the prevalence of comedy in mime, but was also a deliberate choice to make the subject matter accessible. We don't want to depress people, but to give hope, and present new viewpoints and maybe options. We often use comedy in our work, because we often tackle emotionally charged subjects. In time we may choose to use less comedy, but humour as a vehicle to make points for young people is very important. We don't want to progress past our audiences.

Is the Women's Troop a feminist theatre company?

The feminist label is not something I necessarily attach to me or my work, though I don't deny it either. It's almost as if being Black makes the word a little bit irrelevant. Staunch feminists might think our work too naïve, or not political enough. We talk about motherhood rather than about 'political issues'. But when I called the company 'Black Mime Theatre Women's Troop' I was told by friends that the name implied politics. And I agreed. The word 'Black' implies politics, as does the fact that we're working with women in the mime troop. And when we add to that mime is still such a 'white' art form (there is still an appalling lack of Black people, or women, working in mime), then what we're doing is very political, very challenging, even provocative.

It's amazing that in a multi-cultural society, an art form (mime) still remains almost exclusively white, and largely male. So Black Mime Theatre Women's Troop has to be political and also feminist, in some sense.

Is the Women's Troop treated differently, or reviewed differently, from the mixed-gender group?

Oh yes. Very much so. Many audiences who like the men's works say 'the women aren't as good.' Well, these women have trained for four weeks. What they have learned in those four weeks is amazing. What they have done in *Mothers* is far superior to what the men did at this early stage in their work. So the comparison is unfair. These women are amazingly good. They are dealing with subjects of such an emotional depth, and the men took a long time to work around to being able to handle subjects like this.

I have really enjoyed working with these women, and hope to continue the work. There's been a closer relationship, a personal determination pulling us together. Much more so than with the men. But I can't help thinking that there are so many more Black women out there who have not yet been found. I hope we can get proper funding — to find them, train them, help them learn to express themselves.

What is your funding situation?

In 1992 we were awarded our first-ever three-year franchise by the Arts Council of England. This, alongside the revenue funding given by London Arts Board and London Boroughs Grant Unit enabled Black Mime to establish The Ensemble, the first-ever permanent Black ensemble. 1995 has brought BMT a second award of three-year franchise funding. Although this means we are substantially better off than a lot of theatre companies, we have found that our operations have increased to such an extent that we are still currently underfunded with a very small administrative base.

The Mime Theatre does use some spoken language. Do you find that the women use language (body language and spoken language) differently from the men?

The women's method of working tends to be more detailed than the men's. They appear to have a greater commitment and investment in the work than the men do. I think the men need the approval of the audience more, the laughter especially, which can sometimes cause problems. If a scene is devised with a strong emotional content and the audience are seen to laugh at it, the male actors immediately want to play the scene for laughs, irrespective of whether it creates an imbalance in the piece, making the scene ineffectual and a nonsense. Clowning seems the order of the day for spoken and physical work.

The body language of the men tends to get very set in patterns, which takes a while to break down in order for the men to develop their physical vocabulary. Whereas the women are more willing to explore those arenas that are new to them and unchartered. Everyone reaches blocks at one point or the other but with the men there is a greater resistance to trying things new.

What is the most important thing to say about Black Mime Theatre Women's Troop, or the opportunites for Black women in mime in general?

So many of these women haven't worked much, and it's not for lack of talent or energy. Black women are assessed in certain ways, by white people with a white vision of what Black people are, or what 'Black roles' should be. Some groups now try for integrated casting, but then Black performers will tend to be rewarded for not disturbing the balance, not standing out too much. Multi-racial productions need Black performers who can conform, blend in and just be noticeable, but not agitate. This kind of approach will make British theatre stagnate. Black culture can add a whole new dimension: maybe it's too great a threat.

What are the future plans for the Women's Troop?

With the establishment of The Ensemble in 1992, the Women's Troop has been confined to the annual Women's training project which takes place during the summer. However, the Women's Troop is simply waiting for the right moment to relaunch itself as there are still so many stories to be told. Funding is our main problem, but I'm sure we have enough resolve to overcome this.

What's the future for women in the theatre?

To unearth new tales, create stronger links throughout the community, allowing women's voices to be heard, and to impact on the society we are living in. We've spent too long seeing the world through men's eyes; a woman's perspective is greatly needed. Saying that, I am aware we will meet with a great deal of resistance and even give up on the ideal. It is right we should take our place in the management, creative and technical areas of theatre/the arts. They can all learn from us in a non-threatening way, which doesn't mean we are passive, just more determined.

What's the future for Black *women in the theatre?*

To create new art forms, develop greater accessibility, while allowing for increased training provision for all in the arts. Basically to throw open the doors for all art forms. It seems to me that Black women's creativity is not acknowledged as being equal but something less so, to the dominant culture. This can be turned around with documentation of our work and a critical analysis which is not eurocentric in its application. These are all fields of evolution that Black arts in Britain need to take on board.

In the same way that Black music has inspired and influenced generations throughout the world, so can the work of Black women in the theatre. Their stories have the possibility of uniting us through our differences, with their immediacy and innovation in comparison with a theatre built on classical orientation.

Lizbeth Goodman
Interview conducted in London, April 1991; updated for publication 1995.

KRISTINE LANDON-SMITH OF TAMASHA

Tamasha is an Asian theatre company formed in 1989 to bring contemporary Indian-influenced drama to the British stage. Its permanent members are Kristine Landon-Smith and Sudha Bhuchar, who employ a full production team for each play. Their productions include: Women of the Dust, House of the Sun, Untouchable, *and* A Shaft of Sunlight.

What does Tamasha mean, and how did the company come about?

Tamasha means spectacle. Some people have also translated it as a 'knees-up' or a hullaballoo.

Tamasha was formed by myself and Sudha Bhuchar as a result of our working together in the theatre as actresses. I went to India on a British Council grant and staged an Indian adaptation of the book *Untouchable* in Delhi. I took a video of that production and when I came back to England, I met Sudha and we set up the company to produce it here. Since then the company has gone from strength to strength. We have been approached by various other companies wanting to collaborate with us — Theatre Royal Stratford East, Bristol Old Vic, and the Birmingham Rep.

There are very few Asian women's companies or even plays about Asians (women or men) in England, though the Asian population here is quite large. Why do you think that is?

Until recently there have been so few of us in the arts world, that we have had no presence there. Playwriting is a specialist skill: it needs money to be developed and it needs opportunities for nurturing. Since there has been little money available up until now, there has been very little substantial new Asian writing.

Do you foresee any improvement in the status of Asian theatre?

Yes... I think things are beginning to improve. Funding bodies are aware of the Asian voice and are recognizing good Asian work and talent. There is also some positive discrimination. Once the mainstream picks up on Asian work, things will improve.

What are the origins of your play, Women of the Dust?

We did the play because we were approached by Oxfam, who wanted to do a profile-raising exercise as part of their fiftieth anniversary commemorations. They had already put small amounts of money into our productions because they recognized the human rights issues in our work. Oxfam gave us material on their projects, although the play did not have to be about Oxfam itself, and we came up with the subject of migration. Then Sudha saw photos of women on construction sites, and we decided that the sites would make a good setting for a drama. The impulse to do the play was that visual one. We found a writer — Ruth Carter — and the three of us went to India to do research.

What was the research process which led to production of the play?
        We went to construction sites all over Delhi, interviewing men and women workers, middle men, contractors and the upper hierarchy. Then we went to the villages the workers came from and compared how people felt in the villages and on the sites. We took photos and videos of much of this. When we did the research, the women came to the forefront: they do the hardest work for the least wages, and also bear children, cook the meals and so on. The women always go to work, they never miss a day, because they feel the responsibility more than the men do.
        We talked to the women more than the men, because the women wanted to talk to us (the men less so, which may have been partly because we were women, but there were other factors as well).

The set for Women of the Dust *is very striking. Would you describe it?*
        The set was designed by Sue Mayes (who has designed all Tamasha projects). She had been to India with us previously, though not on this particular research project. We brought back a lot of photos and visual material, from which she came up with a replica of a construction site.
        When we first went to India for this project, we thought we might do a play about rural development projects, but once we saw the construction sites against the urban landscape, that was so much more powerful an image, it was obviously the place to start. In the end of the play we represent the village for contrast, symbolized through the unrolling of large swathes of fabric in blues and oranges: the bright colours of open air and the colours of the earth and the village.

The use of costume very effectively provokes an awareness of cultural and gender difference attached to the wearing of certain garments and colours. How did you decide on the costumes for the piece?
        Colours were also carefully chosen in costumes, and costumes were related to character and to environment. The way middle-class women behave and what they wear is very much part of their personality (there were

many joking references to handbags within the production). The costume is very important on the sites as well — the jewellery is very important, even in hard labour which is in some respects degrading work. The jewellery and traditional dress, ornaments of life, may work to some extent to keep women's dignity high, to symbolize their status and help them to get past the dirt and the dust. For a Westerner to see this heavy work being contrasted with draped scarves and traditional feminine attire is striking, visually and emotionally.

Are there thematic issues, cultural differences, of more substantial kinds, which you wanted to bring out in the play?

Yes. From a Western perspective we see the dowry system as limiting, as a trading in and of women, but the bracelets which work in the play to represent the dowry system aren't seen as chains by the women who wear them — that's a Western way of reading the image. Speaking of Western interpretations which aren't always accurate or helpful, we've had some quite odd responses to the play: some people have said that they don't have sympathy for these women, why don't they stand up and fight, etc. which is a very limited and biased way of imposing Western values on the lives of Indian women.

It's surprising to me that the cultures aren't translated and understood. It's so important to make that imaginative leap, not to stand outside as westerners and judge from that perspective only. The theatre helps to make that imaginative leap.

What 'messages', if any, did you want to convey through producing this play in England?

One of the things we're doing in performing this play in England is trying to say to audiences that the Western perspective isn't the best place to start in looking at the lives of Indian people, women and men. You have to look at the culture from its own starting-point, the audience members have to do some work and make that leap for themselves.

You have performed Women of the Dust *in India. How was it received ?*

We received mixed reactions because we were doing it in English and the play didn't fit the usual genres of English-language theatre in India, which mainly consist of sex comedies and farces, or translations of 'classics'. Doing an English play about rural people was also controversial, because that sort of thing is usually only done in dialect. People said, 'Who are you British Asians to come and talk to us about the poor?' Our response was that we had done a great deal of research, and so believed ourselves qualified to

13. Sudha Bhuchar in *Women of the Dust* by Ruth Carter, produced by Tamasha Theatre, directed by Kristine Landon-Smith (1993); photographer: Kristine Landon-Smith.

do this play. We felt that we should not be restricted to doing plays about our own country [England].

Ultimately it was a rewarding experience: people did come, and they enjoyed the play despite their preconceptions. They were drawn into the story, so it did work. People did come up and say thank you, and that they were ashamed to have lived almost side by side with these people, but never given a thought to how they lived. Also, the visit made international contacts for Tamasha.

India, in a different way from Britain, is a class-conscious society. How do you bring out the parallels in your work?

The class theme emerged in the process of staging *Women of the Dust*. It wasn't imposed from a British perspective, though it's true that the class parallel helps translate the experience of the play for an English audience — it gives them a point of comparison. But of course you're right to say that class is a central issue in India. It's all very well that mechanization speeds up work, as one of the male characters in the play points out, but it also puts people, mainly women, out of jobs which they need to survive. It's all complicated; we met development workers, stayed with middle-class Indians and heard their stories, saw how they lived. The class theme emerged naturally within the Indian context, and what helps to translate it for performance in England is that parallel to British society.

Does Tamasha produce 'women's theatre'?

I don't know how to answer that. I don't like categories, Indians don't have to do Indian theatre, women don't only have to do women's theatre work. We, Tamasha, aren't a women's theatre group, in that all of our plays before *Women of the Dust* have involved more men than women. For the first time, we've given lots of Indian actresses good opportunities and of course that's important, but personally, I don't like exclusive ways of working — in terms of gender or culture or race. So we wouldn't call this a 'women's theatre piece', though other people may. Partly I stay away from labels because they tend to come with so many associated assumptions. I don't want the work stereotyped, but I also don't want it claiming authority or 'representativeness'.

Are there non-Asian women involved in Tamasha's work?

Yes. In fact, *Women of the Dust* was written by an English woman. Many people have asked, rather critically, why we hired an English woman to write an Indian play. Why not? Ruth is an experienced woman writer and journalist. We interviewed many other writers (including many Asians) and she was the best person for the job. Exploding those categories is part of what the play does.

What plans do you have for the future?

We plan to go on producing plays as a project-funded company. Our next project is an adaptation of Lorca's *Yerma*, which was set in Spain in the 1930s, but we are going to set it in the Punjabi community in urban Britain today, because we see very strong parallels between the two. We are going to use a British-Asian cast, and we plan to perform it in Britain and then take it to India.

Lizbeth Goodman and Jane de Gay
Telephone interview by Lizbeth Goodman November 1992, updated in 1995 by telephone by Jane de Gay.

THE HAIRY MARYS

The Hairy Marys is a women's physical theatre and dance company based in London. The current company has three core members: Carmelle McAree, Siân Stevenson (director) and Susan Swanton, who work as an ensemble to create theatre which entertains, stimulates and invigorates its audiences. The first incarnation of The Hairy Marys was a larger group, formed of women with Irish roots or interests in Irish dancing and comedy. Shows have included the acclaimed Travels on Testos *(1993).*

What kind of work does The Hairy Marys do?

Our work is extremely visual and energetic, employing an evolving theatrical language, embracing physical-based theatre, speech, humour, music and Irish dance. The company delves into the world of gender and sexual politics, producing work that invites its audience to view issues from an alternative perspective: illuminating through laughter. The company tries to deal with the complexities of issues — never to see them as black and white. People often find it difficult to pigeonhole us. We hope to deal with issues in an original way, using different art forms. We have also been called outrageous. We are not a traditional theatre company and our work often challenges the status quo and may make people feel uncomfortable at times, but our first aim is to entertain and encourage discussion.

Over the last few years, we have started to work with directors we've hired in from outside the company. This has allowed us the opportunity to push our artistic style in different directions through exploration into a variety of ways of working. We felt this was important, as we were keen to avoid becoming complacent. For instance, we were questioned a lot about our decision to work with a man, Eric MacLennan, as director of our production *Travels on Testos*. Our answer is straightforward: in this production, we were dealing with male behaviour and felt that as a group of women who have no experience of being male, it was important to work with a man. This production was a big turning-point for the company. We realized that while we still wished to work with comedy as our main focus, it was also possible to use comedy while dealing with issues at a more serious level, such as gender relations and power relations.

14. The Hairy Marys, in *Bitches on Feet* (1995); photographer: Sheila Burnett.

Would you agree with the statement that The Hairy Marys play with gender roles through comedy and physical theatre?

Absolutely. We're making fun of sex roles and stereotypes in *Travels on Testos*, but we're also showing how dangerous those stereotypes can be. There's a very serious side, even to the comedy. We're not exactly showing an 'androgynous' image, but really we're looking to see what happens when stereotypes about women and men are represented and exaggerated on stage.

What's the typical audience for your work?

We have now established ourselves as a national touring company, drawing on a broad-based audience. The traditional audience of women and Irish people has expanded to include a large lesbian and gay following, as well as many people interested in theatre and dance.

I know that you did a new show in 1994, choreographed by Emilyn Claid. Did the work with Claid take The Hairy Marys in a new direction?

The company had already started to move in a different direction, towards physical theatre and movement work, as opposed to lighter comedy and cabaret. But this production encouraged us to move further in that direction, and to make fundamental decisions about the way the company might develop.

Is The Hairy Marys a feminist company?

Yes. Our artistic policy states that quite clearly. Writing, devising and choreographing collectively, we're committed to generating and presenting new material from a female perspective. We aim to create a new forum for women performers and audience members. In company policy, and public performance, we aim to redress the gross imbalance in representation of men and women in mainstream culture as reinforced by the mass media. However, we aim to be true about what women are and show women in *all* their splendour. We offend women as well as men.

We also have an active Educational Policy: we offer workshops in conjunction with the shows, or as separate projects with groups. In the past these have included workshops for people with special needs, schools and older women.

Lizbeth Goodman

Interview conducted at the Oval House Theatre, London, 7 March 1993; updated and edited in 1994 with Siân Stevenson.

EMILYN CLAID

Having begun her career working in traditional dance forms — ballet and contemporary dance — Emilyn Claid broke away to become involved in radical dance and New Dance at X6 Dance Space and the Extemporary Dance Theatre, where she was Artistic Director. She now freelances as a performer-director and choreographer and hopes to set up her own touring group.

Does gender matter in the theatre?

I can only talk about what I do. I live what I work. I believe that the energy of human beings is very sexual. And so as a woman my sexuality is a woman's sexuality. So sex, sexuality and eroticism underlie all the performance work that I do.

Are you aware that the position of women in the theatre has changed in any way over the years?

In the independent dance theatre scene, women have a very powerful role, particularly now that the emphasis is on the maker/performer role. Many women in this field are successfully creating and performing their own work now, so in that way things have changed.

However, we work within a very small area — that of independent dance/live art/theatre. Within that area I feel that I have a powerful role — but it's a very small area, and if I look outside of that, I would feel that my position and that of most women artists is absolutely negligible.

Is gender-bias in the arts one of the possible reasons why your work (and other women's physical theatre and dance work) is not more widely recognized?

It is easy to say that gender is a problem out there, but it's not that simple. Generally women have a harder time in the arts than men but that has to be defined more closely. Women work in a very different way from men, and women's work doesn't always fit into the metanarrative context of male theatre. However, there are a lot of women who do work like men (there are male and female ways of working) and I think those women do have a big place out there in the scheme of things.

Are you aware of 'dancing, performing and choreographing as a woman'?

I'm very conscious of dancing and directing and performing and making work as a woman — and in a very positive way. The issues that I am involved in — like redefining what eroticism is for women in performance, looking at the dark side of women's sexuality — are incredibly positive for me.

In my last show, *Laid Out Lovely*, I worked with the themes of beauty and death, contrasting the romantic beauty of the last century with the androgynous, down-to-earth sexuality of the 1990s. To flip women's beauty in this way, to see the dirty, dark and powerful sexual side as positive always provides exciting material for me.

Do you feel strongly either for or against working collaboratively with other women in the theatre?

I don't like collaborating at all — I prefer devising. I like to work with a group of performers where I'm drawing material out of them, but I like to work quite clearly as a director.

The gender of the people I work with does not matter. I like to work with wild, energetic, passionate people and I love working with men. I need the male energy. I have a lot of that energy myself. I love the conflict of the those two energies — masculine and feminine — or you might say that there's *three* energies, including lesbian energy.

How, precisely, do you find that these three energies work in the theatre?

It is these three energies I am working with in my next show, *Fifi La Butch*. I am fascinated by the idea of the androgyne, a powerful being with infinite sexual choice, playing the balance between male and female qualities, between sweet and dangerous, charming and manipulative. For me, gay and lesbian sexuality comes closest to this androgynous state of play yet neither incorporates exactly the qualities I am searching to define. The theatre is a wonderful place to express these ideas, 'play' being the key to the relationship between myself, the audience and the stage. There's nothing like a little theatre magic to put across some profound ideas. It's a great playground, but then I love performing!

How would you define 'feminism'?

I hate the word 'feminism' and I hate the word 'feminist'. I was one of the leading feminist dance people of the seventies, and for me the word 'feminism' was for the seventies. It's very much about hammering the nail on the head and I feel that I don't want that title anymore. It's a much more exciting vibrant time now — young women are working around the edges, installing things, subverting ideas. There's a lot more play and I think the word feminist is still stuck in a heavy angry title. I would love to see it redefined but I think we need a new word really.

15. Emilyn Claid in *Laid Out Lovely* (1994: Arts Council funded tour); photographer: Steve Hanson.

Have you any idea of what the word would be?

The word 'gender' has taken the place of feminism quite a bit because gender does not exclude men. Feminism excludes half of us.

Would you ally yourself politically with this new vibrant attitude to gender?

Yes. There's a lot more playfulness today, a lot more courage in terms of looking at the male ways of doing things, taking on male gestures and ways of working, and subverting them. We — women working in physical theatre — used to try to present something which is totally different and totally female. But the boundaries aren't so definite any longer. In my work, I incorporate a lot of that maleness — I love it and want to play with it.

Did the earlier form of feminism affect the theatre; and has this new movement affected it?

Feminism definitely affected the theatre. The hard work that we all did in the seventies and the eighties has paid off. In the dance world the image of women has completely changed and so has the whole idea of aesthetics. What has happened through feminism is that the old aesthetic of 'up', the Victorian idea of going up to God and the spirits, has changed to 'down' — throwing yourself down on the floor, looking at the emotional, sexual and animal in oneself. That's a whole new aesthetic that has happened over the last ten years in dance theatre, and feminism helped to create that change.

Can you trace a development of feminism in theatre, decade by decade, since the seventies?

In the 1970s, feminism in dance had two strands. One was political, connected to liberation issues of class and race, issue-based and 'personal is political' work, devising and collective working and developing mixed-media performance. The other strand affected the movement itself, stripping down hierarchical methods of teaching technique and ways of making, working, deconstructing the 'choreographer as god' myth and the content climax, looking at new structures, collage styles, new non-hierarchical movement techniques. And, of course, the body aesthetic. Doing away with the sylph. Different artists emphasized different strands in the seventies, but in the eighties the strands came together, the concepts became refined and developed, women building their confidence and individual styles of making work.

Of course, the negative side of all that is, as I said before, feminism became stodgy, lost its sparkle — one of the worst areas to be affected was lesbian style. I always felt feminism dictated that entertainment was politically wrong. Hopefully now, we are back on track. The best directions of feminism have been retained, but also we have recovered our 'bite', our 'flirting powers' and our glamorous, ambitious selves.

What's the future for women in the theatre in the UK?

If women take the initiative, play with risk and do not dig themselves into trenches, then there is no stopping us. There's good work and there's bad work. Good work for me is when there are at least two or three levels speaking and if there are two or three levels speaking it's likely that you're not going to be left with just one side of woman. I would rather think of it like that than think that we are in for a deep and depressing year 2000. I think there's enough of us making very vibrant, sexy, powerful work. Passion, power and play are the three areas for me — as long as those things are really being addressed then the work will be erotic in a new way rather than falling back into the old tracks.

You choreographed a dance piece by The Hairy Marys — that's quite a combination of styles. How did it all come together?

I directed a theatre piece for them which had some choreography in it. It was great fun. They came to me with very definite ideas about witches and virgin births, wanting a more physical and deeper approach than they were used to. We worked together for five weeks and created a dangerous, sexy and humorous piece of theatre, which involved text, movement, singing, acting and visual image[1].

Do you believe that the theatre can affect social change?

I think the media does affect social change and the media and the theatre have got very close, especially in terms of videos, pop videos and song text. The more video affects theatre and theatre affects video and media the better. A lot of theatre needs to address what's happening in the media and take it on if they want to be heard. Ideally, I'd love to be able to back up performances with film and documentation. These would get at the issues behind the performance, so the entertainment is just the cherry on the cake.

What's most important to you in considering the performance context of your work?

Relationship with the audience is very particular in my work. So much of theatre is about creating work which then has a distance between itself and the audience, I feel that for me the emphasis is to relate directly to them. A love affair of the most honest kind.

---

[1] See page 209 for The Hairy Marys' account of this project.

Does the gender of the audience matter?

It doesn't matter at all to me. I'd hate to play to women only. To do without men's energy in this world would be just drastic — bastards as they are!

Jane de Gay
Interview recorded on audiotape, London, July 1994; updated for publication January 1995.

MORWENNA BANKS

Best known in the UK for writing and starring in Absolutely! — *a very popular TV show which had run for five seasons when this book went to press in 1995 — Morwenna Banks has also made an academic study of comedy. With Amanda Swift, Banks co-authored the book* The Joke's on Us: Women In Comedy from the Music Hall to the Present (*Pandora Press, 1987*). *This interview was conducted in Los Angeles, where Banks worked in 1993/4 on a new television pilot.*

You've been remarkably successful in the comedy business so far. How and when did you get your start in comedy?

I started when I was at Cambridge University. I began writing and performing in Footlights (the student comedy club) after being persuaded by the then President Neil Mullarky that that's what I should be doing rather than a lot of very serious dramatic stuff which I wasn't very good at.

Were you one of only a few women in Footlights in your time with the company?

Yes. Initially there were two of us: myself and Kate Duchenne, who's now an actress with the Royal Shakespeare Company, I believe. When she left I was the only woman on the Footlights Committee, and then I was the only woman in the show that year too.

You worked very much as an ensemble in Absolutely!, *but again with you as a lone woman in a group of men. How has that worked out?*

It's interesting that it happened again — working with men — but it's worked out just fine. We're often questioned on this fact and sometimes attacked for it, but my answer is always that there would never be another *person* in *Absolutely!*, female or male. It's not a gender-specific thing, it's just that the six of us started writing and performing, and thought 'this is it!' The six of us *are Absolutely!*. It's an organic process. That's how we've always wanted the show to be. But I take the point that the gender imbalance is representative of the way things are in comedy.

You do have some wonderful parts in Absolutely! *which you've written for yourself. There's an amazing range of characters which you play: some hideously ugly and some quite beautiful and some very physical and some very verbal. What kind of characters do you most enjoy writing and playing?*

I really don't care what I look like on television. One of the things that I really love is being able to play grotesque characters. It's very liberating to exploit a character for three minutes and see how far I can go with it.

Do you make conscious decisions about not looking glamorous on stage and screen?

I'm not sure whether it's a conscious thing. Like I said, I guess I just basically don't *care* what I look like. Maybe I've accepted that I'm never going to be a whispy, beautiful actress, so I may as well just have fun doing what I *can* do...

Do you ever find that people don't recognize how much you contribute to the show?

Unfortunately yes. One of the things I find hardest is that there is a basic assumption, more amongst people in the industry, that I just write the 'Little Girl' monologues. It's often assumed that I don't write very much, and that's a very hard one to fight, particularly given the co-operative nature of our company. I think it's very good for the spirit of the show that no-one really knows who writes what. But on the other hand it's very difficult being the only woman and having people assume that you only write the women's parts. I've certainly been guilty of making assumptions about other women performers: that maybe they don't write their own material, and — to serve me right — that's what I've often come up against.

You've also got an academic background. In your book, you and Amanda Swift look at preconceptions about women in comedy as well as the history of women in comedy from the music hall to the present. How has your academic research influenced your perception of the situation for women like yourself working in comedy?

It was very useful writing that book. Amanda and I decided to write it because we were often the only women performing wherever we worked. We were always discussed in terms of being 'the next so and so': the *next* Pamela Stephenson, the *next* Julie Walters... as if there's only allowed to be one successful woman comic at a time. That, of course, sets you in competition with other women; bills you as taking the spotlight from someone else. So we decided to write a book and provide the historical basis for what we were doing, in order to show that women had been funny for a long time, and we were not just 'the next' someone, but were actually part of a tradition.

What kind of response did the book receive?

The response was odd: some people were actually quite hostile towards us for writing it, and others (mostly women) would say to us, 'Well what do you know about it?', as if we didn't have a right to the subject. Some people said that they didn't 'just' want to be classed as 'women performers', which wasn't the point of our book at all. But I think the situation's really changed, and now I think it's gratifying to have the book as a document of what was going on in 1987.

And where are we now?

Well, looking at what's happening now [in the 1990s], there are actually many more women around, and certainly more women in the vanguard, excelling at comedy. When we wrote the book, Victoria Wood was everybody's icon. Now it's French and Saunders, and Jennifer Saunders especially has made history with *Absolutely Fabulous*. Josie [Lawrence] has become famous, as has Sandi [Toksvig], Jo Brand, Caroline Quentin, Helen Lederer, Jenny Eclair... All of these people who were kind of bubbling under a few years ago are really making names for themselves now.

It's difficult to name many women who are involved in the mid-1990s in writing as well performing situation comedies. What's the difference between writing and performing sitcoms as opposed to, say, stand-up or sketch based comedy, and why do you think fewer women are involved in writing for sitcoms (in the UK)?

Well the exciting thing about sketch-based comedy is that it allows so much room for experimentation. But in a sitcom, you have to create sustainable characters which will reappear week after week. And with sitcoms you have to guard against crassness, because so many sitcoms are just unbelievable. What they talk about constantly in the sitcom business out here [in California] is REALITY. Maybe women are simply too in touch with actual domestic reality to turn it into the simple-minded rubbish that so often finds its way onto our TV screens. Or maybe not. Who knows?

Why is the situation comedy so difficult to do well?

I think it's because — both in the USA and the UK — people are trying to represent a way of life and a sense of reality that actually doesn't exist. In the USA I've found this kind of endless cheerfulness, this view that things *have* to be alright and that you *have* to say 'I love you' two thirds of the way of the way through every show... While at home in the UK, sitcoms depict situations where everybody's bumbling around inanely, but we're all going to pull together in the end. And I think that sitcoms succeed when people can identify other people's weaknesses. Take a loser like Basil Fawlty [in the hugely popular television show, *Fawlty Towers*] now that character was hardly 'realistic' or overtly sympathetic, but John Cleese made it work brilliantly. In the USA there does seem to be more emphasis on creating characters who are sympathetic and who look good, are pretty or handsome and know how to say nice things to people. Apparently, that's what the public wants to see. But I simply don't believe in that kind of simplistic formula. *Seinfeld* and *Roseanne* are two of the most successful sitcoms in the USA at the moment, and neither is about beautiful or nice people…

If you think about the Roseanne show and its immense popularity, do you think that its success may not only be to do with the fact that the Roseanne persona represents real problems like compulsive eating and working class situations, but also that she's subverting images of women which have been so popular: taking the Lucille Ball image of the beautiful-feminine-funny-person stereotype, playing with it and taking it to an extreme…?

Oh absolutely! I think that it's a triumph that a lot of people love Roseanne, and that a lot of people identify Roseanne's success as a personal triumph, and as a symbolic success for the blue collar sector *and* for women. Roseanne is one of the most powerful woman in American television, and in fact one of the most powerful women in America, and she's *not* a traditional model of femininity.

You've obviously found success… but do you think it is any easier for women working in comedy today?

Yes and no. If we take our book [*The Joke's On Us*] as a gauge it's easier to answer that question. There are certainly more women comics around now than there were when we wrote the book in the mid-eighties. More role models. But there's still a reluctance in Britain to allow women to have the same amount of freedom in terms of writing as men have. That's because there have been certain notable failures, and with women the failures are always notable.

So individual women are still seen as somehow representative of each other, of ALL WOMEN, rather than as individuals?

Unfortunately, yes. Too often that's still true. You can see why that happens. It's very hard because the failures amongst the men aren't judged in the same way. I've always been very very reluctant to attribute any lack of success or any stumbling blocks to my gender. I've always believed that if you're good and you're funny that that will actually win out. But the longer that I work in comedy I think the more aware I am of the difficulties facing women. It is extremely rare to be funny and to be taken seriously as a writer, particularly for women, and I would say that's more a case in Britain than it is in the USA.

Lizbeth Goodman
Recorded on audiotape for the BBC in Hollywood, 1993; version of this interview was first published in Second Shift Magazine, *1994.*

VICTORIA WORSLEY

Victoria Worsley is an actor and writer and occasionally a director. She co-founded the women's performance company Tattycoram in 1986. With Tattycoram, she co-devised and performed three shows. She founded her own production company, Jade, in 1992. Her writing credits include: And All Because the Lady Loves... *and* Night Train *for Jade, and* Lift and Separate *for Soho Theatre's '(Small) Objects of Desire' season of new work. With Caroline Ward, she also co-devised a solo show,* Make Me a Statue *(1990).*

Does gender matter in the theatre?

Yes, clearly gender does matter in theatre. A writer, director or designer will bring their particular experience to their work and that experience will be partly determined by what sex they are. Also, more obviously, one can say that gender matters, looking at the still poor showing (numerically) of women in top positions in the theatre in comparison to men. And the situation for female actors is still more difficult.

Are you aware that the position of women has changed in any way over the years?

Yes, in that there are more women working in the theatre now than previously. Women are now holding artistic directorships and being acknowledged as writers, directors and designers; in greater numbers and at higher levels. However it is still possible to total the number of women directors running buildings on one (possibly two) hands. While the entire administration, stage management, and even a significant number of the technical crew in a rep theatre might be female, the artistic and executive directors will still, in most cases, be male. I also find it interesting that artistic directorships are being ceded to women at a time of crisis in the theatre when anyone who wants to earn serious money is leaving it for television.

Are you conscious of 'acting, directing or writing as a woman', and, if so in what ways?

As a writer, my experience as a woman clearly affects what I write and how I go about it. I have always consciously acknowledged that and furthered it, using my own emotional experience as a woman and examining it in a social and political context. I also question the presentation of women on stage and the traditional functions of female characters in plot. I do feel, however, that there has been a tendency to decide what it means to 'act/write/direct as a woman' — not only by men but also by different feminist traditions. I often find myself working against both these sets of expectations and assumptions.

As an actor, I have turned work down on the grounds that it is offensive to women. In taking responsibility for the women characters I play, I have sometimes had to challenge a writer or director's vision, though it is not always appropriate or possible to do that. Sometimes the need to earn money, make a career step, work with someone you particularly want to work with, leads to unfortunate but necessary compromise. Moreover, as an actor you are never in control of the context of your work, which might render any effort at a particular reading of a character redundant.

Do you feel strongly for or against working collaboratively with women in the theatre?

I have found the support in collaborating with women extremely important in finding my own process and freeing me to look at my own experience, in order to see its social and political background. Indeed, in the days of Tattycoram, I found it essential. However, I have since had very good experiences collaborating with men and now, while I still look to women on the whole, I feel able to pick men to work with when I choose to. I can benefit from their different experience and attitudes and to let it enrich rather than subsume my work.

How would you define 'feminism'?

I still define feminism as working towards the liberation of women. The question now is liberation from what? Clearly much has been done but in many cases old attitudes and beliefs either remain or have adapted themselves to still constrain women within the new status quo, or to produce new problems. Added to that is not only the 'backlash' phenomenon but also sometimes equally constraining pressures left over from some early forms of feminism. I feel that the collaboration of men in examining and under-standing their sexuality and cultural position is now necessary for the progress of women, even though that path may appear retrograde at times.

According to your own definition, would you call yourself a feminist?

Yes.

Would you say that feminism has affected the theatre in any major way? If so, in what way?

Yes, I would say that feminism has affected the theatre — there have been advances in employment — but there is clearly still a long way to go.

Feminism has also had an impact on the kind of work being made and the representation of women on stage. There has been an increase in the number of plays looking at the experience of women and using central female characters, although, as ever, not enough and still often with limitations. The stereotyping of women on stage is at least recognized as an issue now and there is a significant if not vast body of work addressing it. Feminism has also played a part in challenging the idea of what a play is in terms of its form, where it is performed and how it is made, in providing the impetus for some of the agit prop, collective devising, performance art, and other innovations in writing and performing since the late 1960s. It is still possible on occasions, however, to visit the West End, regional touring theatres, and even some repertory theatres and to feel as if feminism has had no impact at all.

Do you believe that theatre can affect social change?

On its own I don't believe the theatre can affect social change. I think that when it is an integral part of a culture it can help achieve social change by being another voice in the crowd that constructs social beliefs and attitudes. Moreover, the interaction between live performers and audience and its potential for bringing a multitude of art forms together to reach that audience on a number of levels can make it an extremely potent voice.

In Britain at the moment I don't think the theatre is capable of contributing much to social change, if anything. It is no longer a significant part of the culture, having been usurped by cinema, television and now video and having largely cut itself off from a popular audience as well as being demoralized by lack of funding.

What's the future for women in the theatre in the UK?

I find it difficult to dissociate this question from that of what future there is for the theatre in this country AT ALL; which I view very pessimistically at the moment. One back-handedly positive thing I can say about the future for women is that as there is less and less money available for the theatre, more and more women will no doubt be allowed top jobs in it. However, conservatism in the current chronic conditions does nothing to help women writers who do not fit the predominant 'male' mould, while women artists are generally no longer considered a funding priority which means women could lose both ways.

I do see women freeing themselves increasingly to make the work they feel really speaks for them. And I see some male work becoming increasingly sensitive to female issues — examining male experience in a useful way. I suspect, though, that many practitioners will have to look to television or the continent to earn a living — as is already happening.

Jane de Gay
Written interview, edited June 1994.

MARA DE WIT

Mara de Wit is a performance artist, choreographer and dancer, and the founder of the Research and Navigation Dance/Theatre Company which is based in mid-west Wales. She also lectures in Performing Arts and is currently finishing her PhD in Dance at Middlesex University.

Does gender matter in the theatre?

Yes, of course. Gender matters especially in theatre because it's a medium that works in symbolic language and concrete images: in representations. Theatre is a field where gender issues are central, especially for a woman practitioner who concerns herself with the physical embodiment and projection of characters, or personas. The body of a man or a woman cannot be placed innocently in a theatre space without having social, historical and cultural resonance because the body represents gender. The question of identity becomes a question for the spectator too.

Are you aware that the position of women in the theatre has changed in any way over the years?

I have been conscious of gender and feminism from the seventies onwards. Sometimes I wonder if anything has changed. In terms of an economic base-line structure I don't feel much has changed: most women I know who are involved in performance are part-timers or are working freelance. In TV, the popular media and the world of pop music there seems to be a much broader presence of women. In the theatre retrospectives women are largely invisible.

Why do you think the position of women in theatre hasn't changed?

Maybe in the end women do not invest in the staying power that is necessary. Our lives are not as linear as male lives—we may or may not have children for example. Also in a socio-political sense the existing structures in the theatre industry are not women-friendly. I am not talking here of blatant sexism but of the Old Boys and Young Boys networks! Those young boys are part of the old boy network whether they realize it or not. There is no written code for advancement in the theatre, it is simply a quiet facilitating movement beneficial to men, which is still in place.

Are you conscious of 'writing and performing as a woman'?

All the time. And I am increasingly aware of being a woman performer, perhaps because I am increasingly aware that things haven't changed all that much. If I'd been a man my life would have taken a completely different shape and form. The roles remain determined by gender. I am present but still excluded.

I am forever developing women characters. For the last three years, I have been working on a piece, called *Self as Source*, involving movement, voice, writing, song and the body. I am exploring female conditions. I go back ten or twenty years in the lives of my characters, I look at the decisions they make, what moved them to love, to go places, what makes them end up here and now. They are womanly models for me.

This 'piece' has been a working process I've been engaged in over a long period (some six years). In presentations and preparation, I open up this process. I may start with fully occupying one image, which could be perceived as stereotypical in terms of costume, hair, make-up, shoes. Added to this are expressions and occupations such as certain love songs, longings and dreams. By exploring these (often romantic) clichés 'live', I find myself at times, tripping over, falling, sometimes crashing through, conventions and expectations, both my own and the onlookers'.

As a multi-lingual person, how do you see language (spoken, written and body language) affecting your relationship to performance?

As a performer I have an ambiguous relationship with verbal language. This is perhaps because I am a second language user and most happy when dancing, or moving in silence without speaking. I desire a text with enough space to listen, see and imagine, rather than verbal inundation in densely set phrases. Mostly, I have to force myself to literally come to grips with verbal language, especially in public performance, I experience this getting my body, mouth and tongue around these meaningful articulations. I have had to learn to adopt and adapt, to employ sentences and words as a functional skill, to mediate meaning this way. Indeed, as if I 'mastered' a foreign language.

Do you feel strongly either for or against working collaboratively with other women in the theatre?

I'm not strongly for or against. I do tend to work collaboratively with women, but in areas of specific skill I am happy to work with men and feel equal from my own angle of experience. I am more wary of working with a male director unless I know I can trust him.

I feel that with women, collaboration can be a more exploratory process. You can explore boundaries, with men involved one may not end up exploring the same boundaries.

How would you define 'feminism'?

I see feminism as a historical term now. Feminism is a term used to mediate a lot of meanings across many territories. I don't say 'this is a feminist issue', I say 'this is a gender issue'. I prefer the word gender, but no doubt this will change.

I don't think I'd call myself a feminist. It seems like an outdated term. It's not a word I find useful in positioning myself now because you can't use the term without going on to talk about the whole range of its historical implications.

Would you say that feminism has affected the theatre in any major way?

Feminist thinking has affected nearly all realms of present thinking in theatre and is still evolving. It has definitely affected dance and the performing arts. In the mainstream it has broadened the images of women generally. Space has been created that no longer has to be fought for and argued about. Whether this has been the feminist movement or a broader awareness of women's issues I find hard to answer.

I would relate feminism to other cultural structures: gender, race, class, religion, age. When ground is gained it has to be fed into other arenas as well. I can't see women gain all the ground without cultural and racial advancements too. There is an overlap, a woman's identity is made up of many facets.

Do you believe that the theatre can affect social change?

Yes. In a broad sense the question puzzles me. But in an immediate personal sense it is a transforming, potentially transcending activity and practice. If this can happen on a personal level it must be true on a social level too.

What do you understand by transforming and transcending activity?

I am talking of theatre in terms of moving the boundaries in the perception of oneself. During the creative process one enters a playful state, you allow a journey through yourself. Initially you are sense and body-bound, but you might end up in a different state of mind. Theatre is about sharing and audience exchange, it has an inter-active quality. One hopes that something happens for the perceiver, that they go through a transcending as well.

What's the future for women in the theatre in England/the UK?

    I hope they keep their jobs and that more jobs will be created so that women can continue to dance, make theatre and survive financially. It is the saddest thing not to be able to do what one wants to do, needs to do. For four years I have been witnessing a very hard time in theatre. I see the economic restrictions on women's lives all the time. They want to change their lives and can't. They're working to pay off mortgages and have no room for manoeuvre.

    I cannot talk of theatre without talking about education. Academia, arts in education are whole territories that need to be defended, as does the very right to an education. This is especially the case for dance; aspiring dancers are still not entitled to a mandatory grant.

Is there anything you hope women in theatre will develop or do?

    I hope that women will be able to create more networks to accommodate access to the theatre whether it be dance, performance art or any aesthetic practice. Women need access to imaginative, creative theatre-making processes, to engage their envisaging faculties. Women need nourishment and role models in the fight against the odds. Most importantly, women must remain visible in the public realm.

What motivates you as a female artist?

    I'm not consciously looking for role models but I do look to other women's lives. My work is about what fuels me as a woman, what motivates me for the next day. I try to locate the unpredictable in myself and to encourage myself into territories involving risk. Sometimes, it is easier to explore all this through the characters I invent. Theory is another territory, an additional tool. I feel I have made myself adept at it in order to move the subject on.

Mary Luckhurst
Interview conducted May 1994; updated January 1995.

DEBORAH LEVY

Deborah Levy is a playwright, poet and novelist. After working with visual artists and sculptors, and performing her poetry in pubs and galleries and on the cabaret circuit, she wrote her first plays: Pax *and* Clam. *In 1986, she wrote* Heresies *for the Royal Shakespeare Company, directed by Lily Susan Todd for the RSC Women's Project. Levy has also worked as a writer and director with the Magdalena Project, for whom she directed a devised theatre piece entitled* The B File, *based on her own fiction,* Swallowing Geography. *Her recent theatre texts have included* Walks on Water *(1992),* Call Baby Jane *(1992, ManAct Theatre),* Honey Baby: 13 Studies in Exile *(1995, LaMamma, Melbourne),* Pushing the Prince into Denmark *(1993) and* Shiny Nylon *(1994, Women's Playhouse Trust). During 1995, she will be working with the languages and autobiographies of five performers from non-English speaking backgrounds in a theatrical event for Playworks in Sydney, Australia. A collection of Levy's poetry,* An Amorous Discourse in the Suburbs of Hell, *and two novels,* Beautiful Mutants *and* The Unloved, *have been published by Jonathan Cape.*

Looking back at your earlier work, would you say that your interests have changed? For example, it seems to me that both in Pax *and* Clam *one can trace the beginnings of a post-modern kind of theatre that was later developed in* Heresies.

I wrote *Pax* in 1984 — it was my first commissioned play. Before then, I had been devising work with visual artists, sculptors and composers who were asking me to write texts. So my earliest beginnings were in performance — in collaborating with the particular languages of music, image and text and seeing how they work together.

That changed with *Pax*, which was commissioned by the Women's Theatre Group. They asked me to write an anti-nuclear play and I remember sitting with a collective of eight women and taking out my notepad. They told me what issues they wanted me to include in the play, so I wrote all that down, but I knew that I was never going to be able to write in that way.

All the same, I was very lucky with *Pax*. This was my introduction to Lily Susan Todd as a director, and Lily Susan respects a particular kind of creative process. She knows how writers work, and she knew that that was an impossible way to work. She said to me: 'Throw that piece of paper away, what do you want to write about?' No writer with their first commission could have been luckier. Had it been a different kind of director who had wanted me to take on all those suggestions, I don't think I would have been able to write.

I said to her: 'I want to write about Europe in the last hundred years'; she said: 'Go off then and do it'. In addition, I should give due credit to the

Women's Theatre Group for making the production of *Pax* possible, because not very many theatre companies would have had the vision, or the money, or the will to do it, but they did it. *Pax* transferred to the USA in 1985.

I asked for the composer and designer to be there from the first day of rehearsals, the composer was Camilla Saunders, and the designer was Wendy Freeman. I also asked for somebody who was visually and physically articulate, who had a kinetic understanding of the theatre space, which is an insult for a director, because directors feel they can cover all that, but I knew that for the sort of theatre I wanted to make I really needed such a person. It was quite outrageous to ask for these things, but I was a beginner and I asked for them.

We kind of had two directors on the scene. Lily Susan worked with the actors and the language of the play, the meanings and nuances, while Anna Furse was responsible for working with Lily Susan on the floor, visually realizing the piece. Those were the best creative conditions possible for that piece.

Clam was impeccably directed by Anna Furse, and performed by Mina Kavlan and Andrej Borkowski. Three more plays for the stage followed. I was having to write very quickly at that time, and when we got onto *Heresies*, (which was also directed by Lily Susan Todd) I don't think I was that much more aware of postmodernism, maybe a touch. When I really began to think about postmodernism, I stopped writing for the theatre for three years, from 1987 to 1990. *Heresies* had something in common with *Pax* in that they were both ambitious, epic pieces. *Heresies*, I think, was more formally confused than *Pax*. I was, for a number of reasons, landed with a plot and notions of 'character' that just did not fit me.

I get this sense, most of all, in Heresies. *Leah, the music instructor, and Violet, the teacher, go to the East to find a new self. This self is juxtaposed with Pimm's constructed, western self. So to me you are juxtaposing two worlds. Is this your way of doing political theatre with a 'leftist' ideology?*

What interested me with Cholla and Pimm was the idea of the western man desiring the 'Other'. Also of interest were the parts of himself that he understood least — the notion of imperializing a heart, a country, a female psyche, all themes I go on to explore in my fiction, *Swallowing Geography*.

What was the thinking behind the composer and teacher characters in Heresies?

The irreverent composer and teacher were based on people like Dora Russell and Rosa Luxemburg. I have a great admiration and affection for those elderly feminist women of the left who really were so brave and so outspoken.

What was behind the creation of the characters in Heresies?

I think the notion of how we describe ourselves in the world. How we invent ourselves will always be a major theme in my work. I never really believed that there is one true authentic self or that there is an authentic homeland. I tried to believe it in earlier work. The beginnings of those ideas were sown in *Pax* and later developed in *Heresies* via Cholla and Pimm. The man releases all his misplaced needs and anger by wanting to get the child from the woman. All the ways in which he had constructed the exotic Easterner are graphically analysed in *Orientalism*, by Edward Said. After *Heresies*, I read Spivak, Kristeva, Cixous, Stuart Hall, and of course they had found a theoretical language to talk about the things that I was exploring in a very naïve or confused way in those early plays.

Do you feel that realism as a theatrical device can be useful to women's theatre?

I think that naturalism, for the theatre anyway, is dead. As far as I'm concerned, naturalism lies to me all the time: it promises so much and it lets me down every time. In the end, if you are talking about writers, it depends on what kind of imagination you have.

The artifice of the theatre is what makes it, ultimately, a transgressive medium to work in. The kind of work I wanted to make for the theatre was always a struggle to put on, and I yearned for writerly colleagues whose concerns were similar. It seems obvious to me now that I should have directed the work rather than battle it out with directors who thought, 'I'll chuck in a bit of this and a bit of that', wrongly believing that they were making 'physical theatre' or 'visual theatre'. You see, I didn't study English literature at university. I had a physical theatre training at Dartington College of Arts, where I trained with dancers like Steve Paxton and Mary Fulkerson, plus the odd brilliant workshop with Bill Gaskill. So in a sense, I was trained to direct, though I increasingly long to surrender my theatre texts to appropriate collaborators.

Do you feel that as a playwright there are many obstacles to overcome whenever you want to use a different form for the theatre?

Implicitly, if you are a writer for the English theatre a certain kind of form is required. But there are more imaginative languages with which to articulate my cultural position, and it just so happens that for me they are not naturalism.

16. Jennifer Potter and Sean Than John in *Shiny Nylon*, text and direction by Deborah Levy, produced by the Women's Playhouse Trust, Royal Docks, London, February, 1994.

On the other hand, I'm not saying anything new. Artaud was going on about form long before me and lots of other artists you could name, but what those people had to do was to create their own structures to make theatre work. What I was doing up to 1987 was somehow managing to make it happen — albeit queasily and often flawed — within existing structures. At the RSC for example — and I think that was a real first, work in that form at that time had never been put on there, and I'm glad it was.

Now I'm finding that if I don't create other structures for my theatre work, it will be silenced. My writerly voice has changed so much in the last four years. I'm really looking forward to working in the theatre again.

Would you say that a woman playwright can write about men?

I think that if you are going to create a character for the theatre, you have to make it complicated — whether it's a man or a woman or a pig. There is no simple reductive male or female persona.

When you write plays, how do you find your way?

Every situation is different. I can only tell you how I *have* written plays. I probably prefer just to sit down and write, but beforehand over a period of time, I will have cut out a whole lot of images, news-cuttings, articles, quotes that interested me. I don't know why I have collected them at the time, they appear to have no binding themes, but suddenly the enquiry, atmosphere, argument, obsession reveals itself, and I'll pin them all up and begin.

I often map out what I know should happen. The pleasure is finding out *how* it should happen. Form is everything. All meaning, all ideology, lies in form. The composition of my theatre is using the language of the theatre for all the meanings it can give me. It might be that you have one image and a sound-track for five minutes, for example.

In your view, is creating a female voice or women's language essential?

Yes, indeed. But if you talk about a female language for the theatre, all you're really talking about is attention, not intention. It's where your attention is as a writer. A lot of women's writerly attention is in a very different place from that of male writers.

To me, your art is intertwined with politics. Do you believe that art should be intrinsically political?

I believe that it should let in the world. If art doesn't, then it is pretty boring to me. On the other hand. I would say that there is a kind of utopian language in my early work, a kind of false bravado that I would not repeat now. I would say that the plays you are talking about are political in the sense that they take on some of the things that upset me and make me unhappy, and I attempt an analysis of them.

Do you think that saying you're doing women's theatre, labelling it like that, is useful for other people but not for artists?

It's probably useful for academics. I think artists will always try and move out of those definitions. There are all sorts of 'women's theatre', for example, that I don't think is representative of the work that I make. So being lumped together with other women playwrights with whom I do not share an aesthetic seems very cruel — it would never happen to a man. Perhaps this is done partly because there are so few of us, but that's another question altogether: why do women writers not take on that public arena? Because the theatre is the most public of places to put the female subject in. But since there are very few women in the public arena of the theatre, I guess it is tempting to herd us all together.

All in all, would you say that things have changed for 'women's theatre' in Britain since the 1970s — and where are the 1990s going to lead?

I suspect that very little has changed. In the 1970s there were a lot of collective theatre companies funded by the Arts Council, then in the 1980s much of that funding was cut and theatre companies had to find public sponsorship — had to market their work, to package it. This is the scenario. Experimental work on the whole fell by the wayside. Theatres, mostly run by men, produced very safe, well-made naturalistic plays.

If you were serious about your work, you had to create structures ingeniously to make the work happen at all. If you were going to be working with a different kind of theatre language, you had to be very clear about what that language was, who it was for, how to get funding for it — and that had its own kind of energy and impetus, so in this way some very interesting, very polished, very articulate, avant-garde work was made. I mean by people like Annie Griffin, Rose English, Neil Bartlett, Claire MacDonald, Keith Kahn, Forced Entertainment.

There is the view that we now live in a post-feminist era. If we say there is a post-feminist kind of theatre in Britain nowadays, is this a way forward?

The fight is still on, and we still don't have equality in the streets or public places. But women are more confident and less grateful. The contribution of women who have pioneered for so long is that they gave us a language to talk with, to build on, and to take somewhere else. Feminism keeps making and remaking itself. Ideas get dumped or have other incarnations.

Do you consider yourself a feminist, then?

Oh yes, and I consider myself a postmodernist because, as Nancy Reilly of New York's Wooster Group says, I make a career out of my own confusions and inconsistencies. What postmodernism has contributed to feminist thought is that all those contradictions, the collapse of absolutes and so on, can be embraced. Some women are frightened to describe themselves as feminist because they think it is old-fashioned, that somehow they are more beautiful and desirable untainted by the word!

Do you think that feminist theatre is as strong today as it was in the 1970s, although there are so many problems and constant struggles?

Stronger. Less didactic. Sexier. Riskier. Bolder in film than theatre for reasons we have discussed. The American performance artist Karen Finlay does it the best. To quote from my introduction to *Walks on Water* (Methuen, 1992): 'The keen questions for artists in the 1990s are to do with survival. To explore the contours of the centre and the margins, power and powerlessness, the gap between imagined worlds and the real world.'

Irini Charitou

This interview, originally published in New Theatre Quarterly *(Vol. IX, issue 35, August 1993, pp. 225–230), was edited and updated for this publication by Deborah Levy in 1995.*

NINA RAPI

Nina Rapi was born in Argos Orestiko, Greece. She has written three full-length plays: Ithaka *(1989),* Dreamhouse *(1991) and* Dance of Guns *(1992); and two monologues,* Johnny is Dead *(1991) and* Dangerous Oasis *(1993). She researched and scripted the documentary 'Greek Love and Sapphic Sophistication', (Channel 4, 1990) and has had a variety of critical work and poems published. She is the editor of the lesbian and gay theatre journal* Glint*. She is also a translator, a tutor at Birkbeck College, and a visiting lecturer at Goldsmiths College, London University.*

Does gender matter in the theatre?

Yes, though this is problematic to answer because the question is so general. Perhaps I should say that sexuality matters more to me. 'Gender' normally refers exclusively to heterosexual women.

My experience of working in the Fringe over the past few years has led me to believe that the so-called liberality of the theatre is just a myth. When it comes to the average heterosexual thespian, they still hold on to absurd, outdated notions about lesbians. These they communicate to you either insidiously through body language, looks and silence, or directly. I prefer the latter form of discrimination. At least you know what you are dealing with and can respond to it, without instantly being further pigeonholed into 'aggressive' or 'paranoid', two adjectives favoured by straights when they want to dismiss dykes.

Still the 'direct' comments I have heard from 'progressive' young actresses about lesbians (somehow the directors are comparatively more aware), have never ceased to amaze me. Straight actresses can relate to you, as a lesbian playwright, in the most predictably inappropriate ways. To start with they act as if you are going to pounce on them. Once it sinks in that you *don't* fancy them, however, their attitude changes. They become flirtatious and start bombarding you with questions: how do lesbians do it?; do you think I am a femme or a butch?; which of us do you think is a potential lesbian?, etc. etc. This stage can be very amusing. Not so when they'd easily spend days of precious rehearsal time discussing whether a kiss between women is necessary in the script, and even at times arguing that a character I had written as a lesbian, is not really a lesbian. They would know, of course.

It is ironic that in general I have encountered less prejudice and had more support from straight men than straight women in the theatre.

Are you aware that the position of women in the theatre has changed in any way over the years?

Yes, I am. I've been working in the theatre for five years. Back then the female playwrights I knew were Caryl Churchill, Pam Gems and Sarah Daniels. Now I could name another ten women. The number of female directors and lesbian directors in the public eye has also risen. Yet before this interview I went through *Time Out* and out of 45 directors on the West End I counted five women and two or three women writers. For the fringe the ratio was about the same. So certain individuals have 'made it', but women as a force have not made a huge leap. What has changed is that women are becoming more confident. But even on the gay scene what I see are more plays by gay men — lesbians still remain largely invisible.

Are you conscious of 'writing as a woman'?

Yes, but I have to say that I have been commissioned by two companies who both wanted me to write solely female characters, and this had a restrictive effect on my imagination. One play was about the Greek Civil War and it seemed definitely wrong not to have any male characters at all.

Do you feel strongly either for or against working collaboratively with other women in the theatre?

I don't feel strongly either way but I don't believe in situations where roles are not clearly defined. Firm guidelines are essential, otherwise 'collaboration' becomes a power battle and a nightmare. Directors and actors should remember they are *not* writers. If they want to be they should go ahead and do it. Meanwhile, they should let *us* write.

Giving credit where credit is due is also very important. Often in 'collaborations', a false collectivity is assumed which ultimately denies individual women the recognition they deserve. There are cases where, say, six women do the work but only one gets the credit, but the opposite is also true. Both are wrong. Mutual respect and clear boundaries are the key really.

How would you define 'feminism'?

When I thought about this four predominant strands of feminism came to mind:

a) Feminism as a weapon for radical sexual and political transformation. This was my first contact with feminism: wild, sexual and rebellious. It is about sexual freedom and *direct action*; not the armchair feminism we see so much of now.

b) A bourgeois, selfish and uninspiring feminism. Equal opportunity is useful but I find myself asking equal to whom? I don't admire men, why should I want to be equal to them? I don't feel that this form of feminism questions the status quo. I aim at transformation, not equality.

c) A puritanical, hysterical feminism. I use the word hysterical consciously. This is a feminism which is anti everything: anti-sex, anti-pleasure, anti-beauty. Coming from a Mediterranean culture beauty is actually very important to me.

d) Another currently dominant form of feminism is the theoretical and academic. This form can reflect any of the previous three. At its worst it can be incomprehensible and irrelevant jargon: at its best it can be intellectually exciting.

According to your own definition would you call yourself a feminist?

I feel I have a feminist consciousness but wouldn't call myself a feminist because of the negative associations. Political correctness seems to have got way out of control, has become pedantic and lost touch with the real issues. Yet I wonder — society continues to be male-dominated, misogyny still rules by passing as 'natural' and women still predominantly perceive of themselves as either 'victims' or 'martyrs' — yet at the same time it is so fashionable to be anti-feminist, that calling yourself a feminist can be a brave thing. But perhaps that is the best thing, as long as you explain what it [feminism] means to you, rather than allow the presumptions of the bourgeois/liberal or the restrictive/prescriptive kind of feminisms to dominate.

Would you say that feminism has affected the theatre in any major way?

Yes, primarily theoretically. This isn't a bad thing. I believe in theory quite strongly. But it is important to link theory and practice. Theatre has been helped through the introduction of new concepts and new perspectives in term of representation and aesthetics. The search for a female aesthetic is very exciting, doing something unique and different rather than just regurgitating old forms.

Do you believe that theatre can affect social change?

I have doubts about this in England. At the moment the theatre audience is mainly middle-class and smug. This audience is not the agent of radical social change. But the potential for change is there in theatre. In Eastern Europe theatre was fundamental in bringing about change. I believe that the so-called minority theatre: black, lesbian, perhaps TIE [Theatre in Education] can bring about change. The dominant theatre is not interested in social change — just in big names and money. Certain male figures in the theatre world are treated as though they are beyond criticism — Peter Brook, Robert Lepage. This has got to be bad for theatre. Alive, relevant theatre that can actually bring about change, can only exist in conditions that incite questioning of dominant forms, structures, contents and 'leaders'. That is why 'feminine' or 'androgynous' or 'queer' theatre can be potentially subversive.

What's the future for women in the theatre in the UK?

It's important to have more plays by women at the centre of the dominant theatre. More importantly we need laboratories for experimental work. Changes have occurred, they are slow but they will continue. I am optimistic — with reservations. I see a new confidence in women and that makes me optimistic.

Something that interests me is playwrights who are bi-lingual, it is an area I would like to explore. I am a Greek but write in English — that tension is a constant for me.

How does your multi-lingual perspective affect your work in theatre, especially in terms of your approach to spoken, written and body language?

This affects both my writing and the reception of my work. I often find that when it comes to acutely painful realities, writing in English creates the necessary distance that allows me to verbalize them. For example, writing about the Greek Civil War in *Dance of Guns* was a minefield of conflicting emotions — in terms of language, representation and loyalties. Other people are brought up with fairytales and lullabies; I was brought up with stories about the civil war. It was a deeply personal experience, even though I had not gone through it. My mother and father had, and I was dangerously close to both. I had to write about it in a foreign language — English.

The result was contradictory. I have had people describe that work as both 'curiously unmoving' and 'deeply moving'. I suppose the people who think the latter are those who cross the distance I have created out of necessity, while those who think the former don't make that leap.

Structurally, I find that writing 'as a foreigner' I almost always write on at least two different levels, often at once. Usually those levels are to do with 'seriousness and engagement' and 'detachment and wit'. When I write about English realities I tend to be somewhat 'removed' and sardonic, when I write about Greek situations I'm more 'involved' and sympathetic. The balance is, however, very precarious.

As a writer I feel more 'in control' when dealing with Greek stories and situations. Surprisingly, however, *Ithaka* and *Dreamhouse* were

17. Victoria Hazwood and Sharon McKevitt in *Dance of Guns* by Nina Rapi (1993); photographer: Katrina Slack.

appreciated by many precisely because of their 'witty and surreal' quality. The balance shifts... Ultimately, the surreal approach can be limiting, can lock you into cynicism and a sense of superiority towards your characters. On the other hand 'sympathetic engagement' can lead to plain old naturalism, which is not very appealing. I struggle with the acrobatics of the forms but meanwhile I wonder what would I come up with if I wrote in my mother tongue? And am I ready for that yet?

In terms of acting, I invariably imagine my work acted as either tragi-comic, passionately dramatic or 'heightened reality'. English actresses and directors may miss the humour altogether (I suppose Greek humour is much more overtly cruel or philosophical and the English are likely to think 'This is *not* funny!') or they can misinterpret passion as melodrama and 'heightened reality' as hysteria! Naturally there are exceptions.

Writing in a foreign language also creates conflicts in terms of audiences. I often feel guilty in that I think if I have anything to offer I should be offering it to Greece — even though Greece has forced me into self-exile here. One of my biggest satisfactions in terms of audience reception was when *Dance of Guns* was performed in a Turkish community centre in London. The centre was packed and at the end the people not only applauded wildly but gave a standing ovation. And the Turks are supposed to be the Greeks's worst enemies! It's at times like these that I believe in the power of theatre to bring about social change.

Mary Luckhurst
Interview conducted May 1994; updated January 1995.

DEBORAH BADDOO

Deborah Baddoo is a dancer/choreographer who devises her own performances. She works both as a solo artist and in collaboration with other poets and dancers, as well as performing with her own company, State of Emergency. She is a Senior Lecturer in Performing Arts at Hackney Community College (London).

Why did you chose the name State of Emergency for your company?

The title was not meant to be directly political: though some time after the company was named, South Africa was declared to be in a state of emergency. The title of the company refers to the need of dancers/performers to produce work quickly, to work with little or no funding, to make work when it is needed. It also means that the company is on alert, ready for any eventuality regarding performance.

It is a music and dance production company, co-directed by Steve Marshall and me. We have done a large-scale live jazz production, *Dance for Life*, at the Womad Festival, the Chisenhale Dance Space and at the Jazz Café. We used jazz with roots in African music, and elements of Latin American and Caribbean music as well as contemporary influences in that particular show, which was a dance and music collaboration.

Can you explain the thinking behind your solo piece, in Defence of Identity *(1993)?*

I had something I wanted to say with this project: it was a semi-autobiographical piece, asking the question: do I or don't I want to have children (and also, of course, is it the right time?; am I in the right relationship?; am I ready to change my life and priorities for a child?; would I be having a child for the right reasons or because it's the thing to do or because I'm running out of time?; etc.). Common questions for many women. So while it's a personal piece, it speaks to the experience of many other women as well.

Can you describe how you brought the piece together?

I have been working on this piece, on and off, for four years. It began with the fundamental fact of being a mixed race woman. (I am half Ghanian and half English). I have always had the idea of working on the mixed race issue, that question of identity, in my work. Then, more recently, I had the idea of exploring women's identity in relation to child-bearing.

At first I thought the two would come together in this piece. But it didn't work out that way. I started working with Sally Ridgeworth, a white woman, improvising through racial and cultural themes and tasks. We worked on many of the movements together. However, after a time, the intensive ideas which we developed at the outset of the piece gradually changed.

As the duet developed, it became more about her and us than about me. I lost the focus of my own identity, as we began to work on similarities between us instead of differences. We were women of different cultures, and the work we made was interesting, as it explored the points where our experiences met. We performed together, in a piece called *Penalty Fayre* at Chisenhale and at Chat's Palace in 1989.

However, I still wanted to work on a piece about my own identity. So we eventually decided to work separately.

And so you continued working on the piece by yourself?

On and off, but meanwhile I was studying for an MA, and my academic/practical project involved working on a two-woman piece which explored female stereotypes in soap-opera. I was looking at women's realities and women's myths; asking whether fictional representations of women sometimes seem more real than 'real life'. In this project, I used video, dance, theatre and music, and looked at the academic issues behind this kind of work. Then I worked on *Dance for Life* with State of Emergency. And after that, I returned my attention to the piece about identity, this time solo.

How important are issues about race in your work?

In addition to looking at the question of motherhood, I was looking at question 'What is Black Dance'? People assume that I'll do African dance because I'm black. If I were to label myself in that way I'd get more funding, but it's too easy to play to those assumptions, and it's too easy to get pigeonholed. These are all forms of separatism. I'm black and I'm white, Ghanian and English. I have many influences in my work: jazz, African, Caribbean, English, European.

I did one piece about a journey back to Africa (though I've never actually been to Africa); *Dream Vignette* in October 1992 at the October Gallery. It also used images: scarves and vibrant colours. But my work isn't all about those origins. It's about all the different sides of me.

How did the solo piece develop once you parted company with Sally Ridgeworth?

I started performing the solo piece in the summer of 1992, in the USA (Washington and Pittsburg). I began with the images and ideas, developing as I went along, performing different versions. I used video to help me see the work as I couldn't hire a director as an outside eye.

I would like to work on another solo piece. I've found a lot of inner strength in working alone on *In Defence of Identity*, which I performed in London at the Oval House Theatre, Highbury Roundhouse, Tom Allen Centre and Chisenhale Dance Space. The piece is still developing .

In Defence of Identity *builds on a series of repeated movements and gestures. What are the main images and ideas behind the piece?*

The piece represents a journey, a process of thought and decision. It depicts the process of thinking the same thing over and over, and gradually getting a bit further (just as in thought processes, you reach decisions little by little, not all at once). I was tired of not deciding, not making the major decisions in my life. I wanted to 'bite the apple' So that's the image I started with: wanting to bite the apple of the decision about whether or not to have a child. And that image, of me biting the apple, standing by a chair in a spotlight, is central to the piece. The apple is a symbol with all its rich connotations, and that idea shaped everything else. I always knew I wanted to end the piece with that image. And in real life, I did the same. I was one month pregnant when I performed the piece. I bit the apple, and had already bitten it before I started dancing this piece.

The briefcase was also a symbol: of career, which I use in a similar way to the apple in the piece — two choices, represented by symbols. It couldn't have been a word processor or typewriter: it had to be something flexible, that I could lift and move and manipulate [see front cover image].

It was interesting to perform this piece knowing that I'd bitten the apple. I felt that, once I'd had the child, I wouldn't want to do that piece any more. Even though it does speak to many other women and in that sense would still be relevant, it wouldn't be so relevant to me. I'd want to do something else.

Is your work 'feminist' in any sense?

Not in an obvious sense. However, I consider myself to be a feminist, and my work is derived from my perspective as an independent women. My work reflects my thought processes. Therefore my work deals with a number of important issues that are central to me as a woman and relevant to many women. In that sense, my work may be considered feminist.

Do you believe that theatre can affect social change?

A number of years ago, I might have said 'Yes', but in the current social and economic climate, it is easy to be more cynical. I feel that theatre

18. Deborah Baddoo, *In Defence of Identity* (1993); photo credit: State of Emergency.

does raise a number of important issues for consideration and debate in people's lives. But as far as affecting change, this depends on audiences taking new meaning and inspiration from performance work. Audiences for this kind of theatre are mainly people already interested in black performance, or physical theatre/dance, or perhaps 'women's theatre'; I haven't yet reached a 'mainstream' audience in any sense. While community audiences are very valuable in many ways, it does sometimes feel like I'm 'preaching to the converted'.

Lizbeth Goodman
Interview recorded in London, March 1993; updated December 1994.

ANNA O

The company Anna O devises and performs physical theatre/dance work exploring issues of gender, language and power in interdisciplinary and multi-media form. The company is comprised of two women, Janet Hand and Tessa Speak. They have worked with other women, and with one man, John Gange.

Who is (are) Anna O?

Anna O was the pseudonym of one of Freud's patients, in one of his most famous female case-studies. Janet came up with the name Anna O for the company, with the link with psychoanalytic criticism in mind. In 1987 she composed a performance piece on Dora, another of Freud's case studies. In both choices of focus — Anna O and Dora — our interest is in the relations between psychoanalytic case study in its narrative complexity with the concern for interdisciplinary performance work. Complicated ideas and relations arise by working through different media. In our work, the relationship between autobiographical identification, the representation of the 'self', poetic language, the slippages inherent in language, and conceptions of 'self' are all explored in terms of performance.

Why did you focus on those two characters in particular: Dora and Anna O?

There were many reasons for choosing Dora. Gender was only one angle which made that choice interesting. It was also challenging to engage in a debate between the written text and possible choreographies within the performance text.

Anna O was the pseudonym for Breuer's analysand. Breuer named the 'talking cure' after her absences, or 'hysterical amnesias'. 'Private theatre' was a term she made up herself to account for when she was 'absent' — or awake, but not conscious. Sometimes she spoke in languages she had learned as a child, but had believed she had forgotten. 'Anna O' — or Bertha Pappenheim, her family name — became a famous social worker in Germany. She translated Mary Wollstonecraft's *Vindication of the Rights of Woman* into German, and has been commemorated in Germany on a postage stamp. She became a symbol for the divided woman, hysterical and rational, active and passive, like Dora.

How many shows has Anna O devised and performed?

We've done six shows, all told. One show, called *The Howl in the Afternoon*, drew on Lacan's case study of 'Aimée': a woman who identified with and stabbed an actress. We contrasted her with a contemporary woman who followed people in modern London: a voyeur. Looking at these two women, we studied the unique nature of female voyeuristic relationship (a shift in the usual power relation, in male voyeurism), linking the case study and biography. We imagined the story of the female voyeur as ours, as if we lived her encounters in the city. This kind of work is something we call hyperdocumentary. We incorporated slides, to show documentary and imaginary worlds together, collapsing 'the authentic' in both. The other early shows also used this form, in various ways.

How would you describe the creative process which Anna O invokes in devising performances?

In *Howl* and all our other work, we repeatedly address the question of how we construct the body through language, in relationships, abstractly, performatively. Janet Hand and Tessa Speak have been with Anna O from the beginning, John is always in the periphery of our work, supporting it in one way or another. He took a central role in the work when we came to do our sixth show: *Twenty Ways to Learn a Language*.

Twenty Ways to Learn a Language *is your best-known show. What does the title refer to?*

We thought of three words which were intriguing to us. Each of the three was about issues of language and was also choreographically provocative. The three words were: translation, transition, boundaries. From there, it was a very structured process. We made a list, came up with 'twenty ways' which were devisable, visual, physical, and also critical, engaging. So the piece is twenty segments, some much fuller than others. One is actually titled Body Language — the section titles are listed on the wall, undercutting or underpinning the physicality of each segment of the piece. We each took sections and set them up to devise from. Some were worked from text, some from images.

We drew a map on the floor representing national borders, but also representing other kinds of borders or boundaries. Tessa devised the map, which was always integral to the work. It would have been too grandiose a gesture to try to really take on the changing face of Europe in a direct way. But it couldn't be ignored. It underlies so much of the piece: changing borders, bodies rubbing out the outlines on the floor, rubbing out lines between states, alluding to transience, tourism. For example: we used postcards (pictorial images, connected to ideas of travel and crossing borders, making conections) in juxtaposition to international current affairs items conveyed through the spoken words of the play and in a multi-media montage.

Another starting point for *Twenty Ways* was the question of how one plays with signification and meaning. The performance piece incorporates a video of images and performed sequences. The video was made very early on by Andrew Robbins. We used it in thinking out the live performance, so that the two fed off one another. The video with the live performance work brings up some of the cemented complexities of language: dictionary style aspects, semantics, which contrasted so well with other performance aspects. Of course, the video also brings in that different spectator relationship with the piece.

The most interesting work comes from experimentation, not explanation. We don't start by articulating a line of thought and working through it, but by setting up situations, dynamics, observations, and then reworking, revising, rewriting, moving from there. It's most interesting to see whether you can be surprised by what you come up with.

How did the collaboration with John Gange come about?

Anna O has a strong psychoanalytic source: Janet and John Gange have discussed the psychoanalytic dimension of their work regarding gender and performance at length. But the time came to do some work together when a woman we had been collaborating with, Mutsumi Yagi, ran into real problems with 'transitions and borders' when she was denied re-entry to Britain and we had to carry on our work without her.

I suppose that answers my next question, which was to be: have you encountered any difficulties, practical or artistic, in the collaborative process?

Of the most extreme kind. The collaboration with Mutsumi fell apart at Christmas (1993), only months before *Twenty Ways to Learn a Language* was due to open. Her absence was a feature of the piece. We kept her physically present even in her absence, by including visual images of her in several different forms: within the multi-media aspects of the piece, and also in textual terms (we read a text, a fictionalized account of being denied re-entry to the country, into the 'script' of the performance). The text was, in fact, written by Janet. It juxtaposed Mutsumi's story with a kind of 'love at first sight' tale, twisting the convention of the latter with the absurdity and 'muting' consequence of the former. Mutsumi's border story was a very invasive, very personal experience for her. It was also, sadly, a story which many other people have 'lived' in some sense, symbolic or real.

What is the story behind that particular 'border issue', in brief?

Mutsumi Yagi, a Japanese woman who had been working with us to devise *Twenty Ways* for some time, was intended to be a key performer. Mutsumi was prohibited from re-entering the United Kingdom, due to problems with work permits; she was detained at Customs at the airport when returning to England for rehearsal and the opening of the piece. Her diary was seized, translated and read.

The performance piece was obviously affected by Mutsumi's absence, but it also developed out of this experience. Video and slide images depicted Mutsumi. In one sequence, Tessa Speak reads immigration codes to the audience.

So Anna O's work is partly autobiographical, personal as well as political?

Yes, very much so. We work in a particular way, though. For instance, you could contrast our work with that of Mara de Wit; she tends to begin with minutiae, starting from personal experience and working that experience into a much larger and more complex picture, reflecting on culture and performance itself. Our work also involves autobiography, but it's there in a different form. It's not treated as recounted experience, but rather as another version of events.

Mutsumi's story, for instance, is 'real': it has happened. In our writing of it (the text which we read/perform in *Twenty Ways*), the Customs official and Mutsumi have different views of that situation. There's also a double edge in the form — writing trying to describe something which happens between words, at a junction between written form and memory. It's important to present different versions of the same event. Autobiography is no more truthful a representation than any other kind of representation. Someone's life becomes a performance. A real person becomes a fictional character through interpretation and reception. With autobiography, there's always this premise of knowing, which is itself dubious.

Like Mara de Wit, Emilyn Claid and others, Anna O is exploring the connection between self/body/writing. But what's most interesting to us is the attempt to represent 'self', when self itself is vulnerable to not knowing, to not understanding 'itself'.

Do you think there is a 'women's language' or a way of communicating which is specifically gender-orientated? If so, or if not, how does this work itself out in your piece?

The question of 'women's language' is such a complicated one — it's very central to our work. Language is gendered, but that's not the same thing as saying there's a 'women's language' Of course, because our work is tied

19. Anna O, *Twenty Ways to Learn a Language* (1994); photographer: Janet Hand.

up with psychoanalysis, the issue of language is very important, always under consideration.

In a political sense, perhaps it is necessary to argue for a women's language, for women and men are subjects within language, and tend to use language differently from each other. That is, categories of 'femininity' and 'masculinity' have different values in our culture, and this needs, still, to be addressed and critiqued. 'Women' and 'men' as categories, are also not fixed, nor are they easily definable. Yet gender is institutionalized, and affects performance in theatre and life, in terms of power situations, and in terms of intersubjectivity.

But there are a number of double-binds with that idea of a women's language. Gender and language are predicated on each other. I'd be nervous about the possessive ('s) in the phrase women's language. Language can't be possessed, can't be owned. 'Women Language' is a more workable term. We sometimes address disenfranchisement, the difficulty of trying to speak in a language not 'your own' (possession again).

Your work, as you say, is strongly influenced by your interests in and knowledge of psychoanalysis and feminist theory. Ten or twenty years ago, would you have been in the same position to combine these academic/intellectual ideas and practical performance work?

For me, us, no — but to say it was impossible would be to deny the influences of Hélène Cixous, Jean Genet, Marguerite Duras, who *did*. It would be more appropriate to applaud the greater possibility of educational research today.

How is feminist theory affecting the theatre?

Feminist theory affects the theatre in many and various ways which can not be isolated from feminism's impact on other representational modes, and ways of expressing ideas in and through performance, both conventional and experimental.

Lizbeth Goodman
Interview conducted March 1993, and updated in 1995.

JACKIE KAY

Jackie Kay is a playwright and poet. Her first play, Chiarascuro, *was first produced by Theatre of Black Women in 1986. Her play* Twice Over *was first produced by Gay Sweatshop in 1990; and her latest play,* Twilight Shift, *was produced by 7:84 Scotland in 1993. She has also published fiction in* Everyday Matters 2 (1984), *and* Stepping Out (1986). *A selection of her poetry is published in* A Dangerous Knowing: Four Black Women Poets (Sheba, 1983), *and her best-known collection of poetry,* The Adoption Papers, *is published by Bloodaxe (1991).*

Does gender matter in the theatre?

Gender matters a lot in the theatre. You can tell that just when you switch traditional plays. For instance, if you were to do *Macbeth*, and have Macbeth played by a woman and Lady Macbeth played by a woman as well, it would change the whole meaning of the play. This is, in itself, quite a revolutionary and dynamic thing to do.

I think changing gender in the theatre is dramatic in the true sense of the word. It also makes people think of the constructs of 'male' and 'female', and makes us think of what kind of importance or stereotype we might attach to each gender role. So yes, we can question lots of very basic fundamental things through gender in theatre.

Are you aware that the position of women in the theatre has changed over the years?

The position of women over the years has changed quite dramatically in the theatre. We have got more women playwrights now — we've had Sarah Daniels with a play on at the National Theatre, although she was the first woman to make it onto a main stage there, and the play wasn't that long ago and there haven't been that many women at the National Theatre ever since.

So every single change there has been you have to qualify and say: 'yes, it's happened, but it's not actually that huge a change and perhaps more could have happened.' I do think that the male writers are treated with a certain kind of assumption of importance. There isn't the equivalent of a Pinter among women, or at least, there isn't that equivalent treatment. Even Caryl Churchill, who is probably the most famous and the most well-respected woman playwright in the country, doesn't get the kind of status that someone like Pinter does, even though her work is just as pioneering as Pinter's.

So I think there have been changes, but there are not enough changes. Somehow, women — actors, writers, playwrights — and women's theatre companies, women's productions, still aren't getting the same kind of attention. The theatre is still fairly male dominated.

Are you aware of 'writing as a woman'?

When I write anything, I'm always conscious of what I am (a woman). That's true even when I'm writing as a male character, which I did in my last play, *Twilight Shift*.

In that play, for the first time, I created two male characters — a barber and a miner. Even when I was writing, from the point of view of these men and inside these characters, I was still conscious that I was a woman. I think that my men are different from a man's men. My male characters probably were more vulnerable and more open and more emotional than, perhaps, most men are. But I wanted them to be like that; I made a deliberate choice.

Do you feel strongly either for or against working collaboratively with other women in the theatre?

I don't feel strongly one way or the other, for myself personally. Generally, I think that collaborations can work wonderfully well if the people who are collaborating are used to working with each other, if they know exactly how each other works, and if there isn't competitiveness or jealousy or misunderstandings (which can be fatal). Caryl Churchill, for instance, seems to get on well with Max Stafford-Clark, and they've done many collaborations over the years, as well as improvisations, and all of it seems to work. On the other hand, I have heard of collaborations which have been absolutely disastrous.

I have never found collaborative theatre good for me because it's just not the way I work. I suppose it's because I think of myself as a poet first and foremost. I find writing in a solitary way better for me. So when I go into a theatre and I suddenly have to take into account what everybody else thinks and what everybody else wants, I find it a bit disconcerting. I have not yet found collaborating really truly dynamic and exciting in the way that I have heard it can be. Maybe it's just that I haven't met the right people yet.

When you write a play, and then it is performed for the first time, do you still feel attached to it, as your creation? Is it difficult to let go?

I feel a mixture of things when I have written a play. I do still feel involved. I always attend rehearsals, but that's always a peculiar role to be in. It gets embarrassing in some ways because you do not know how much you

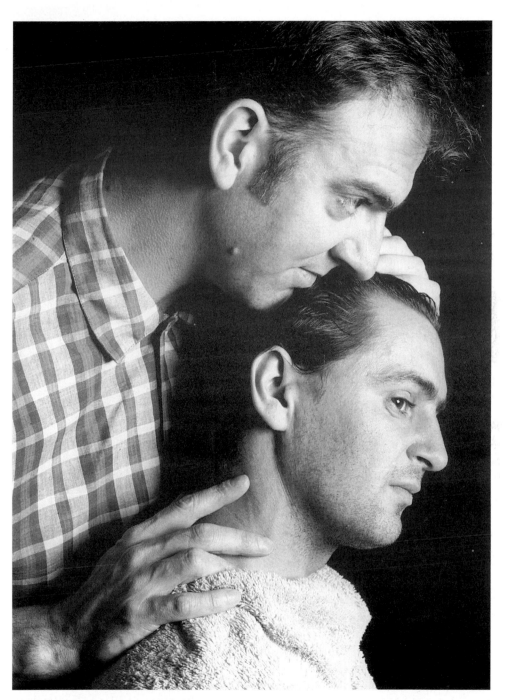

20. Steve Wren and John Kazek in *Twilight Shift* by Jackie Kay, for 7:84 company Scotland (1993); photographer: Iain Reekie, Theatre Workshop, Edinburgh, 1993.

are meant to say, and you don't want to step on somebody else's toes. So I'm always very conscious that once you have done the work of creating a play, then it's somebody else's job to create on top of that. I see the whole process of theatre as involving all different people sharing the making of this huge cake. One person puts in the eggs and another person puts in the flour and if you try to do somebody else's job, then...

I think you can have an input, but you've got to be aware of how much of an impact you can make; you've got to be open to letting other people use their imaginations in the way that you have — you shouldn't stunt anybody else's imaginative growth. That means in a sense giving up your play: you must be able to hold it, but hold it loosely so that somebody else can come and take the balance of it and hold it too. That is really important — you've got to let other people use their vision and their creativity and their imagination, to do something that you perhaps hadn't envisaged. To do it completely differently from what you had wanted. You have to allow that, as a writer. I know that a lot of writers have different ways of working, and a lot of writers don't want to let go. For example, Eugene O'Neill's stage notes went to enormous lengths, right down to telling you about where a flag should fit on a table or whatever. I think that is restrictive ultimately: it hampers people's imaginations, although you do need a clear idea of your overall intention, and need to present that to the theatre company. Then, it's up to them to either try and continue to follow your intentions or not. It's a bit like leaving a will.

How would you define 'feminism'?

I think our concept of feminism has changed from the mid-to-late seventies, to now, the middle nineties. In the last twenty years, the idea of feminism has changed quite radically. In order to define feminism you have to go back to its basic roots. The basic idea of feminism was about women's equality: about women having an equal right to pay, to work, the right to choose different things — to choose an abortion, to choose a sexuality, to choose what to wear. All these basic things.

Now in the 1990s, when people talk about post-feminism, it seems to me a very strange concept. Feminism itself hasn't been achieved, and even very simple things like crèches for working mothers don't always exist. Very simple, basic women's rights don't exist, and yet people talk about 'post-feminism' which seems to me a complete anachronism. I think that feminism, as well as being an intellectually stimulating set of ideas and theories in its most complex form, is also a very simple menu of things. When I think about feminism and how I would define myself as a feminist, I like to go back to these basic principles of feminism. It's the same with socialism actually —

going back to these basic principles and thinking 'what are they?' When you ask yourself these basic questions and you want to remind yourself about what it means, then you get a direct answer. I like things to be stated clearly. I like to see the basic ideas behind things.

According to your definition, would you call yourself a feminist?

Yes, I would call myself a feminist. Not a post-feminist — a present-day, up and running, current feminist!

Would you say that your feminism has affected the way you write?

I think your outlook generally affects the way you write, and everything you believe in affects what you write — whether you are conscious of that or not. I think it is important to remember that a lot of what you write isn't necessarily totally conscious — you do use your subconscious when you write. Anybody who really tries to go into the depths of themselves has to try and explore the side which you might call spiritual. My whole outlook and what I think of the society we live in, and the way it operates, and its past and its present, and its possible future, informs everything I write. Sometimes my outlook also chooses my topics for me, although again, that's not a hard and fast rule. Often you can find yourself writing about a subject which you never imagined you would ever be interested in. It's important as a writer to keep your visions and options open and not to trap yourself in an area or perspective which you can't get out of, so that you're writing yourself down various dead ends and corners and you can never get back out into an open landscape.

I do definitely feel that my outlook and my feminism, my socialism, my awareness of my own race and country and age, and my awareness of being adopted — all of that affects practically everything I write, in both subtle and complex ways.

Do reviewers tend to label your work in particular ways, or to put your writing in pigeonholes or categories?

Yes, I think reviewers do review your work depending on who you are. That's annoying for me, particularly because I have a whole set of labels which reviewers could put after my name — like Scottish, woman, black, lesbian, socialist, adopted…. It is very irritating for me. In my children's poetry books, for example, I write lots of poems about lots of different topics, but reviewers still find a reason to name me as: 'Jackie Kay who is black and adopted and was brought up in Scotland'. And that won't necessarily have anything to do with the poems. I wrote a whole book which didn't have anything to do with adoption at all and all the reviewers said it was about adoption and that the child in it was adopted, and the child wasn't. That kind of thing is very annoying because it means that people are not reading your work properly or carefully or even intelligently. Similarly with *Twilight Shift* which was a gay play, a lot of the reviewers reviewed that from the point of view of me being a poet — because they all know me mainly from being a poet in Scotland — and kept forgetting about the drama of it, which actually restricted the reviews of the play.

Would you say that feminism has affected the theatre in any major way?

I think that feminism *has* affected the theatre, but that it had a particular impact in the mid-eighties that it is not having at the moment (but that impact might come back in some way). In the mid or early eighties, there were huge Take Back the Night Marches through the streets. Every time that there was terrible violence or abuse or rape, people would take to the streets in these huge candle-light processions. We don't have that kind of activity anymore, and it's really noticeable when you see cases like Karanjit Ahluwalia's, or of women who have been imprisoned for murdering their husbands after years and years of violence. These cases have had campaigns around them, but the campaigns have been much much smaller than they might have been in the early eighties. That is similar to what is happening generally, politically, and it has also affected theatre so that there is a kind of moving on from certain ways of dealing with politics. Some of those changes are regrettable, and some of them are good.

When you go to see a play that is informed by feminism nowadays, it's much more likely to be sophisticated; it doesn't have the raw edges of say Gay Sweatshop in the early eighties or Monstrous Regiment. But that rawness is exactly to me what theatre is all about. What I like about theatre is its raw energy, not the polished edges, not smooth, comfortable, slick theatre. I like theatre that makes you feel slightly embarrassed when you are watching it, involved and awkward, so that you are affected by the genuine, powerful emotions of it. Theatre is all about experimenting all the time — trying to find a form for what you're trying to say. So it's constantly changing, it's more fluid than any of the other art forms. And that very fluidity is interesting to trace.

I think feminism in the 1990s in the theatre is completely different from what it was even a few decades ago. And the kind of plays you see that are affected by feminism are different. I went to see a play by the Black Theatre Workshop written by an American woman, Bonnie Greer. That was a 'bad' play because it was dated. So you can see plays which remind you of plays that you have seen years ago, and you don't want to do that either. In all writing, you want to use the language of your time — that's your tool.

Theatre is the same: you want to use that contemporary language and use 'now' and try and transform 'now' (and even the future) into theatre. I haven't seen any theatre recently which made me think: 'Wow, that was a great feminist play'.

Would you say that you were in any way influenced by plays in the 1980s and 1970s? I find it interesting to trace generational change.

If anything, I have been influenced by much earlier theatre. I like playwrights such as Ibsen and Eugene O'Neill, and I like Arthur Miller, and I like claustrophobic drama that puts a lot of people together into a room, like *Long Day's Journey into Night*, where you go through that journey with those particular characters. I suppose when I write, each one of my plays is trying to get that sense of people changing each other in a very short space of time. I still haven't managed to do that — *Twilight Shift* was the closest I've got so far. The thing that's difficult about writing for the theatre is its active nature: you watch it, it happens in front of you, to you; it's up and running. Theatre doesn't work in such an exciting way if it relies too heavily on reported action or reported monologues. Some playwrights of the past knew exactly how to strike a balance between reported action and real action on stage — think of *Hedda Gabbler* — but many modern playwrights don't seem to know how to do that (and I certainly don't). So all my writing, basically, is an attempt to try and get that balance right.

I don't think in that way I've been helped particularly by other modern playwrights, because I think every play that you go along to see is flawed in some very deep way. Plays are the most difficult thing to get right — harder than short stories, or novels or poems. Plays have to *work* at so many different levels, if they're to really affect people, visually and emotionally and intellectually. I find that kind of writing very difficult. Even when I see contemporary plays by the playwrights I most admire, I'm often disappointed. And I know I'm not alone — often what you hear on the way out of a theatre is people saying, 'Oh but such and such really let it down'. That's what people do when they go to see a play today — they've seen so many and have such high expectations, that they talk most about what didn't work.

Do you believe that theatre can affect social change?

Yes, I do. I think that theatre can affect social change — it can be very influential and it can affect individual change and social change. I can remember going to see 7:84 and Wildcat, two famous Scottish theatre companies. I used to go along to see these companies at work, and they actually changed my way of looking at things. 7:84's landmark play *The*

Cheviot, the Stag, and the Black, Black Oil completely changed my way of looking at Scottish history. It made me interested, it made me want to know about my past, it made me read books on the highland clearances, and it made me think of wealth and ownership. I was one person the play affected, but it also affected people across the country. That show played in the highlands and the islands and the wee youth clubs and community centres as well as big theatres. And when theatre companies do that — go from community centres to mainstream metropolitan theatres — that's when they are really *effecting* change because they have taken something to every place where you could possibly have theatre. That's what theatre should be about — you should have it everywhere; it shouldn't be an exclusive thing where you have to pay £25 to go to the West End.

So much about the theatre today is commercial: it all seems to depend on where the theatre wants to place itself, how much the tickets cost, what the audience is like, how much marketing they do to get people into the theatre. Often you can go to see plays which are about racism and black people in some way, yet you'll find yourself in an all-white audience (composed of people who could afford to buy the tickets). That to me is a terrible pity because something just isn't getting through.

Or often you might write a play for a particular audience — like I wrote *Twice Over* for schoolchildren. Initially it was for the Theatre Centre and it was meant to tour schools. What I wanted was a play for young teenagers, to go around schools and get young people to think about sexuality. But the company lost their nerve at the last minute because Clause 28 was in the air, posing a real threat to organizations which sponsored lesbian work or 'promoted' lesbian or gay sexuality. So, Theatre Centre cut the play. They had spent £2,000 promoting it and spent another several thousand pounds paying me. So altogether they must have wasted about £6,000 on that play, and they never showed it. That to me was tragic, because it meant that the play didn't reach the audience it was intended for, and therefore it didn't get to do whatever it could have done in terms of change. So the play, any play, needs to get out into the right medium. Then, after it has found its way there, it can very deeply change people. Just as I believe books can change your life, I believe the theatre can.

You can be in some audiences in certain places where a response to a play is just electric. Think of *Torch Song Trilogy* and *Bent* — these plays for their time made a huge impact on people, and made them actually think about all complicated, controversial issues like sexuality. That is *affecting* social change. Some plays might even get people to think about the law or about Clause 28, for instance. In that sense, theatre may be affecting legal issues, and possibly affecting social change. There have been plays about

AIDS, right from the beginning, when HIV-Positive People and People with AIDS were still treated like lepers. Those plays effected social change in that they got people to think about how they were responding to AIDS as a disease. That's an example of a kind of theatre which is really doing its job, by initiating or pushing for social change. Theatre isn't just for entertainment value or for a good night out — although it should offer those things too. There's nothing to say that politics and entertainment should be mutually exclusive. Feminist theatre can also be 'fun', and sometimes funny as well.

Lizbeth Goodman
Interview with Jackie Kay, assisted by Mathew Kay, London, January 1995.

PETA LILY

Peta Lily is an Australian performance artist and teacher who lives and works in Britain. For a time she was a member of Three Women Mime, and she has collaborated with David Glass, but she has most often worked solo. Her performance pieces include Wendy Darling, Dogs I Have Known, *and* Beg! *(1992).*

Do you address feminist issues in your work?

I've always wanted, in my work, to express things which are private, important, real to me. And within that, there are also what might be seen as 'feminist issues'.

Much of your solo work is concerned with the representation of women. Would you call your solo work feminist?

Yes and no. Whatever repercussions my work may have, my approach to it is quite individual. For instance, my decision to do my piece called *Frightened of Nothing* was related to reading some feminist fiction. It was inspirational for me to read of women detectives, because so many heroes — when I was growing up — were men: men were the figures who were emulated, respected. There were very few active, powerful female models in my experience, and I was very much aware of that lack. I wanted to address it somehow.

Did the under-representation of women in the field influence your decision to pursue mime and physical theatre work?

Yes. And also, you've got everything open to you with physical theatre. You've got fantasy. Now that I'm starting to write more, to write plays, I'm still writing and creating my own particular field of vision. To show what women could be, or show women's experience that has been hidden.

Much of your performance work takes fairy tales and myths and well known female characters and re-creates them. Where did you find the source for your 'mythic women'?

When I was studying mime, it occurred to me that everyone was doing 'Everyman', even the women. There was heaps of material to be explored, in memory and imagination, about female characters, women's responses to situations.

Wendy Darling comes from the story of *Peter Pan*, of course, but she was also a character in my imagination almost ever since I can remember — a character which has always had its own resonances and associations for me[1]. The show which includes that character, simply called *Wendy Darling*, was a very important piece of work for me.

Wendy Darling is a very powerful piece: in its shifting characterization, shifts in fantasy/reality, shifts in gender and power on stage. As the performer on stage, you seem to enter all those characters and simultaneously to re-enter your own childhood. Does the piece work for you at that double level?

The process of getting to that complicated response was very complex. I had thought of Wendy and subverting the story from her point of view. So I thought of Wendy's role in the original story, all to do with the theme of unrequited love. Well unrequited love is such a waste of energy! So at first I decided to try to give Wendy something better to do with that energy.

At the end of Barrie's *Peter Pan*, Wendy has a daughter, who has a daughter. I thought I'd try to trace those characters through time, so that Wendy could become a bluestocking figure in the 1930s, a bit like those Victorian women travellers who would walk to Tibet and learn to fly in the Yogic way so she wouldn't need Peter at all! And then I thought she could be visited by one of her daughters in the 1970s....

But, after reading and re-reading the book several times, I realised that what I liked so much in the story of *Peter Pan*, was the unrequited love story — exactly what I had been trying to get away from.

In the end the piece became, as you've suggested, an exploration of childhood. Childhood is not just a happy simple place. There are very dark threads there which need to be explored for all of us.

There seems to be a similar dynamic at work in Wendy Darling *and* Beg!, *both in terms of the power dynamics on stage (manipulations of reality and fantasy, power and status, gender relations, etc.), and also in so far as the pieces focus on central female characters (extreme, grotesque, frighteningly possible) in their struggles to come to terms with memories and events from her own childhood. How important is the exploration of these childhood memories?*

---

[1] Bryony Lavery discusses her own version of *Peter Pan*, page 44.

Very. *In Beg!* the central character coming to terms with incest.... Her psychopathy comes from that trauma which she's buried.

Beg! draws on fairy tales in particular: Rumpelstiltskin, Red Riding Hood, etc. How did you come at those stories, in the process of devising Beg!*? Did you begin with the idea of incest, or of a woman psychopath, or with the characters in the fairy tales (or all of the above)?*

Beg! began as an imagistic fetishistic thing: again, I took a lot of inspiration from my dreams. I write down my dreams and work with them. And often I start with a poem based on ideas or images from dreams. But once it's written I'll move miles beyond it, come back to it and structure it in terms of story telling.

In your work you take familiar stories and images from the collective unconscious which we all share and can tap in to, and physicalize them in and through performance. Do you make the stories somehow personal to you in the process?

I take my own concerns, my own experience, into those stories when I interpret them, bring them to life. My work has been a way to help me look back at the past, oddly enough. So often when I'm working on a piece, usually once it's up and running, I'll come to a personal realization as well. In that sense, all my work is in some sense autobiographical, or linked to autobiography.

The image of woman and dog was at the core of *Beg!* It was about a power struggle, a situation of control and exchange. I knew that was central to the piece, though I only worked it out in detail as the work progressed. At first, I only knew that I was fascinated by this question of getting the upper hand and what that was all about, but that got worked out as the power struggle attached to a sexual relationship, to representing adult sexuality on stage and the power struggle involved there.

I wanted to represent sexuality on stage and to create a positive, empowering expression of a woman's sexuality. We, women, are often attacked — sometimes physically, but also in more subtle ways, in daily encounters which attack or undermine our individual power bases. In the basic power structure of the world, women are placed below men. Though individuals can transcend that dynamic, the overall structure is still there.

How did you go about redressing this balance in Beg!*?*

Through making the female protagonist an active, powerful figure, a woman who likes sex and goes for it, who acts rather than being acted upon. But that wasn't the original idea, it developed as we worked.

21. Peta Lily as Dr. Penelope Second in *Beg!*, Peta Lily and Co. UK tour (1992); photographer: Colonel Kwong.

My collaborator, David Glass, suggested that the female protagonist, Dr Penelope Second, should be a murderer. At first I disagreed, because most murderers aren't women. But it made it a much more interesting part for me to play, and more importantly, it transformed that character from a survivor, or even victim, to a person who acts. She's mad, of course. She's a psychopath.

Did you get any strong responses to that very negative portrayal of a woman?
Responses to *Beg!* have been mainly positive, and most women have found Penelope, her activity, her refusal to be the victim, empowering. I'd bet that even a few years ago I would have had a very negative response to that 'negative' character. But things have changed. In the past few years there have been lots of killers on screen who were women.

'Fatal Attraction', 'Basic Instinct', etc...
Yes; these depictions of violent women may be quite extreme and inaccurate, a product of a male paranoia or hatred of women in some cases. But looking at them — and the fact they they these images are looked at by so many people — still means that we have female protagonists who act. That is in itself empowering.

Are your female characters generally active, whether in positive or negative ways ?
No: active female characters have never been my strong point, though I didn't realize that until it was pointed out to me. My protagonists have always been survivors. But often they haven't been active. Wendy is not active. She really is in a state of stasis. She resolves something, but not through acting, rather through reflection.

Because Beg! *is so violent, did you get extreme, audible responses from the audience?*
During the show, audiences responded like they were on a rollercoaster. We had a number of people who walked out, but it's hard to know their reasons. After the show, we discovered an enormous range of feedback, with some people very distressed and also grateful for having seen a piece which touched on what are often considered taboo areas.

Did you hold post-show discussions?
No. Audience feedback came from venue managers or from people I know. A woman who's a survivor of child abuse saw *Beg!* Afterwards, she said that she couldn't say she enjoyed it, but wanted to thank me for it — she found it liberating to see that experience on stage. A lot of men were very

nervous about it, about me. That's wonderful, because my worst fear about the show was about being on stage in knickers and bra, doing a show about sex and violence. I thought I'd feel threatened. But performing in *Beg!* was actually very empowering, because people were staying away from me, they were afraid of me!

There is a lot of very dark comedy in Beg! *How do you use comedy in your other work?*

With Three Women Mime, we used to do short sketches, very visual, with a lot of props (very different from what I do now). In much of our work we found that we could reach people, even on feminist issues, either through the heightened means of visual theatre or through comedy. For instance, a guy came up to us after the show about rape and said that he'd always had trouble understanding why women found catcalling horrible or irritating and now he understood why. The physical theatre made him understand why, made him react physiologically to the piece, as part of the process. Any rhythm you create on stage will be picked up by the audience. Even when I use physical theatre techniques of this kind, I usually use a kind of dark humour as well — it slips under people's intellectual guards. Comedy, like physical theatre, is based on rhythms and unexpected juxtapositions.

Do you often write about gender issues, as in the piece about rape you produced with Three Women Mime?

It depends on what you mean by 'about'. I believe that if you're writing with an issue in mind, it's best to have a heart to your work. The work itself must take priority over any message you desire to convey.

Do you think that performing live, for an audience present in the space with you, is absolutely essential to your work, or could you also do similar work for other media and contexts (film, videoed live performance, etc.)?

For a long time, I was most drawn to work which involved an audience and me alone on stage. But over the years, it was a difficult kind of work to sustain. With the economic climate getting worse and worse, and with other forms of entertainment on offer, so multi-coloured and sophisticated, audiences are getting used to seeing a great deal. They're not so used to using their imaginations to make the colours, the images, the richness themselves. You can see the effects of this in marketing terms as well. A one-woman show these days doesn't sound exciting enough to entice audiences any more. They can make a choice between a big comfortable cinema and a little dingy arts centre.

How do you address these issues of the power dynamics of gender, class, etc. in performance, and of personal space, when you teach less experienced performers or choreograph their shows?

All the techniques I've assimilated about this discipline, everything I've learned about theatre more generally, has helped me to understand the world, has helped me to see the ways in which we can look at our place in the world outside the theatre as well. You can, physically, in a muscular sense, transform the body: through training over a period of years, or in moments, using the imagination. I teach that in workshops because it's the first step to recognizing the relationship between the body and the world, the way we see ourselves overall. Theatre is about transformation.

Where is your work leading you now?

Writing is becoming more important to me now, and my work is moving further into the world of language and a more structured form of story telling. I used to work primarily intuitively. I was drawn by texture, atmosphere, ambiguity. But now I'm very excited by trying to create plays informed by visual elements.

Lizbeth Goodman
Interview recorded on audiotape February 1993; updated for publication January 1995.

WOMEN'S ISSUES THEATRE
Sue Schilperoort, speaking for the company

Women's Issues Theatre (WIT) was co-founded by Sue Schilperoort and Julie Child in 1991. It was set up as 'a feminist co-operative committed to: producing work central to women's lives; presenting experimental pieces alongside more conventionally formatted material; and developing a new "feminist theatre practice."' Their work has included the experimental pieces Remodelling Woman, Judy's Last Punch, *and* Daisy in Bright Lights; *Sue Schilperoort's plays* Mothering Rights *and* Half a Million Women; *and Franca Rame's* The Same Old Story. *They also run drama workshops and theatre-in-education projects.*

Does gender matter in the theatre?

Absolutely. Whether we define gender as fe/male or feminine/masculine, it matters. The presence of women on stage is both practically and symbolically important. It's practically important because women are then working in the field in which they have talent and creativity; and it's symbolically important because women are seen to be subjects in their own right, rather than just incidentals in the expression of Great and Significant matters, patriarchally defined.

We need to acknowledge that femininity/masculinity as social constructs are largely male-defined in a patriarchal system. In my role as an educator, I remain deeply shocked by the prevailing attitudes of young people towards gender identification. Little progress seems to have been made in changing perspectives on elements of the 'self'. Popular culture continues to perpetuate images of ourselves as highly 'genderized'.

Since theatre both reflects society's existing social and political structures and acts as a catalyst for change (we hope), it is crucial that women take a central role in theatre. We have a responsibility to women (past, present and future) to address the impact of patriarchal structures. And this role is as much about enriching and developing the lives of men as it is of women.

So I'd suggest that creating roles for women in theatre is not enough: we should be looking took at gender issues and genderizing issues in creating those roles. As directors, devisors and performers we need to be aware of the creation of stereotypes — stock characters like the butch and the femme, the career woman, the caring mother, the domesticated wife. Useful though these signifiers are, we have a role to play in subverting existing images of Woman, and exploring new representations of ourselves. In practice the final product might be shaped more by a determination to address a particular issue, but we should at least try to recognize gender issues in our work.

Are you aware that the position of women in the theatre has changed in any way over the years?

Since I'm relatively new to working in theatre, my perceptions of how things have changed have been drawn more from academic study than my own experience. However, experientially I'm aware of a great deal of talent and creativity which might have developed far further had there been more equality of opportunity in theatre (as indeed elsewhere). My own contribution to theatre depends very much on the support and encouragement I get from the women's community and from my partner. What I refer to as 'internalized phallocentricity' inhibits many women from expressing our creativity and sharing our experiences. As women we often rely disproportionately on external affirmation and approval, and I'm frequently taken aback at the fragility of my own confidence in my work.

In the 1990s, there are more women out there making theatre, but much of it is on a shoe-string, or costing them a great deal. And what concerns me in practice and in prospect is that so many of our potential audience are 'Thatcher's Children', with their anti-feminist, anti-Left, anti-radical bigotry. But at least one fundamental socio-political shift has possibly worked in our favour — the increasing plurality and fragmentation of society. We might argue that this has democratized, empowering the Little Person with a big voice and a lot to say.

Are you conscious of 'acting, performing and writing as a woman'?

I don't see how we can avoid this. Our lives, identities, experiences are all shaped by our genderized selves. Everything I do is informed by my 'woman-ness', and my work in theatre is no exception.

In writing I'm committed to creating strong roles for women, beginning to redress the imbalance of the dearth of female parts, and to addressing issues central to women's lives in contemporary society.

When I direct for Women's Issues Theatre, I play the role of the 'outside eye' or 'facilitator' in work devised by the company, just as often as a 'direct' plays. I've worked with my colleagues — including Julie Child and Dooni Akonanda — in developing a new theatre practice, based on feminist principles. Our practice aims to support company members in personal growth and awareness: seeking to work with them in moving from phallocentric spaces to ones in which women-centredness defines who we are and what we can be. We seek to create a space we can truly call ours, in which we're encouraged to explore new ground and new identities.

As a performer there are times when I might be working with material which draws on essential 'human-ness'. At other times material may be particularly focused on the experience of being a woman. In both cases I'm aware of 'acting as a woman', of bringing to performance something which is uniquely 'me'. Exploring what it means to be a woman is central to my own performance pieces like *Women, Sex, and Passion* or *Half a Million Women*. I am acutely aware of 'acting as a woman': drawing on my own very personal experience of someone disenfranchised because of her sex. And by acting my own story, I'm saying to other women, 'You're not alone. It happened to me too. Come and talk with me.' And they do.

Do you feel strongly either for or against working collaboratively with other women in the theatre?

Working in collaboration with other women can be wonderful. There are all kinds of risks (of self-expression, exploration, and self-development) which women may be prepared to take in single sex groups. Furthermore, we can develop a shorthand and language, arising from our common experience, which facilitates clear and effective communication. In terms of working processes this can be extremely effective.

But let's not fall into the trap of believing that segregated groups are definitionally free from all the crap that's associated with working with mixed gender groups. In my experience, while exploring new working processes, avoiding hierarchy, authority, delineated responsibility, formality, we might lose many of the things that work towards making groups effective and coherent. It seems to me that what we need to recognize is that authority, responsibility, formality all might have a place in any group. We should not be afraid of employing a variety of means to achieve our aims as long as we agree on certain basic ground rules that we aren't prepared to compromise.

How would you define 'feminism'?

My own philosophy is relatively simple: as women, many of us find ourselves suffering from internalized phallocentricity, and we might recognize this to a greater or lesser extent. For me, feminism is about moving from this to a woman-centred experience in which I stand centre-stage. I don't want to be there, in the wings, by dint of being someone else's appendage, the Other. I want to be there in my own right. Feminism is about empowering both women and men in their attempts to transgress the socially-constructed roles in which we are seemingly entrapped.

According to your own definition, would you call yourself a feminist?

I strive to be — as a mother, teacher, theatre-practitioner, lover, as myself in many guises and roles. But this is always within a system that annihilates the family, makes impotent the teacher, impoverishes the arts, censors lovers and disfigures the self. But if we cease to strive, what hope is there for the future?

Would you say that feminism has affected the theatre in any major way?

Feminism has affected every institution, and has certainly affected the theatre. It has given women a belief that they have a right to be seen and heard. It has given women spectators a notion that they might not be alone in their experience. It has given funding bodies the threat of a rap across the knuckles if they aren't seen to be making at least a minimal effort to support and promote women's theatre. And it has given the other 49% of the population the suggestion that there just might be certain issues, particular experiences over which they don't have the monopoly of insight.

Do you believe that theatre can affect social change?

Emphatically yes! If I didn't believe this, I wouldn't be in this business.

What's the future for women in the theatre in the UK?

This question leaves me with a heavy heart. With a shift to the right in British let alone international politics, I fear for the future of anyone in British theatre. The one thing that bothers me is not the state's attempt to cut our funding, silence our calls and discredit our work. What worries me most is that the wo/man in the street has been led by the pocket (mistakenly) to the right of the field (that is, to areas where financial rewards are greater: mainstream and commercial theatres, television and film). Of course, these media tend to be less political as forms, so we lose our grasp on politics in the attempt to survive. This is the greatest threat: that we are striving so hard to be heard in a society in which those who should be our allies are bowing to Mammon.

I see two prospects for women in political theatre in Britain. The first is a continuation of our present role. In times of censorship, whether through administration or cash controls, there will still be some pioneers of change who seek reaffirmation. I trust that these will remain as an audience, creating some measure of demand for women's work. The second prospect is that our role will grow, develop and become richer as society swings back towards some place in which idealism focuses on something other than another Porsche, a villa on the Costa del Sol and two lovers. I dream of a future

Britain in which women are equally represented in theatre — whether in writing, performing, directing, acting, sound, design or whatever. My hope is that the dream will prove to be a vision.

Lizbeth Goodman
Written interview by Sue Schilperoort: October 1994, edited 1995.

SHARON MORGAN ON WELSH WOMEN'S THEATRES

Sharon Morgan is an actress who has worked mostly in Welsh language theatre. She started her career in the early 1970s with Cwmni Theatr Cymru, Wales's first professional theatre company, and went on to co-found Bara Caws and Hwyl a Fflag, a Welsh-language company which foregrounded sexual politics. She has also acted in mainstream and English-language theatre and TV, particularly after becoming a mother and finding it more difficult to tour. In 1994, she devised and performed a solo piece, Gobeithion Gorffwyll *(Desperate Hopes), based on a story by Simone de Beauvoir.*

Let's start by looking at the background to women's theatre in Wales. What needs and characteristics are peculiar to the theatre in Wales?

There has been a professional theatre in Wales for less than thirty years and we are still trying to establish a feeling of confidence in the theatre, both within and outside Wales. As a country, Wales has its own cultural background and needs which are very different from those of England. Due to an extreme lack of funding, Welsh theatre is very marginalized and until we gain a measure of control over our own affairs, the theatre and indeed the arts in general in Wales will not be able to fulfil their potential.

Although we get more funding per capita than English theatre, it is still not sufficient, firstly because Wales is a bilingual country, and secondly because the theatrical tradition is so young. As we see, *Under Milk Wood* (Dylan Thomas, 1954) at the National Theatre (April 1995) and *One Full Moon* (an adaptation of Caradog Pritchard's novel, *Un Nos Oleu Leiad*, 1961) at the Young Vic — both set in the past, both perpetuating a particular image of Welshness — it becomes clear that we need to struggle to free ourselves of stereotypes of what is seen to be Welsh.

Does gender matter in the theatre?

There are two ways of answering this question. Firstly, I can't imagine plays or performances where gender doesn't come into question. As soon as you have male and female characters, then all gender issues and the long complex history which has separated men and women come into play. The second way in which gender matters concerns relations between practitioners. Theatre is more open and democratic than many other institutions, but no-one can escape their conditioning. And of course, particularly if a company is trying to redress the balance, then gender matters a lot.

Are you aware that the position of women in the theatre has changed over the years?

Yes, but change has been spasmodic and it has been the work of isolated individuals.

In the mid-sixties, Wales' first professional theatre company, the Welsh Theatre Company (based in Bangor working in Welsh, and in Cardiff working in English) was run by men. Since then, an enormous number of companies have grown up, still run mostly by men. The building-based Theatr Gwynedd in Bangor and the Sherman Theatre in Cardiff, experimental companies like Brith Gof and ManAct, and writer-based companies like Theatr y Byd and Y Cwmni are run by men. But mainly since the mid-eighties, the presence of women has become more marked. Made in Wales working in English and Dalier Sylw working in Welsh, both new writing companies, are run by women, Gilly Adams and Bethan Jones respectively. Theatr Clwyd is run by a woman, Helena Kaut-Hawson. Even more recently, new women's companies such as Jesus and Tracy, founded by Eddie Ladd, and Alma Theatre, both experimental companies, and Y Gymraes, founded by Sera Moore-Williams working in Welsh and performing plays by Sera, have emerged. Women have a strong presence in Theatre in Education (TIE) and community theatre: Fran Wen in Gwynedd has consistently been run by a woman, and Sara Harris Davies and Manon Eames are leading members of Theatre West Glamorgan. Also, Volcano Theatre Company has a strong woman member.

It disturbs me that, apart from devised shows and translations, we see very little writing by women. Apart from Sera Moore-Williams, Menna Elfyn, a feminist poet, has written a play for Dalier Sylw: *Y Forwyn Goch*, (The Red Maiden) based on the life of Simone Weil. Angharad Tomas, a well-known Welsh-language activist wrote *Tanddaearol* (Underground) for Hwyl a Fflag and Mair Gruffydd worked as a writer in residence for Bara Caws for a year. Branwen Cennard wrote *Mysgu Cymyle* (Mixing Clouds) for Dalier Sylw and Siân Summers *Un Funud Fach* (One Small Minute) for Hwyl a Fflag. In the English language, Made in Wales has performed two plays by women, *Wanting* by Jane Buckler and *Waiting at the Water's Edge* by Lucinda Coxon, neither of whom is Welsh or lives in Wales. Other women writers — including Helen Gwyn, Siân Williams, Siân Evans, Christine Watkins — have had plays workshopped at the Made in Wales writing festival, 'Write On'. Phil Clark, the (gay) artistic director of the Sherman Theatre has encouraged several women to write for the lunchtime slot, including Helen Griffin, Elizabeth Morgan and Lisa Hunt.

Phil Clark has also employed several new, relatively inexperienced women directors; this year in this slot — Morfudd Hughes, Menna Price, Allison Gearish (who runs the Sherman's youth theatre) and Yvonne Murphy. This last development is extremely positive as there are so few women directors. Bethan Jones of Dalier Sylw and Gilly Adams of Made in Wales and Sera Moore-Williams of Y Gymraes direct new writing. In TIE, Carys Huw, Menna Price, Jill Ogden and Llio Silyn direct. Gwen Elis has directed for Hwyl a Fflag, Falmai Jones for Bara Caws, and Janet Aethwy for Canol y Ffordd and Chwarae Teg. Helena Kaut-Hawson directs for Theatr Clwyd. Alison Hindell, a BBC radio director who has encouraged many women writers, also directs theatre.

I feel frustrated that we lack a strong focus because there is no one strong women's company. The Magdalena Project, run by Jill Greenhalgh and based in Cardiff, is a very important development, but because it takes an international perspective and is concerned with experimental theatre, it tends to be on the fringes of Welsh theatre as a whole.

Change has been haphazard, because of a lack of a body with a focused overview. The Arts Council reacts to proposals and can't and shouldn't, of course, dictate policy. Also, after sixteen years of Tory rule (and Wales has never voted for a Tory government!) the theatre in general is struggling for survival. Networks are not so easily formed, as individualism rules and women don't work together as much as they should. Women as writers, performers and directors need tremendous encouragement, and it's sometimes only practical coercion that propels women into taking assertive positions.

Are you conscious of 'acting as a woman'?

I am not conscious of it when I am acting, because I am steeped in a character, but I cannot be anything but a woman. Doing shows like *Gobeithion Gorffwyll* (Desperate Hopes) felt right because I understood de Beauvoir and related to the piece. That has never happened before because I am usually in plays by men, acting the parts of women created by men who are often stereotypes. That means that I have to pretend to be something else. Or, if I put my own interpretation into a piece, that may conflict with the script. I was once playing the part of a woman who was so aggressive that I felt I was being asked to play a man. When I complained to the director, Edward Thomas, he said 'This is the woman I've created'.

When I was younger, I played a lot of 'dumb blondes', who were the sexual object of the man in the piece. I was perfectly aware of how ridiculous it was. Men's sexuality is distorted by capitalism and the media. Women's sexuality is thus exploited, so that actresses cannot explore their sexuality.

The answer is to do my own work, but I cannot make a living doing that. In my solo piece, I was trying to discover my own way of working, but the money did not allow sufficient rehearsal time. There were so many different ways of working which I had to leave unexplored. It's not a satisfactory working practice, but I still think that moving away from the mainstream will help me to find a more suitable — and different — sort of performance.

Do you feel strongly either for or against working collaboratively with other women in the theatre?

I did a lot of collaboration in the mid-seventies, with various theatre companies. I would love to work only with women, but the opportunity never arises. In TV, I am often the only woman in a scene and on the set. Women are always working in isolation, which is sad, because we have so much to learn from one another.

How would you define 'feminism'?

I define it as a belief in the right of women to fulfil their potential as human beings — *not* their right to equality with men because lots of men cannot fulfil their potential either. All women are oppressed and treated as second-class citizens (however rich they are), in every society, to different extents, throughout the world.

According to your definition, would you call yourself a feminist?

Yes, I am a feminist, although I am concerned many women seem afraid to use the word. Words are unsatisfactory, but we have to express ideas in some way!

Would you say that feminism has affected the theatre in any major way?

Inevitably. It has expanded opportunities for women, giving them more confidence. All the changes I talked about earlier would not have happened without feminism. Also, more women are talking about gender issues now. The roles women play have been affected to a certain extent, although until more women write plays, we will not move forward as we should.

We need to be aware that it's taking longer for feminism to get to Wales. It is still a dirty word here and feminists are still isolated individuals. Wales is a patriarchal society — there are huge prejudices. The backlash had arrived before the first wave took effect!

Do you believe that theatre can affect social change?

It's important that it does and it can, but it's more likely to shift consciousness than create revolutions. Theatre reacts to society as it is, but it should also educate, enlighten and open up attitudes in people's minds. Sometimes it is the only place where marginalized voices are heard. It should be a platform for discussion of issues not heard in the media — a moot point here in the Welsh language, in which the dominance of S4C [the Welsh channel] is massive.

Hwyl a Fflag dealt with sexual politics in its early years. The plays *Diwedd y Saith Degau* (The End of the Seventies) and *Unwaith eto yng Nghymru Annwyl* (Once Again in Dear Wales) focused on women's dissatisfaction with traditional roles. *Wastad ar y Tu Fas* (Always on the Outside) was the first Welsh-language play about a gay relationship.

The company ground to a halt last year, because it lost its Arts Council grant. Basically, personnel changed and the company seemed to lose impetus. Dedicated to new writing, the company struggled to find suitable, relevant work, and standards fell. There was also an element of marginalization and the problem of geography, in that there were two other companies in Bangor competing for the same pot of money.

What's the future for women in the theatre in Wales?

The future for women depends very much on the state of the rest of the theatre in Wales. We need self-government and a Ministry for the Arts. An Arts Council survey has been commissioned to look into the position of women in the theatre. It should be used to redress the balance by addressing the problem of encouragement and positive discrimination.

A strong feminist, bilingual theatre company would be wonderful; but is hardly likely at the moment. The existence of Alma Theatre, Y Gymraes and Magdalena is encouraging, however. I am an optimist and believe things will improve, although change will inevitably take time!

How do the conditions of women's lives create difficulties for their work in the theatre?

The fact that women are still almost completely responsible for child-care is a big problem. Attitudes towards child-care need to change. There are no crèches and no sympathy for flexible hours in most theatre companies, except at Magdalena and Y Gymraes. And, of course, there is still no tax relief on child-minders. Many women feel guilty and suppress their own needs, their own creativity after having children. So, apart from the practical problems (which are huge) there are many psychological problems which arise for women with children. Magdalena will be dealing with these issues in 1995 in a project called 'Mothers of Invention'.[1]

Also, I think women's creativity is different from men's and so not as highly valued. The problem is that men set the standards by which work is judged. Only women can address this issue, but it will be a long slow process.

Jane de Gay
Telephone interview, February 1995.

---

[1] Held at The Point Arts Centre, Cardiff, September 1995.

CHARABANC THEATRE COMPANY ON IRISH WOMEN'S THEATRES

Charabanc is a women's theatre company based in Belfast, Northern Ireland. Its Artistic Directors are Carol Moore and Eleanor Methven. Working since 1983 and still going strong, Charabanc is one of the first and longest running women's theatre companies in the UK.

What does the name 'Charabanc' mean, literally and metaphorically?

Charabanc means tour bus, holiday bus. Metaphorically, the term applied to our very first production, which was written for and about the female mill workers. Those women had a tradition of taking the occasional and much-earned day off, hiring a bus and going out for a good time together. The term 'charabanc' is generally associated in Northern Ireland with the idea of women together, out for a day of fun. We used the term as our company name for that first production, as we weren't immediately thinking of ourselves as a company with a long-term future. But when we continued, the name stuck.

When was Charabanc formed?

Our rough beginnings would have been the initial discussions about the mill workers' play. So we first started working together as a group, kicking around ideas, in March and April 1983. Our first production was performed on 15 May 1983. We've been together ever since.

Does gender matter in the theatre?

Of course. How could one be a feminist and not believe that gender affects the workings of every institution from government to, in this case, theatre? Male and female administrators, directors, writers and actors all bring to theatre a view of the world via the gender lens.

Are you aware that the position of women in the theatre has changed in any way over the years?

That depends on what you mean by 'position'… Is the definition one of numbers of jobs in theatre taken by women, or the profile of women directors, writers and actors over the years? As within all male-dominated structures, individual women have come through, although in the past more successfully as actors than as directors or writers. The position certainly in

Ireland over the last 20 years has seen more women establishing themselves in all the various areas of theatre practice. But, the biggest change has to be women who have begun new companies where the image is one of committed, creative, professional and political groups who continually throw up challenges to the rest of the arts community. Women writers, however, still struggle to be acknowledged and accepted as 'mainstream', particularly if their work has come from a feminist stable.

Are you conscious of 'acting, directing, designing, writing, as women', and if so, in what ways?

Yes, our individual and collective choices within Charabanc as artistic directors, actors, etc. are consciously coloured by the perspectives we bring to those roles as women. Charabanc's artistic policy has meant choices that create strong roles for, and give opportunities to, women. Prior to Charabanc, these strong roles for women were just not available in the majority of theatre in Northern Ireland. As researcher/actresses, we are personally aware of creating and playing roles — not as mothers or girlfriends, but as central protagonists. We feel we have given historical and contemporary women a voice.

Do you feel strongly either for or against working collaboratively with other women in the theatre?

Charabanc's work has always been fired by the collective energy that comes, in the main, from women. But, our success is also due to a business style that differs from traditional hierarchical structures. We work more effectively in positive environments where communication is central to confidence, morale and performance. We focus on the end result and how we can work collectively to achieve it.

How would you define 'feminism'?

'Feminism' is female centred. The lens through which the world is viewed has a female gaze. Whether our plays explore the demise of the Northern Irish Labour Party in 1949 or the impact of the Community Care legislation of the 1980s, they are viewed and reflected through the eyes of women. So, of course, we would call ourselves feminists.

Would you say that feminism has affected the theatre in any major way?

It is remarkable to think that women are often still regarded as a minority grouping. The mainstream theatre often views 'female-centred' or 'feminist' plays as they would gay plays or Asian and other ethnic minority plays. They have 'their moment' and then the establishment retreats to its familiar male-centred territory.

Feminist theory still holds much challenge for contemporary society but, I suppose, 'liberal' attitudes within theatre have meant a reluctant acceptance that at least the door should be seen to be open.

Women forming their own companies is the present reality and we look forward to that continuing and developing. Sexism and discrimination continue in the workplace and government legislation works slowly to demand equal pay, equal opportunities and promotions for women. Feminism offers women in the theatre today several choices: to continue to work in a male-dominated environment, but to decide to battle from within that organization and/or through the Courts; or to seek out employers who are striving for equal opportunities and fair employment in an open and honest way; or to create their own working environment by creating their own companies and/or their own opportunities.

Do you believe that theatre can affect social change?

Theatre can pose questions and offer dilemmas to audiences which are both personal and political, but social change and attitudes towards change are slow. Theatre, by its nature, is as much a participant in that push as is any institution. All of Charabanc's commissioned plays have addressed to some degree the legacy of the 'Northern Irish State'. The Republican, Loyalist or Unionist politics of our characters reached the ears of audiences in theatres, leisure centres, hotels, community centres and bars. Perhaps old and difficult questions presented by 'likeable' characters did and do evoke a different response — if only one of 'I'm enjoying myself, so I'll stay and listen.'

What is the relationship between feminist theatres made in Northern Ireland and those made in the Republic of Ireland?

Feminist theatre is feminist theatre; it's all about being woman-centred, concerned with women's issues and experiences, and working to present a female gaze in performance. But of course there are major differences between the work of women in Northern Ireland and the Republic, mainly because there are major differences between the societies, and the life experiences of women. Most importantly, we in Northern Ireland live in a military or paramilitary state. That affects our lives and work in very fundamental ways. We have to approach our work from a woman-centred position whilst in a state of war, just as if we were trying to make Palestinian or Israeli feminist theatre. So, in our early work, we felt ourselves to be feminist but we had to begin from a more general, political place: we couldn't jump right in and examine one woman's conflict with her sense of family or self, as first we needed to consider her sense of safety in a community and

22. Michele Forbes in Charabanc Theatre Company's production of *Bondagers* by Sue Glover, produced in 1991 at the Ardowen Theatre, Enniskillen, followed by an Irish tour; photographer: Jill Jennings, Chris Hill Photographics.

culture. We had to look at the effects of the political situation on women generally, rather than individually.

By contrast, women's theatre which is made in the Republic can begin at a different place, with closer focus on women's domestic and emotional situations: a personal-political rather than a cultural-political starting place. There isn't very much feminist theatre in the Republic, but what has been made has tended to look at issues of importance to that culture, such as legislation on abortion, contraception and divorce.

Is feminist theatre in Northern Ireland comparable in any way(s) to that made in England, or Scotland, or Wales?

Even per head of population, there's not much feminist theatre to speak of in Northern Ireland. In fact, Charabanc is and always has been the main women's company in the country, though there are individuals working in similar terrain, such as the playwright Christina Reid. Other companies in other nations have colleague-companies; there are many feminist companies in England, and at least a reasonable number in Wales and Scotland and the Republic of Ireland (though many of these are very small and largely unfunded, and of course they are far outnumbered by male-centred companies). The result is, that while feminist companies in the rest of the 'United Kingdom' can go straight to feminist issues in their work, we start from a broader place. But, having worked together for twelve years, we've developed as a company and are now beginning to move into more personal-political material.

Our next play, *A Wife, a Dog, and a Maple Tree* by Sue Ashby, is about domestic violence. The title is taken from the seventeenth-century anonymous (and it should remain so) rhyme: 'a wife, a dog and a maple tree, the harder you beat them the better they be'. The play is powerful and very relevant to women of all ages and experiences, but it starts for us at a wide cultural level and focuses on individual women within the culture, rather than vice versa.

How would you define Charabanc's 'political' agenda?

Consciously making a woman or female character the central protagonist is a political statement. The so-called 'Troubles' have hijacked the political agenda in Northern Ireland. So, women's issues have either not been properly reflected in the media or have been marginalized. Contemporary women *do* want a voice and theatre needs to reflect that.

Lizbeth Goodman
Interviews conducted and updated, September 1994–January 1995.

THE MSFITS, ON SCOTTISH WOMEN'S THEATRES

The MsFits is a Scottish women's comedy/theatre company, founded in late 1985 by its two members, Rona Munro and Fiona Knowles. Both women write independently as well as performing with the MsFits on tours of Scotland and the UK.

How did the MsFits come together?

Fiona: I met Rona when I did a play of hers (*The Salesman*) with the Edinburgh Playwrights Workshop. Then Rona was commissioned to do a play for the Tron Theatre, Glasgow, called *Fugue* (published in 1983) which was her first commissioned play. Rona and I had worked together before, and had remained friends. We were both very interested in women and theatre, and issues in feminism in general, so we decided to experiment with writing. Rona had also performed as a student and then after university in her own shows at the Edinburgh Festival. We both decided we'd like to write and perform. An organization called Women Live — which in 1985 was a big movement for women in the arts — gave us a platform and encouragement to write and produce our own show. So we wrote a short sketch about being female Picts, standing on the battlements. We were women on the inside, with men outside, trying to get in. And as the show developed, all the sketches revolved around these two women talking about the men and their problems with them.

Sounds a bit like Lysistrata? ...

Fiona: Yes, but it was stand-up comedy with a serious intent. The format was quite radical for its day: sketches linked with rap songs and poems. The show covered all sorts of issues about politics and feminism. We had a tremendous response to that first show, so we plucked up the courage to audition for the Tron Theatre Mayfest in 1986. Our Mayfest gig was our first performance as the MsFits.

After that, our reputation grew and spread, mainly by word of mouth. I think we may have gained so much popularity early on partly due to the novelty factor: there was nothing like it at the time.

Why did you call yourselves the 'MsFits'?

Fiona: I came up with the name initially. We had to invent a new name on the way to the audition at the Tron. Because we're Aberdonians,

23. The Msfits: Fiona Knowles and Rona Munro; photographer: Roddy Simpson.

we say 'fit' instead of 'what' (so it's 'Ms-What?'). 'Ms.' obviously because it was feminist (although, even now, it's often mis-spelled as 'miss' by the press).

Also, we were talking about women as the 'msfits' of society, and we wanted to express that sense of women not 'fitting in' as equal human beings. We'd always felt 'msfit' in mainstream theatre. What we were doing was more independent.

Speaking personally, for instance, the kind of work we do is relegated to outside the mainstream. There's a ground-swell of approval and support around Scotland, so I can make a living, just. But we are always seen as the exception to some rule, which seems to be about men. Maybe that's why our comedy shows about women turning the tables were so popular, and so unusual.

Does gender matter in the theatre?

Rona: Yes, it does. But how? — that's what I don't know, because women and men's experiences of the world are so different. I'd define myself as feminist in feeling that these different experiences matter. What we're getting with women's writing now is the addition of a new realm of experience into the theatre, and what the effect of that will be I don't know.

Are you conscious of writing and performing as women?

Fiona: Yes.

Rona: Yes, definitely. It makes a difference. Gender is not invisible in any situation.

Do you feel strongly either for or against working collaboratively with other women in the theatre?

Rona: I feel strongly *for*, though when it happens it's not always a positive experience. We all know the Maggie Thatcher syndrome: beat the boys at their own game, etc. I think it's most energizing to work with women, but some women are exceptions. We can't generalize too much. But I like to think of the gender situation in theatre (or any art form) as a game of musical chairs. The game's been going on for ever, and only once in a great while does anyone add a new chair. But no matter how many people are playing and how many chairs there are, there's only ever one *one* chair for women. Now we've added more chairs but not really enough. I'm an incurable optimist, and things have always gone reasonably well for me. But still, I think, the establishment is slow to change, in the theatre and in academia and critical circles. Yet audiences out there are *very hungry* for reflections of women's stories which haven't been told.

How would you define 'feminism'?

Rona: It's making women's experience visible without being judgemental about what it should be. It's *not about* reforming men — that's their job (I wish they would do it themselves!).

According to your own definition, would you say that the MsFits is a feminist company?

Rona: Yes. The MsFits has always been a feminist company.

Do you have any trouble combining comedy and serious material?

Fiona: No trouble at all. The shows are both funny and sad. The comedy communicates the serious points very well, probably better than 'feeling' theatre. Comedy makes our theatre absurd. We always use a story-line format, including a range of characters and situations. It generally seems that audiences can find someone or something with which to identify in the material.

Who are your main audiences?

Fiona: Our audiences are mainly women, but men do come along, especially in the past three years. Reactions from men have been quite good, perhaps better than we expected them to be. Some come because they're sympathetic. I haven't had any negative feedback — to my face, anyway, but I can see it can sometimes make men uncomfortable. Often, women will say that 'our husbands should have seen that'. We aim to write about women and women's lives for women. If men listen and can hear what we're saying, that's great, very important.

Would you say that feminism has affected the theatre in any major way?

Rona: Yes, I think so. I can write plays that might have seemed screamingly radical ten to fifteen years ago, and no-one bats an eyelid now.

Do you believe that the theatre can affect social change?

Rona: I don't know. I doubt it on a large level. But on a personal level, perhaps. This is where we examine ourselves, share dreams and ideas. In its day, *Cathy Come Home* was very successful as issue-based work, produced at the right time. That had a major social impact, but such work is not very common, and in any case the hope of really affecting social change will necessarily involve a very gradual process.

Fiona: Yes, I think theatre can affect social change, but only on a very small scale. You can only change yourself. Women, individually and as a group, are changing, have been changing since the 1960s. Validation of women's experience on stage is very important in that process of change.

Could you give some examples of work which validates some Scottish women's experience on stage?

Fiona: The first one-woman show I did (1992) was called *The Seven Ages of Woman*. It was about women's status and it was a comedy. In 1993 I did a show called *Rabby Burns yer tea's oot*, which is a Scottish expression taken from the phrase which many women yell at their kids. This show, like all our MsFits work, is largely about the invisible women of history. The most recent one-woman show, *Burying Dad* (1994) is about three generations of women at a funeral. I link the show together with stand-up comedy and songs — trying throughout to reflect women's lives and to empower women in the audience.

What kind of work are the MsFits doing at the moment?

Fiona: Still comedy. Our shows are one hour to one and a half hours long, always comedy sketch shows. But the change is that I'm now the solo performer and Rona writes. She's always worked in theatre, TV and now film. Rona retired from performing in 1991, but still contributes to MsFits shows. I tour the country performing. Each year I do a new show for international women's week. I tour *all* year, but don't get *reviewed* until I get to the Edinburgh Festival Fringe. (And the reviews so far have been great.) But the Arts Establishment doesn't pay much attention.

Now that you don't perform together, are you still collaborating on the writing ?

Rona: Oh yes. We're still a team.

Fiona: We (Rona and I) both wrote half of each of these shows. Rona writes the sketches and I write most of the linking material.

Fiona, when you do your solo tours, what kinds of audience response do you receive?

Fiona: I travel to far away places where people don't see theatre generally — village halls in the highlands, and islands and school halls. I mainly perform in Scotland, but I have done England too. In 1993 I did a Union conference in Blackpool, and Theatre in the Hill, Bradford, for instance. When Rona and I where touring together as the MsFits, we did four gigs in England and they went very well. My accent is very strong (especially the dialect I use in performance), but this doesn't seem to be a problem with audiences so far!

What is the general position of women in Scottish theatre?

Fiona: There are many women working in Scottish theatre, but of course most are not in secure jobs. As far as I know, there are no full-time female directors of theatre in Scotland. Maggie Kinloch left Scotland to lecture at the Central School of Speech and Drama in London. Jenny Killick was at the Traverse, but is now gone. For years, Joan Knight was at Perth Rep., but no more.

There are young women freelance directors, but predominantly theatre is very male. There are a lot of actresses around, and especially older actresses, but, as we all know, once we reach our mid-thirties, the parts run out in theatre and television.

Perhaps because traditional and mainstream theatres don't offer enough good big parts for (older) women, and because the employment situation for women directors is also unsatisfactory, there's a movement afoot. A lot of women are starting their own companies now. For instance, Gerda Stevenson started Stellar Quines ('quines' is a Scots word for girls), which is a new company designed to create parts for older women. New groups are important for younger women too, as younger women need a platform to get their work seen, just as we (Rona and I, in the early days of the MsFits) did with Women Live.

Slowly the mainstream changes in response to initiatives by women, but we have to keep pushing ahead on our own. Women slowly win more stage time in the mainstream, but only as we continue to make women's shows and feminist shows. Both work together eventually. *Dancing at Lughnasa* and *The Good Sisters*, although plays by men, have excellent parts for women. So things are changing. Actresses won't just accept bit parts as mums and grans any longer, or at least if we do, we know and we make sure that others know that we can do much more than that, too!

Is the position of women in Scottish theatre comparable to that in England?

Rona: Well there are a lot less of us. It's difficult not to be paranoid. But in terms of the status of our work, I do think we're under-represented. The men seem to be treated more as a solid mass, part of an established living culture offering new voices for posterity. We, women, often get bigger audiences, and yet are seen as less important, more like soap opera rather than great drama. So we have to ask who is doing the valuing here...

The general perception of Scotland is of hard macho men, in the context of a working-class culture. Apart from caricaturing the experiences of a very diverse country, this view ignores the experience of women almost entirely. Being Scottish, being a woman, working in England, working towards defining a definite place in culture: all of these are possibilities to me — not labels but areas to be explored, open questions.

Lizbeth Goodman
Written and telephone interviews, December 1994.

CAROLE WODDIS

Carole Woddis worked as a Press Officer with the RSC, the National Theatre, the Round House, and the Royal Ballet before becoming a journalist at Time Out *and for six years at* City Limits. *Now in her fifties, she is a freelance writer who teaches and reviews regularly for a number of publications, including the* Glasgow Herald *(for whom she is the London theatre correspondent),* What's On in London, *the* Jewish Chronicle, Everywoman, Capital Gay, *and* New Statesman and Society. *She has been co-editor of two volumes of the* Bloomsbury Theatre Guide *and has also edited her own collection of interviews with leading actresses:* Sheer Bloody Magic *(Virago).*

Would you call yourself a feminist?

Feminism is something which has certainly grown on me. My mother always said she was a feminist, without, I think, always knowing what that meant. Mostly it was to do with anger against men and opportunities for herself, without the realization that it could also mean solidarity with women. That was totally missing. But I was one of that generation whose feminism came slowly, very slowly and was developed through experience — what I saw, what I felt, what other women told me — rather than just reading.

It started to come to the fore during the seventies though I couldn't then have articulated it. I was very aggressive in a suppressed kind of way, with an enormous rage against men from time to time which, again, I couldn't put into words or analyse. As the years went on, I began to be able to make some sense of what I was feeling through feminism; it gave me a kind of context.

Was theatre an important part of that process?

Hugely — and in many different ways. But one play which made a significant impression on me was *Hedda Gabler.* That always spoke to me, not so much about my own predicament as about my mother's generation and their frustrations. Quite often, you begin to understand yourself through other people and identification with them. At least, that's how it's often worked for me.

Your theatre career began as a Press Officer: what made you decide to become a critic?

I was kind of pushed out by the Royal Ballet. I think, looking back on it now, that I was obviously in conflict with the Royal Ballet establishment, which was very chauvinistic. They saw women in a certain way. Not that there weren't women working in quite important jobs but if you were a woman who spoke your mind, it was difficult. Leaving was a very painful part of the process of beginning very slowly and tenuously to find my own voice, my own words and views. Being a press officer — which I was good at — you have to service other people.

Does gender affect reviewing — for instance if you're reviewing a play by a man which seems chauvinistic?

That's an easier one than reviewing women's plays about women. There are many things to be taken into consideration, but if I feel that a play is chauvinistic, I will say so. You don't often come across that these days — though John Osborne was unrepentantly misogynistic to the end. But then he was pretty misanthropic generally about contemporary life.

It's not that I particularly want to shackle writers, whether they be male or female. It all depends on the context and intention. If I feel a male writer has created a three-dimensional female character with a full and truthful emotional life, even if it shows her in a poor light, that seems okay to me. We're hardly saints! By the same token, I get a really uneasy feeling in my gut when women dramatists overdo the 'positive' qualities. I think we've gone past the 'positive' images bit though they do still have their place. It's something you can't always put your finger on. But I'd rather have contradictory truthfulness than saintly feminism.

I sense, though, that things are on the change again. Male writers want more freedom — as indeed do women artists — from self-censorship.

Since, at least, the early eighties we've all been under a terrific yoke, certainly on the left, as we were trying to get alternative voices heard. At *City Limits* we were always taking up postures about how writers should be expressing certain things (and what they should be expressing) in their writing. We had an altruistic intent, but there is a cutting edge between politics and Art and we probably pushed the politics thing as far as it could go. We felt that theatre could be used as an instrument for change, and the only way that we could do that was to come down hard on middle-class white male writers who were still constantly writing about their middle-aged angst. While I think that was a good thing to do, another 6–7 years on, one can see that it can be quite a restrictive programme for men and women alike. I've always felt that art and artistic freedom are important. Therefore, while I write as a lesbian feminist critic, I hope I am fair. If art has been created and speaks to me on a personal level and a human level, I will say so, whoever created it.

You were saying it is difficult to criticize women…

There's a huge problem as a feminist criticizing women's work. Both *Time Out*, initially, then subsequently *City Limits* tried in the 1970s and 1980s to be supportive of minority groups and new writers addressing new issues in a different way — whether it was to do with Black and Asian work, gay and lesbian theatre, left-wing agit-prop, or performance and live art. If you're supportive sometimes you cover your tracks and operate something of a double standard. I think it's fair to bash the RSC and the National because they have the resources for it. If it's a small company working on no money in a pub theatre and you see sparks of life in it, then you're going to overlook negative aspects. That certainly applied in terms of women's theatre.

The other big problem is, I am a woman who has come through a male educational system and most of my views of what was good were seen through my father's eyes, through my brother's eyes, through the newspapers I read as a teenager, with agendas set by men. What I see as 'good' is still male-dominated on a subconscious level, I think. There's always that big question. How do you differentiate between good and bad when something is new and going against the mainstream: is this new company, play, writer, really trying to do something completely fresh which is worth supporting or is it just a pile of old dogma and you ought to say so? When is a new interpretation ahead of its time — or when is it misconceived and just plain bad? How far down the 'extenuating circumstances' line of financial and other limitations are you prepared to go? These are questions you have to ask yourself every time you sit down to write. No wonder it sometimes feels so tiring. You're re-inventing the wheel, every time!

Even the language and the way women journalists are supposed to write is still mediated through that male principle. There's a whole new vocabulary we've been trying to create over the last few years — words that *The Sun* wouldn't use, words that are a way of expressing who people are (mis-named and re-appropriated as 'political correctness'). There has to be a way of embracing the vocabulary of the moment, which doesn't continually put people down, but is a simple language that speaks to people directly. I haven't managed it yet. I constantly look at my colleagues like Claire Armitstead and Lyn Gardner of the *Guardian* and I believe they have found ways of being direct without indulging too greatly in what I call male-speak.

Would you say that this process of trying to find a new language is relevant to theatre, the sort of plays that are being written?
Absolutely. This feeds precisely in to what women trying to find their voices have been about. I can remember seeing a production by Scarlet Harlets and you could absolutely feel that women were trying to find a new language which was more wide-ranging, that wasn't Aristotelian, that wasn't linear. Anna Furse and Blood Group were trying to do that sort of thing in the mid-1980s. So were Women's Theatre Group when they did *Pax* by Deborah Levy; they were trying to juggle a huge number of issues — history,

nuclear destruction, the position of women in society — through specifically female-related eyes and trying to find a language to reflect that.

Do you think that lesbian theatre struggles with language and power in particular ways?

Productions that I saw by people like Siren were certainly trying to find a different language and trying to reveal what they felt to be the patriarchal system, trying to get out from underneath what patriarchy does to women and I guess they were taking the most abrasive attitude to all of that. What is interesting is that the things which they took an abrasive attitude towards eventually do seep into the mainstream. It's very curious.

Can you expand on that a bit?

Sarah Daniels, *The Devil's Gateway:* Sarah was coming from a fairly radical lesbian perspective. She showed a mother becoming politicized and going to Greenham Common. And you get that image not very many months later, turning up in David Edgar's *Maydays* for the RSC where he had a scene at Greenham. Who knows whether Daniels influenced Edgar or not? But she was the first to show the possibility of 'an ordinary housewife' becoming politicized, that journey — and putting it on stage. And she has continued to do so in later plays: the politicization of ordinary mothers, wives and aunts — a very important image when political consciousness and activity often still tends to be seen and written as a male prerogative.

What is the most unique and influential aspect of lesbian theatre?

Lesbian theatre is, on the whole, prepared to take more risks. It's prepared to say the unsayable, which feminist theatre still hangs back from saying. I think a lesbian perspective can push ideas that crucial one step further. And, more dangerously, it can make jokes about men and patriarchy.

What is interesting is that plays by young lesbians are few and far between, far fewer than there were 5 or 6 years ago. Lesbian theatre companies have almost dried up and this is very curious. There are several reasons: there is a new generation of young women who are not interested in the lesbian theatre they see. Another is Arts Council cuts. Most of all, I think, it's to do with changing fashion. Young lesbians would rather spend their money elsewhere — in clubs, pubs, buying videos, CDs, seeing films — than in the theatre. Some lesbian theatre-makers who were active and influential in past decades are still making good work today, including: Bryony Lavery, Lois Weaver and Peggy Shaw's Split Britches. Phyllis Nagy, their young American counterpart, is everywhere! But where once lesbians on stage were seen as a way of reinforcing a positive image in a landscape in which they were largely invisible, those images are now available elsewhere. The likes of Lea de Laria have spawned a whole new industry: in-your-face stand-up. Claire Dowie, Donna McPhail, New Zealand's Topp Twins are all crowd-pullers. Maybe it shows a kind of maturity. But I feel rather more pessimistic about stand-up; I see it as more of a retreat than a theatrical advance. That's probably just my prejudice, though, because I do love Claire Dowie's work. I love the way she breaks the boundaries of what's male, female, lesbian, straight. It's great, radical stuff.

What general comments would you like to make, regarding the development of women's voices in theatre over the years?

There are two things I'd like to say. What's interesting is the amount of self-analysis people of my age, like Gloria Steinem, have gone through. Everything constantly goes through this internal mincing-machine, in a way that probably doesn't happen for men. I do think some women arrived at a point of tremendous wisdom and therefore can be of service if anyone is prepared to listen.

The other point is to do with competitiveness and ambition. It is very hard for women because women don't like to talk about competitiveness, even less acknowledge it (particularly if they are socialist). But I think competitiveness has to be acknowledged by women: it is a very destructive but real dynamic which comes out of frustration and a sense of scarcity — not enough to go round. I don't know the best way forward for women except to acknowledge that it's there.

Perhaps that's why women's theatre foundered — torn asunder by internal bickering and the thought police. Actually, I don't believe that. Whilst the socialist collectivism of the 1970s and 1980s proved rather more problematic in practice, it was the institutional rigidities that proved harder to crack. Much as I hate to lump a complex bag of social and personal realities together — a lot of women's work recently, for complicated reasons, has often just not been very good. Patriarchy does still reign. Women's work is often the product of impoverished and reduced circumstances. We've also lived through fifteen years of hard-line Thatcherite policies, the consequences of which can hardly be over-estimated.

Notions of socialism or collective working became dirty, outmoded words as the cult of individualism soared. Companies have not survived; individual performers have moved more and more towards solo work. Maybe some 'women's theatre' was pretty 'worthy' when you look back on it. Even so, for someone of my generation, you can't help but feel that the last decade or so, 'backlash' and 'post-feminism' notwithstanding, has been characterised by a sort of censorship-by-stealth. The politics of the market-place and 'economic necessity' have pushed innovation and experimentation to the wall. It's therefore hardly surprising if women artists took the easy way out — opted for safe, popular choices, chose to work in smaller groups, on their own, or gave up altogether.

Still, I take heart from a number of hopeful signs. Sure, nothing is enough. As a woman artist, you still have to be twice as determined, twice as gutsy, twice as pushy to make your way; women are still under-represented on the TV screen in terms of type and number of roles. But with the likes of Deborah Warner, Katie Mitchell, Phyllida Lloyd, Anna Furse, and younger women such as Abigail Morris, Denise Wong (Black Mime Theatre Women's Troop), and Cat Horn around and a whole batch of executive directors and administrators in influential theatre positions — Genista McIntosh at the National Theatre, Jude Kelly at the West Yorkshire Playhouse, Jenny Topper (Hampstead), Ruth Mackenzie (Nottingham Playhouse), Lois Keidan (ICA), Mary Allen (Secretary-General of the Arts Council) and her deputy Sue Hoyle — you have to recognize that something has changed.

True, women in these institutions are still subject to the modes of working and thinking these places impose, but I can't help but feel positive. The artistic and administrative choices these women make cannot but reflect the times through which they have lived, and the 1970s and 1980s feminism to which they have been exposed. Beatrix Campbell, socialist-feminist writer and journalist, put it brilliantly at the Sphinx's annual Glass Ceiling Conference in 1994, when she described the historical context of the feminism of her generation and its internalized contradictions. She argued that it was time to recognise that kind of feminism as dated, as the product of the social and political circumstances of its time. So, she said, we should move on. I agree that perhaps the most exciting time is now; this is the time to find a way of re-fashioning, of capturing the best of the spirit of the Monstrous Regiments of old; to build on that sense of kinship alongside the new-found confidence and technology which the 1990s generation have inherited. I see no reason why the two should be incompatible. The big problem for women and for theatre generally in the 1990s is whether anybody out there is going to be interested enough to come and see it... Or has non-musical theatre become an obsolescent art form? Addressing that question — the viability of theatre, and political theatre, as forms — is the *real* challenge of the 1990s.

Jane de Gay
Interview recorded on audiotape, August 1994; updated for publication January to March 1995.

CONCLUSION: AN INTERVIEWER TALKS BACK

'What do you mean by that?' One of the first things you find when conducting interviews is that the answer to any question is very often another question. However, moments of uncertainty in a reply are also the first to be lost in the editing process. When transcribing the interviews, I found that the first few minutes of a reply often consisted of the interviewee thinking aloud about the *question*. In most cases, it made more sense to ignore these opening comments and carry on playing the tape until the interviewee had formulated a more considered reply. During editing, the need for clarity and the lack of space meant cutting down answers even further, to leave the portion which was most directly relevant to the issue at hand. Finally, all participants were sent proofs of their interviews, and several took the opportunity to revise what they had said, often turning an off-the-cuff comment into a finely turned and definitely *written* (not spoken) statement.

In its way, the process of putting together *Feminist Stages* could be read as a microcosm of the process of writing about theatre itself. The more that is written, the more spontaneity is lost, until at the end of the day, the theatre critic/scholar must give up on the attempt to record what happened. S/he is left with two 'traces' of what went on: the 'script' (the interview texts collected here in *Feminist Stages*) and her/his memory of the impression made on her/him by the performance. The interviews collected above form the 'script'. This conclusion will, in a sense, offer a 'review' of these interviews. As we have heard several times during this book (and thousands of times during the history of women's theatres) a critic only writes from her/his own perspective. So, here I will give my impression of these performances, rather than claiming to offer an authoritative statement or summary of what has been said. I shall offer an alternative conclusion (that is, one of many possible alternative conclusions) which instead of providing answers will try to identify some of the many questions which have been thrown out by the interviews in this book.

This alternative conclusion will concentrate on three questions or issues which contributors found difficult to discuss. These questions in effect provoked more questions — and debates which continue beyond the covers of this book. Firstly there is the complex issue of feminism — what it is, how it relates to theatre and (a really tough one) which of the contributors would call herself a feminist. Next, is the question of whether theatre can have an impact on society; and finally, how do the interviewees see women's current position in the theatre, and what do they envisage for the future? I shall present a spectrum of answers to similar questions by different people, bringing some of the voices from this book more directly into dialogue. Of course, this conclusion is but the start of the dialogue process: anyone interested in tracing it further can use the index at the back of the book to compare and contrast contributors' views on these and other topics.

Using the F word

Feminism is never an easy subject to discuss, not least because there are so many different interpretations of the term. To use a cliché, there are almost as many feminisms as there are women. In many of the interviews in this book, we tried to get around this problem by asking the contributor to begin by offering her own definition of feminism. This helped, because it provided some framework for discussion, but it also raised some interesting problems...

The vast majority of the contributors were happy to give their definition of feminism. Each represented feminism as the means of promoting the concept or issue closest to her heart. The concepts were varied: friendliness, choice, self-determination, equality, awareness, liberation, rights, fulfilling one's potential, the belief that women matter, uncovering women's history, questioning traditions, addressing marginalization, understanding how the world operates, and prioritizing women-centred experience. However, several women were uncertain and prefaced their answer with a disclaimer 'I can say what I *think* it is about'; 'it has something to do with ...'; 'I suppose feminism is ...', or, like Michelene Wandor and Claire MacDonald, replied that it is difficult to define feminism at the moment, because it is changing so rapidly.

The problems which the women had in talking about feminism are interesting. Language is an important factor, for many were aware that the word 'feminism' is debased coinage in some circles. On the one hand, the word has, for many people, become firmly attached to the political protests of the early 1970s. Ann Jellicoe (who refused to define feminism, implying that definitions were for academics), denied that she was a feminist in terms which suggest that she regards feminism as a militant, political movement: 'it's not in my nature to be aggressive in that way'. Emilyn Claid complains that feminism is a 'heavy, angry' term and says that we need a new word. Like her, Mara de Wit and Nina Rapi deny being feminists because of the negative connotations which have been attached to the word. On the other hand, as Jules Wright points out, there is a danger that the language of feminism can be corrupted by overuse: when this language is used by men it 'sometimes feels appropriated', leading women to feel that their political views have been 'usurped'. The problem with language is that it is all too easy to *talk* about rights and equality, but harder to translate words into positive action.

The problem is not an academic, semantic one: language can be a dangerous weapon. The word 'feminist' is often used by the media as a derogatory term (perhaps in reaction to the latent implications of anger and opposition to the status quo). The dangers lurking behind the 'F word' can be seen in the interviewees' deliberations about whether they would call themselves feminist. A glance through their answers reveals that the vast majority of women in this book *do* call themselves feminists; but when their answers are read more closely, many are anxious about how others describe them and the dangers of being *labelled* feminists. Sarah Daniels argues that labelling leads to prejudice, although adding that, while she did not set out to be a feminist playwright, she is glad to have added to its influence. The sorts of prejudice which might come with the feminist label are suggested by Michelene Wandor who says that 'every so often, there is somebody who assumes that I am only interested in "women's subjects" or women writers', and Kate Owen, who worries that 'I have got a bit typecast as somebody who sometimes does feminist theatre' (a heavily qualified phrase which suggests that this has more to do with how others see her than how she sees herself). In other words, if you become too closely identified with women's issues, your job prospects are reduced accordingly. To make matters worse, labels are extremely important in the commercial structure of theatre: critics and funding bodies like to be able to pin work down into narrow classifications. Yet, as many women point out, art cannot be dissected in this way. Jackie Kay comments that some critics miss the point of her work because they try to pigeon-hole it; while Deborah Baddoo points to the problem that while she does not want to be categorized, she would get more funding if she described her work (inaccurately) as 'African dance'.

The frustrations of being typecast help to explain why some contributors were careful to make a distinction between their personal political views and their theatre practice. Pam Gems says that it is impossible to be both 'a voice for feminism' and an artist (a statement which seems ironic considering that several of the other interviewees claimed her plays as feminist influences). Clare Venables describes herself as 'absolutely a feminist' but not a 'feminist artist', yet she says that feminism is a philosophy which she carries with her and which informs her work. This subtle but important distinction is shared by many: Harriet Walter and Juliet Stevenson both say that a feminist outlook informs their choice of parts and their approach to characters, but that they cannot use their work to express their politics directly.

The women interviewed in this book come from differing backgrounds and work in many different types of theatre. These differences in perspective have an important impact on their view of feminism. For example, contrast Jules Wright's comments on the importance and effectiveness of feminism to her as an Australian, with Yvonne Brewster's puzzlement about feminism in Britain because of her upbringing in Jamaica, where she notes that society is more matriarchal. Bernardine Evaristo describes the Theatre of Black Women as 'Black Feminist' — the term 'feminist' was insufficient for them because they believed that black women had been excluded from the women's movement — while Tasha Fairbanks, who has worked in both lesbian theatre and theatre for the differently abled, describes feminism as addressing marginalization in many of its forms. Where Evaristo suggests that feminism only addresses one axis of inequality, Fairbanks sees it as addressing several. The problem of feminism competing for attention with other ideologies emerges in several of the interviews. Kathleen McCreery (speaking about theatre in the North of England) and the MsFits (from Scotland), both say that women's rights are marginalized in the local, working-class communities. Sharon Morgan agrees, adding that women's presence is only just being felt in Welsh-language theatre, which has until recently been struggling to establish itself. Charabanc note that the so-called 'Troubles' assume greater importance than women's issues in Northern Ireland. When a community faces social or economic inequalities, women's inequality within that community is relegated to secondary importance.

The equation which emerges is that women in the theatre have, on the whole, less power, less money and less priority than men. Ironically, many interviewees say that regional theatres give women better opportunities than London theatres: the work of Jude Kelly (West Yorkshire Playhouse) and Pip Broughton and Ruth Mackenzie (Nottingham Playhouse) are mentioned several times. However, economic inequality is in evidence even here, for these women directors are given less wealthy, less glamorous theatres in the regions, while the London theatres are still largely the domain of men. And, as Victoria Worsley points out, women's opportunities in theatre have improved now that more men are being attracted into the apparently more lucrative worlds of TV and film. When funds are threatened, women's work is hit first. Perhaps it is this economic threat, more than anything, which makes so many of the participants wary about being typecast as feminists. At a time when even the largest theatre organizations are under threat financially, many of these women feel that the best way to

survive may be to resist marginalizing labels and to describe their wor\
terms which make it sound as 'mainstream' and uncontroversial as possible.

Can the theatre change society? A spectrum of opinions

The second question, *Can the theatre affect social change?* presented as much of
a problem for interviewers when transcribing and copy-editing as it did for
interviewees. The copy-editing problem may seem pedantic: should we use
the word 'affect social change' (that is, have an impact on social change) or
'effect' (actually bring it about)? The written question used the word 'affect'
but, since many interviews were conducted orally, the question was
occasionally taken to be 'effect social change'. Most interviewees felt that
theatre can *affect* people's attitudes and beliefs. There was a resounding
consensus that the bottom line for a play/performance is that it should move
its audience members in some way.

This said, opinion is divided as to what impact theatre can and
should have on an audience. Let us sketch out a spectrum by looking at a
variety of comments on this issue. Diana Quick says that theatre cannot 'lead
change', but reflects the times in which we live. Juliet Stevenson takes this
'holding the mirror up to nature' argument further by saying that theatre is a
place where we can examine human nature and change our view of
ourselves. Sarah Daniels agrees, saying that the theatre can't change lives but
it can make us (re)think our views on certain issues. Louise Page says that
theatre *can* change lives by making people see the world in a different way,
although it is not possible to 'rush out and start changing the world'. Annie
Castledine believes that theatre *can* influence world movements, by inspiring
individuals to be more tolerant and compassionate and to reject certain
unhelpful attitudes.

All of the above comments describe the effects of theatre in a fairly
general way, without stating particular aims or giving examples of results. As
we move towards the other end of the spectrum, we find accounts of times
when theatre has provoked a measurable reaction from an audience. This is
where we begin to move from the domain of 'affect' to that of 'effect'. Nina
Rapi describes how potential racial tensions between Turks and Greeks were
allayed when a performance of her play *The Dance of Guns*, about the Greek
civil war, received a standing ovation at a Turkish community centre. Kate
Owen speaks of hundreds of individuals writing to Blood Group and Gay
Sweatshop in reaction to their plays. From there we move to performances
(or theatre companies) which sought to broadcast very specific messages.
There are examples of performances of Kathleen McCreery's plays
influencing the outcome of strikes (in the case of *The Working Women's Charter*

Show) and causing changes in working conditions (*The Big Lump*). Siren theatre company, which had the radical aim of presenting 'lesbianism as a political choice' caused audience members to 'come out' about their sexuality for the first time during after-show discussions. Similarly, at Gay Sweatshop, audiences responded to plays like Jill Posenor's *Any Woman Can* in 'marathon phone-ins'. Siren and Gay Sweatshop experienced other, less positive reactions, as actors received threats and met with actual violence. This suggests that theatre which is socially and politically effective is almost by definition perceived as a threat by some: Elizabeth MacLennan takes this view when she points to the closure of socially aware and political theatres as proof that they have succeeded in disturbing governments.

From the spectrum which has been sketched out above, it seems as if the comments about theatre influencing individuals still apply today; but that the examples of performances which set out to make a particular point and which have a measurable social or political impact are more rare in recent years. Let's look at some ways in which the theatre is changing.

So what's new?

The process of updating earlier interviews for this collection proved to be an interesting window on changes in the theatre. Occasionally, earlier interviews were reworked to record positive changes. For example, Talawa produced its first play by a woman writer (Ntozake Shange's *The Love Space Demands*), and initiated their scheme to encourage new writing by women. More often, however, trends were not so positive. The interview with Gillian Hanna was originally published in 1990, when Monstrous Regiment were still working together, but the updated piece which appears here takes a retrospective look at the company and hints at events behind their current enforced hibernation. A similar change had to be made to the interview with Bernardine Evaristo: the Theatre of Black Women has now closed, so the interview takes on a historic value.

The closure of women's theatre groups drew mixed feelings from the interviewees. The bitter disappointment of Tasha Fairbanks at the closure of Siren and Gillian Hanna at the inactivity of Monstrous Regiment speak for themselves. Elsewhere, there is a grudging acceptance that times have changed. Michelene Wandor suggests that the fact that women's groups of the 1970s no longer exist means that there has been some progress in women's social status; and Nancy Diuguid says that consciousness-raising theatre groups should not be needed once they have succeeded in their aims. These women are attempting to make bearable the closure of companies by suggesting that political feminist, black or lesbian theatres should be means to an end — some form of gender/race/sexuality blindness — rather than remaining static. In a slight variation on this view, some claim victory in the greater presence of women in the so-called 'mainstream' (the large commercial and subsidized theatres, TV and film). Bernardine Evaristo says that she would not revive Theatre of Black Women, because, while it fulfilled the important purpose of giving black women opportunities in the alternative/fringe theatres of the 1980s, the mainstream is now more accessible to them. This implicit preference for mainstream over alternative culture ties in with the participants' reluctance to be labelled as feminists: it is an expression of their desire to avoid becoming marginalized.

Yet, many women are aware that joining the mainstream is not a solution. Some sense a danger that it can make certain cultures trendy — but only for a time. Tasha Fairbanks takes a qualified view of the visibility of lesbians in TV and film: 'I suppose this exposure is good'. Another problem is identified by Juliet Stevenson who finds (from her own experience as a well-known actor) that women's individuality and complexity are lost because the images of women in popular culture tend to revert to stereotypes. For most women, the greatest hope for the future still lies outside the mainstream: with women pioneers working in the margins, or with those who pursue greater diversity of theatrical form. Comments from some contributors suggest that, in the 1990s, the way forward lies in a breaking down of the old distinctions between 'alternative' and 'mainstream': Claire MacDonald detects a general cultural shift towards diversity (especially in forms of theatre) which promises to be conducive to the non-linear pattern of women's lives and work. The MsFits suggest that a complex economy operates between mainstream and alternative theatre: they describe how women are setting up their own theatres in Scotland because the mainstream cannot accommodate them; but that the very presence of these alternative theatres boosts a gradual improvement in women's opportunities within the mainstream.

Now for the great unanswered question: *What's the future for women in the theatre in the UK?* The lack of answers is a worrying indication of women's position in theatre. By far the majority of replies do not make predictions, but offer prescriptions for how women's situation could be improved. The same basic needs come up time and again: women need more access to money and resources; more women are needed in positions of power; crèche facilities have to be improved; more training in theatre must be given; there must be a change in government; more plays by women should be produced in large theatres; and more adventurous forms, concepts and ideas need to emerge.

The greatest concern about the future concerned the next generation of women theatre makers: who they are and whether they will continue the work begun in the 'feminist stages' of the 1970s, 1980s and 1990s. The hopeful view is represented by Susan Bassnett when she says that while the older generation were motivated by rage, the younger generation start from a position of assurance about their equal status, and bring more professionalism to their work. At the other end of the spectrum is Gillian Hanna who sees that these 'tough sassy young women' are as isolated as their mothers were in the early 1970s.

An anti-conclusion

When I phoned Carole Woddis to set up the last interview in this book, she told me that, although she was happy to take part, she found the questions I had sent her difficult, because she had been exploring these very issues in her own writing for a long time and wondered whether anything new could be said. So, in our interview, we talked about her own experiences as a reviewer and about recent developments in theatre, and through these particular topics we gradually moved on to more general themes. It seems appropriate that a collection of interviews which (as I see it) is characterized by difficult questions, should end with an interview which dispenses with those questions and tries new ones.

For this reason, Juliet Stevenson's advice on the future of women in the theatre strikes a chord: 'We have to keep vigilant, keep asking questions, and also *change* the questions. We should never have any polemic or identity which stays fixed, although there are some questions which we keep having to ask.'

So, let's end the conclusion to *Feminist Stages* with some more questions: Do we need a new word for 'feminist', and what would that word be? Who are the next generation, and what interests them? Will a book like *Feminist Stages* be needed in 10 years' time — and *should* it be needed? Is political theatre still possible or is it now a contradiction in terms? Do we need new terms for talking and writing about theatre, to parallel the new forms which are emerging within theatre itself? And finally — where do we start?

Jane de Gay
Oxford, July 1995.

AFTERWORD: 'GUERILLAS IN THE MIST': SIGHTINGS OF, AND OBSERVATIONS ON, FEMINISTS IN BRITISH THEATRE

When I was asked to provide a title for this paper, I decided upon '"Guerillas in the Mist": Sightings of, and Observations on, Feminists in British Theatre', because at the time, I was reading about apes as research for a play about monkeys. I thought the title was a good one for a paper about feminists in British Theatre — how they seem to appear and disappear like Diane Fossey's gorillas, almost always in mist, on the margins, never in strong sunlight in the centre of the forest clearing or a stage. Then suddenly a piece of information hit me between the eyes. It said that although a great deal of research money has been spent teaching apes to speak human language, no-one has tried to assimilate the communication methods of the ape. It came from a rattling good yarn... *Congo* by Michael Crichton. Here is the blurb on the back cover:

> *Earth Resources Technology Services have sent a geological project into the deep, dark regions of the Congo. Their mission is to discover an ancient lost city known to be the last source of the precious blue diamond. The area is said to have a curse on it, a curse no one believes until the entire party are mysteriously killed one night. Back at the project's base in Houston through a satellite link-up with the wrecked camp, a strange figure is seen walking across the camera, something that looks almost like a gorilla, almost like a man...*
>
> *Karen Ross is the young, highly intelligent scientist sent to the Congo to discover what caused the untimely death of her colleagues. She has joined forces with Peter Elliott, an innovative primatologist who is desperate to bring his own project to the jungle — Amy — a gorilla fluent in sign language, who has been having bizarre dreams about her past in the lost city...*
>
> *Together, they enter a world lost to man for centuries where only primitive instincts for survival can save them from the dangers ahead*

Stirring stuff, eh?

I've quoted it because I have been awake all night trying to write an academic paper. I found it fiendishly difficult. As dawn broke, I realized why. I am The Wrong Species. The more I listen to academics here at this conference on 'Centres and Margins in British Theatre', the more I feel like Amy the Gorilla. I know we were created by the same god as the same species... but somewhere in our evolutionary development, two hominid-strands emerged... those who shape their roots and berries into stories, and those who make their roots and berries into theories. As the sun rose on the far water of Biggesee, I realised that I do not want to give you a paper on the state of feminism in British Theatre. To do this, I would have to speak your language. Let us spend some of our valuable research time here with you learning my language. I want to show you My Gorilla-Guerilla World. For the rest of this session, I will be speaking 'Gorilla'.

I am a play-maker. I create worlds. Therefore when I am at work, I am at the epicentre of creation. I am God. It is a divine but stressful position. The rules and laws and practices are all my own. I can kill, maim, destroy, love, lust, enrage, wreak havoc, cause wars, create mayhem for two hours' traffic as long as by the end of my creation the only change to the audience is internal. It is only when my plays are put on that I am encouraged to believe that my work is on the margins... east of the sun, west of the moon, left of centre, straight on till the outer shores of feminist theatre... Instead of my usual long-distance shouting from the oddly-designated Women's Corner, I am going to stand centre-stage and you are going to come and see me.

Come with me now on an expedition.

Enter The Gorilla World.

I have some roots and berries for you.

As in *Congo*, we are 'on a mission to discover an ancient lost city known to be the last source of the precious blue diamond'.

The Ancient Lost City is Theatre.

The Precious Blue Diamond is your enjoyment.

A few weeks ago, I went to see the Literary Manager of the Royal National Theatre and he mentioned a play of mine called *Bag* which he had seen about fifteen years ago. It is a play about a group of friends on a camping holiday in Scotland and he said how much he had enjoyed it. Then he said 'Oh, and it had that wonderful tree!' This was a touring show: the only set was five bags which the characters carried, which became seaside rocks, tents, landscape. The wonderful tree he remembered was the actors looking up into space, imagining a frisbee caught in the branches. There was no wonderful tree. But he had seen it. He still saw it. On that same day, I was carrying a plastic bag and he glanced at it and said, 'Oh, I see you've been to The London Sapphic Centre. What did you get?' I said, 'Giles, I got some pencils. The bag reads "London *Graphic* Centre"!' There is no London Sapphic Centre. It does not print plastic bags with its name. It does not exist. But he had seen it. What he was seeing was my sexuality.

I do not tell this story to establish The Literary Manager of our Royal National Theatre as an idiot, which he's not, but because it neatly illustrates my premise that we do not always see what is there — which is wonderful, but confusing. We see through a gaze which has lens upon lens, glass upon glass, slotted in front of it. The lens distorts, the glass is smeared. A lens brings out one aspect into clear relief, the detail is precise, but the distance view is blurred and indistinct. It is sometimes hard to see the Ancient Lost City for what it is.

Today I wish to encourage you to take off your spectacles, put down your telescopes, lay aside your microscopes and approach a few pieces of instant theatre with the gaze you first turned upon the world as a newborn baby. This is the gaze which we playwrights, in our hearts, want for ourselves and our audience. We want you to see 'That wonderful tree'. This is why today, I want to give you a gift. It is a piece of theatre especially for you. Look at this piece of battered luggage called 'Bryony Lavery' and if you can, peel a few of those tired old labels off my leathery forehead and gaze gaze gaze gaze gaze. No one will see quite this piece of theatre ever again. You are uniquely privileged.

A description of the piece of theatre specially created for the CDE Conference, Biggesee, 1994

1. I tear up the piece of paper with my academic paper on it. I throw the many pieces into the air. You are delighted. But you are academics! For shame! Why are you so pleased?

2. I ask some of the men to help me clear a space of desks, tables and chairs. I point out that while as a feminist I am perfectly capable of clearing the space myself, it is much easier if the men help me. Again you all laugh. Why? You have all so far sat behind these tables, these desks, on these chairs. Are you so pleased they are gone? Why is the larger world not so delighted by simple acts of feminism?

3. I ask you to come and stand on your own in the space at the front of the audience. Is it frightening? Yes. But it is just standing there in front of people. What could happen? Is it exciting? Oh yes, you feel equal impulses of power and vulnerability. This is how a play starts. So simple, anyone could do it. Why, then, doesn't everyone write plays?

4. I ask you to think about something. Then I ask you where in your body you experience that thinking. Most of you find it is in your head. I encourage you to think like actors... to find your 'centre' and place it in different parts of you... the end of your nose, your left eye, your belly, your buttocks... I show you how my body changes as my centre changes. I tell you how, as a playwright, I change my centre with each character. Amy The Gorilla teaches humans her body language...

5. I burn a ten-deutschmark note before your eyes in this lecture room. You gasp in horror. You roar with delight. It is a waste of money. It is not a waste of money. Which? It is my comment on funding theatre. What am I saying?

6. I pick up my bag. Open it. Take out a litter bin. From the litter bin I take another bag. I open it. From the bag I take out a paper bag. I tear it open. In it is a carnation. I think about taking off its petals but I can't bear to. It is harder to destroy than the paper money. Why?

That is the end of the special piece of theatre. You clap loudly. You smile. You laugh. I notice that your bodies have changed. There is a visible relaxing. Theatre is Magic. Magic is The Art of Making Changes. I can see Physical Changes. For a short time, Theatre has occupied the centre of the room here. We communicated in the same language. We understood one another. The labels dropped off my forehead. Surprisingly I find that the labels I had not realized I was seeing on your foreheads have dropped off too. Magically, we did not see them disappear. Abracadabra!

I am talking about the quality of gaze.

Your eyes look clear.

You have been in The Ancient Lost City.

You have held The Precious Blue Diamond.

Altering margins and centres is so simple.

It is so cheap.

You just turn your body from one position to another.

So that your eyes are pointing straight ahead.

Whatever is before you is the centre.

That is surely the way to look at ANYTHING.

I went recently to an exhibition of sculptures by Picasso. This was at the Tate Gallery, London. In one room are animal sculptures created from old toy cars, pieces of scrap metal, old shoes… junk. And in that room, perhaps eight feet up, on a white, white wall, lit by soft clear light, is a sculpture called 'Bull'. It is the head of a bull, made from a set of bicycle handlebars which are its horns and a bicycle saddle which is its face. It took my breath away. It filled me with wonder, awe and tenderness, love and laughter. As Art is supposed to. If I had seen this piece of Art, physically unchanged, its components and composition unchanged, but on the wall of a bicycle repair shop, it would have left me indifferent.

Here's a final bowl of mixed chopped metaphors.

This is how the two hominid-strands come together on their mission to discover The Ancient Lost City. The Gorillas, The Guerillas, The Playwrights must continue, like Picasso, to trawl through the junk and scrap metal until they find the pieces to weld together into a clear representation of Life. Their roots and berries must communicate.

The Scientists, Primatologists, the Academics and Critics must continue to find that room, that white white wall, lit by soft clear light, where the piece of Art can be observed with wonder, awe and tenderness. This room is both external and internal. The theatre is both outside and inside your head. The two hominid-strands exchange their gazes and understand one another.

It is male and female, right and left, margin and centre, intellect and emotion, word and action.

It is common and it is unique.

For a shared moment they hold The Precious Blue Diamond in their joined hands.

Bryony Lavery
November 1994
This piece was written for the CDE Conference in 1994 and will be published in Germany in a collection
of the conference papers.

SELECT CHRONOLOGY OF PLAYS BY WOMEN: 1958 TO THE PRESENT

Lizbeth Goodman
with Jane de Gay

This is a short list of a much larger pool of woman's work in theatre. This chronology is intended as a reference source. Plays listed are primarily by British women and/or groups, but particular plays by American, Australian, Canadian, Italian, Jamaican and South African women playwrights and companies have been included where they throw light on the overall development of a genre or period in the development of 'Feminist Stages' in Britain.

Chronologies of playtexts refer to plays by men only as co-authors of women's plays. All plays by groups have been cross-referenced by individual authors where possible. Plays for radio, television and film are listed here only if specifically mentioned in interviews in this volume, or relevant to the interviews. Dates refer to the first production dates in the first instance if publication came later, though unperformed plays are listed according to the date of publication or completion.

In instances when an author's name is followed in parentheses by the name a group or company, the 'for' indicates that the play was first performed by that group, but not necessarily that the play was written specifically and exclusively for the group.

W.T.G. stands for Women's Theatre Group, until 1992, when the group changed name to The Sphinx.

1958: Jane Arden, *The Party*; Shelagh Delaney, *A Taste of Honey*; Ann Jellicoe, *The Sport of My Mad Mother*; Doris Lessing, *Each in His Own Wilderness*.

1959: Lorraine Hansberry, *A Raisin in the Sun*; Doris Lessing, *Each in His Own Wilderness*.

1960: Margaretta D'Arcy, *The Happy Haven*; Doris Lessing, *The Truth About Billy Newton*.

1961: Ann Jellicoe, *The Lady From the Sea* (adaptation from Ibsen); student production of *The Knack* (in Cambridge where she co-directed).

1962: Maureen Duffy, *Pearson*; *The Lay Off*; Ann Jellicoe, *The Knack* (London debut); Doris Lessing, *Play with A Tiger*.

1963:   Shelagh Delaney, *The Lion in Love*; Nell Dunn, *Up the Junction*; Joan Littlewood's Theatre Workshop, *Oh What a Lovely War* (London); Maria Irene Fornes, *There! You Died* (later titled *Tango Palace*).

1964:   Lorraine Hansberry, *The Sign in Sidney Brustein's Window*; Ann Jellicoe, *The Seagull* (with Ariadne Nicolaeff, an adaptation from Chekhov).

1965:   Nell Dunn, *Talking to Women*; Ann Jellicoe, *Shelley or The Idealist*; Maria Irene Fornes, *Promenade*; *The Successful Life of 3*; Joan Littlewood's Theatre Workshop, *Oh What A Lovely War* (N.Y. opening); Rochelle Owens, *Futz*; Megan Terry, *Calm Down Mother*; *Keep Tightly Closed in a Cool Dry Place*.

1966:   Maureen Duffy, *The Silk Room*; Olwen Wymark, *Lunchtime Concert*; Sylvia Plath, *Three Women*; Megan Terry, *Comings and Goings*; *Viet Rock*.

1967:   Nell Dunn, *Poor Cow*; Maria Irene Fornes, *A Vietnamese Wedding*; Ann Jellicoe, *The Rising Generation*; Olwen Wymark, *Triple Image*.

1968:   Margaretta D'Arcy (and John Arden), *The Hero Rises Up*; Margaretta D'Arcy (with Arden and CAST) *Harold Muggins is a Martyr*; Maria Irene Fornes, *Molly's Dream*; Natalia Ginzburg, *The Advertisement* (Italian, first English production); Ann Jellicoe, *The Giveaway* (Edinburgh); Adrienne Kennedy, *A Lesson in Dead Language*; Myrna Lamb, *But What Have You Done for Me Lately?*; Megan Terry, *Home* (televised); Olwen Wymark, *The Technicians*.

1969:   Maureen Duffy, *Rites*; Lorraine Hansberry, *To be Young, Gifted, and Black*; Carey Harrison, *Lovers*; Ann Jellicoe, *The Giveaway* (London); Jennifer Phillips, *The Backhand Kiss*; Olwen Wymark, *Neither Here Nor There*.

1970:   Rosalyn Drexler, *Hot Buttered Roll*; Maureen Duffy, *Solo*; *Old Tyme*; *The Investigation*; Berta Freistadt, *The Celebration of Kakura*; Christine Furnival, *The Petition* (unpublished); Lorraine Hansberry, *Les Blancs*; *What Use Are Flowers?* (unproduced one-act fantasy); Ann Jellicoe (revival) *The Sport of My Mad Mother*; Rose Leiman-Goldemberg, *Gandhigi*.

1971:   Jane Arden, *Holocaust*; Nell Dunn, *The Incurable*; Christine Furnival, *The Flame You Gave Me* (unpublished); Myrna Lamb, *The Mod Donna and Sckylon Z.* (and other plays of Women's Liberation); Rose Leiman-Goldemberg, *The Rabinowitz Gambit*; Olwen Wymark, *Gymnasium*.

1972:   Caryl Churchill, *Schreber's Nervous Illness*; *Owners*; Margaretta D'Arcy (and John Arden), *The Island of the Mighty* (for 7:84); *The Balybomgeen Bequest*; Maureen Duffy, *Solo*; Nell Dunn (and Adrian Henri), *I Want*; Pam Gems, *Betty's Wonderful Christmas*; Rose Leiman-Goldemberg,

Rites of Passage; Edna O'Brien, *A Pagan Place*; Mary O'Malley, *Superscum*; Jennifer Phillips, *Bodywork*; *Instrument for Love*; Sharon Pollack, *A Compulsory Option*; Michelene Wandor, *The Day After Yesterday*; Michelene Wandor (for Red Ladder Theatre), *Strike While The Iron Is Hot*; Olwen Wymark, *Stay Where You Are*.

1973: (Chris) Tina Brown, *Up The Bamboo Tree*; Maureen Duffy, *A Nightingale in Bloomsbury Square*; Pam Gems, *My Warren*; *After Birthday*; *The Amiable Courtship of Miz Venus and Wild Bill*; Ann Jellicoe, *You'll Never Guess*; Rose Leiman-Goldemberg, *The Merry War*; Sharon Pollock, *Walsh*; Michelene Wandor, *Spilt Milk*; Michelene Wandor, Sally Ordway and Dinah Brook, *Mal de Mer*; *Lovefood*; *Crabs*; Jane Wibberley, *Parade of Cats*; Olwen Wymark, *Stay Where You Are*.

1974: Caryl Churchill, *Moving Clocks Go Slow*; Pam Gems; *Go West Young Woman* (for the Women's Company); Ann Jellicoe, *Two Jelly Plays*; Rose Leiman-Goldemberg, *Apples in Eden*; *Love One Another*; Mary O'Malley, *A 'Nevolent Society*; Jennifer Phillips, *Bodywork*; Ntozake Shange, *for colored girls who have considered suicide when the rainbow is enuf* (San Francisco); Michelene Wandor, *To Die Among Friends*; Fay Weldon, *Mixed Doubles* (five plays); Angela Wye, *The Rialto Prom*.

1975: Caryl Churchill, *Objections to Sex and Violence*; *Perfect Happiness*; and (with Cherry Potter and Mary O'Malley — produced BBC) *An Unfairy Tale*; Margaretta D'Arcy (with John Arden), *The Non-Stop Connolly Show*; Pam Gems, *Up in Sweden*; Ann Jellicoe, *Three Jelliplays*; Mary O'Malley, *Oh If Ever A Man Suffered*; *A 'Nevolent Society*; Jennifer Phillips, *The Antique Baby*; Sharon Pollock, *And Out Goes You?*; Charlotte Keatley, *My Mother Says I Never Should*; Olwen Wymark, *Speak Now*.

1976: Caryl Churchill (for Joint Stock), *Light Shining in Buckinghamshire*, (for Monstrous Regiment) *Vinegar Tom*; Gilly Fraser, *Do a Dance for Daddy*; Pam Gems, *The Project*; *Guinevere*; *Dusa, Fish, Stas, and Vi*, (and 2 adaptations); Claire Luckham (with Chris Bond and Monstrous Regiment), *Scum*; Rosemary Mason, *Sunbeams*; Jill Posener, *Any Woman Can*; Sharon Pollack, *The Komagata Mam Incident*; *Blood Relations*; Ntozake Shange, *for colored girls who have considered suicide when the rainbow is enuf* (London); Fay Weldon, *Moving House*; Women's Theatre Group (group devised), *Work to Role*; Olwen Wymark, *The 22nd Day*.

1977: Marjorie Appleman, *Seduction Duet*; Tina Brown, *Happy Yellow*: Caryl Churchill, *Traps*; Margaretta D'Arcy, *A Pinprick of History*; Donna Franceschild, *The Cleaning Lady*; Gilly Fraser, *A Bit of Rough*; Pam Gems, *Queen Christina*; *Franz into April*; Bryony Lavery, *Grandmother*

Steps; Claire Luckham, *Yatesy and The Whale*; Kathleen McCreery (with Broadside Mobile Theatre Workers), *We Have the Power of the Winds*; Eve Merriam, *Out of Our Father's Houses*; Melissa Murray (and Eileen Fairweather for Pirate Jenny), *Bouncing Back with Benyo*; Mary O'Malley, *Once A Catholic*; Louise Page, *Want Ad*; Eileen Pollack (for Belt and Braces), *Not So Green as its Cabbage*; Lily Susan Todd (and Ann Mitchell for Monstrous Regiment), *Kiss and Kill*; Michelene Wandor (with Gay Sweatshop), *Care and Control*, (with Caryl Churchill, Bryony Lavery, David Bradford for Monstrous Regiment), *Floorshow*; *Old Wives' Tale*; Fay Weldon, *Mr. Director*; Women's Theatre Group (group devised), *Out on the Costa Del Trico*; *Pretty Ugly*.

1978:   Janet Amsden, *Peril at St. Agathas*; Margaretta D'Arcy, *West of Ireland Women Speaking*; (and John Arden), *Vandaleur's Folly*; Eileen Fairweather and Melissa Murray (for W.T.G.), *Hot Spot*; Gay Sweatshop (devised by the mixed company), *Iceberg*; Gay Sweatshop (devised by the women of the company), *What the Hell is She Doing Here?*; Pam Gems, *Ladybird*; *Piaf*, Susan Griffin, *Voices*; Bryony Lavery (and Monstrous Regiment), *Time Gentlemen Please*; *Helen and her Friends*; Liz Lochhead, *Sugar and Spice*; Claire Luckham, *Trafford Tanzi*; *Aladdin*; Melissa Murray and Eileen Fairweather (for Pirate Jenny), *Belisha Beacon*; Mary O'Malley, *Look Out Here Comes Trouble*; Louise Page, *Tissue*; Megan Terry, *American King's English for Queens*; Michelene Wandor, *Whores D'Oeuvres*; *Scissors*; *Aid Thy Neighbor*; Wendy Wasserstein, *Uncommon Women and Others*; Fay Weldon, *Action Replay*; Victoria Wood, *Talent*; (with Snoo Wilson and others) *In At the Death*; Women's Theatre Group (group devised), *In Our Way*; Olwen Wymark, *Loved*.

1979:   Caryl Churchill, *Cloud Nine*: Donna Franceschild, *Diaries*; *Soap Opera* (for W.T.G.); Pam Gems, *Uncle Vanya* (new version); Sara Hardy (with Philip Timmons and Bruce Bayley for Gay Sweatshop), *Who Knows?*; Bryony Lavery (for Monstrous Regiment) *Gentlemen Prefer Blondes*; (for W.T.G.) *The Wild Bunch*; Rose Leiman-Goldemberg, *Letters Home*; Claire Luckham, *Fish Riding Bikes*; Rosemary Mason, *Sunbeams*; Susan Miller, *Confessions of A Female Disorder*; Melissa Murray, *Hormone Imbalance Revue*; *Ophelia* (for Hormone Imbalance); Sharon Nassauer and Angela Stewart Park (for Gay Sweatshop), *I Like Me Like This*; Louise Page, *Lucy*; *Hearing*; Jennifer Phillips, *Daughters of Men*; Cherry Potter, *Audience of Alice's Hut* (for Common Stock); Lily Susan Todd and David Edgar (for Monstrous Regiment), *Teendreams*; Sue Townsend, *Womberang*; Michelene Wandor, *Correspondence*; *Aurora Leigh*.

1980: Caryl Churchill, *Three More Sleepless Nights*; Andrea Dunbar, *The Arbor*; Tasha Fairbanks (for Siren), *Mama's Gone A-Hunting*; Maggie Ford, *The Rising of the Moon*; Donna Franceschild, *Mutiny on the M1, Songs for Stray Cats and Other Living Creatures*; Christine Furnival, *The Starving of Sarah* (unpublished); Pam Gems, *The Treat*; *A Doll's House* (a new version of Ibsen's play); Alison Lyssa, *The Year of the Migrant*; Dacia Maraini (translated by and for Monstrous Regiment), *Dialogue Between a Prostitute and One of her Clients*; Melissa Murray, *The Admission*; *Nixer's Haven* (unperformed); Louise Page, *Flaws*; *Agnus Dei*; Kate Phelps (for W.T.G.), *My Mkinga*; Jennifer Phillips, *The Canonization of Suzie*; Sharon Pollack, *One Tiger to a Hill*; Christina Reid, *Did You Hear the One About the Irishman?*; Angela Stewart Park (and Noel Greig for Gay Sweatshop), *Blood Green*; Timberlake Wertenbaker, *The Third*; *Second Sentence*; *A Case to Answer*; Victoria Wood, *Good Fun*; Olwen Wymark, *Please Shine Down on Me*.

1981: Marion Baraitser, *Winnie*; Sarah Daniels, *Ripen Our Darkness*; *Ma's Flesh is Grass*; *Penumbra*; *The Devil's Gateway*; Nell Dunn, *Steaming*; Lesley Ferris, *The Subjugation of the Dragon*; Ellen Fox, *Ladies in Waiting*; *Saving Grace*; Donna Franceschild, *Tap Dance on a Telephone Wire*; Debbie Horsfield, *Out on the Floor*; Liz Lochhead, *True Confessions*; Claire Luckham, *Trafford Tanzi*; Alison Lyssa, *Pinball*; Clare McIntyre and Stephanie Nunn (for W.T.G.), *Better a Live Cyril than a Dead Pompey*; Honor Moore, (for Monstrous Regiment), *Mourning Pictures*; Louise Page, *Housewives*; Franca Rame (and Dario Fo, first performance in English), *Waking Up*; *A Woman Alone*; *The Same Old Story*; *Medea*; Sue Townsend, *The Dayroom*; *The Ghost of Daniel Lambert*; Rose Tremain (for Monstrous Regiment), *Yoga Class*, Michelene Wandor, *The Blind Goddess*; Timberlake Wertenbaker (For W.T.G.), *Breaking Through*; *New Anatomies*; Olwen Wymark, *Best Friends*.

1982: Sue Carlton, *Linda's*; Caryl Churchill, *Top Girls*; Andrea Dunbar, *Rita, Sue and Bob Too*; Tasha Fairbanks (for Siren), *Curfew*; Angie Farron, *Lost Property*; Ellen Fox, *Conversations With George Sandburg After A Solo Flight Across The Atlantic*; Christine Furnival, *The Petition* (rewritten for performance); Pam Gems, *Aunt Mary: Scenes From Provincial Life*; Elizabeth Gowans, *Casino*; Catherine Hayes, *Skirmishes*; Debbie Horsfield, *Away From it All*; Charlotte Keatley, *Underneath the Arndale*; Liz Lochhead, *Disgusting Objects*; Claire Luckham, *Finishing School*; *The Girls in the Pool*; Alison Lyssa, *The Boiling Frog*; Libby Mason (with W.T.G.), *Double Vision*; Natasha Morgan, *By George!* (unpublished); Rona Munro, *The Bang and The Whimper*; *The Salesman*;

Melissa Murray (for Monstrous Regiment), *The Execution*; Marsha Norman, *'Night Mother* (filmed); Louise Page, *Salonika*; Christina Reid, *Tea in a China Cup*; *Theatre de L'Aquarium* (translated by and for Monstrous Regiment), *Shakespeare's Sister*; Joan Timothy, *Do You Come Here Often?*; Sue Townsend, *Bazaar and Rummage*; Lou Wakefield (with W.T.G.), *Time Pieces*; Sheila Yeger, *People for Dinner*.

1983   Juliet Aykroyd, *Silver Hercules*; Elizabeth Bond (for W.T.G.), *Love and Dissent*; Caryl Churchill, *Fen*; Sarah Daniels, *Masterpieces*; Denise Deegan, *Daisy Pulls it Off*; Tasha Fairbanks (for Siren), *From the Divine*; Jill Flemming, *For She's A Jolly Good Fellow*; *Lovers and Other Enemies*; Maria Irene Fornes, *Mud*; *The Danube*; Ellen Fox, *Medicine Man*; Maro Green, *Ladders and Smoke*; Debbie Horsfield, *All You Deserve*; *The Red Devils Trilogy* (*Red Devils*; *True Dare Kiss*; *Command or Promise*); Charlotte Keatley, *Dressing for Dinner*; Bryony Lavery (for Monstrous Regiment), *Calamity*; Liz Lochhead, *Shanghaied*; *Red Hot Shoes*; Libby Mason and Tierl Thompson (for W.T.G.), *Dear Girl*; Tanya Myers, *The Fence*; Marsha Norman, *'Night Mother*; Franca Rame, *The Mother*; *I Don't Move, I Don't Scream, My Voice is Gone* (translated from the Italian by La Commune); Franca Rame and Dario Fo (translated by and for Monstrous Regiment), *Fourth Wall*; Eva Lamont Stewart, *Men Should Weep* (revival); Sue Townsend, *Groping for Words*; Olwen Wymark, *Find Me*.

1984:   Juliet Aykroyd, *Accommodation*, Chris Bowler (for Monstrous Regiment), *Enslaved by Dreams*; Caryl Churchill, *Softcops*; Sarah Daniels, *Byrthrite*; Grace Dayley, *Rose's Story*; Tasha Fairbanks (for Siren), *Now Wash Your Hands, Please*; Maria Irene Fornes, *Sarita*; Ellen Fox, *Clinging to the Wreckage*; Sue Frumin, *Vera*; Christine Furnival, *The Jewel of The Just* (unpublished); Pam Gems, *Loving Women*; *Camille*; Maro Green, *Jelly at the Ritz*; Charlotte Keatley, *The Iron Serpent*; Bryony Lavery (for Monstrous Regiment), *Origin of the Species*; Deborah Levy (for W.T.G.), *Pax*; Liz Lochhead, *Same Difference*; *Blood and Ice*; *Rosaleen's Baby*; Rona Munro, *Touchwood*; Tanya Myers (with Common Ground), *The Fence*; Louise Page, *Golden Girls*; *Real Estate*; Jacqueline Rudet, *Money to Live*; Jacqui Shapiro (for W.T.G.), *Trade Secrets*; Heidi Thomas, *All Flesh is Grass*; Sue Townsend, *The Great Celestial Cow*.

1985:   Chris Bowler (for Monstrous Regiment), *Point of Convergence*; Anne Devlin, *Ourselves Alone*; Cordelia Ditton and Maggie Ford, *About Face*; Tasha Fairbanks (for Siren), *Chic to Chic-A Cabaret*; *Pulp*; Maria Irene Fornes, *The Conduct of Life*; Sue Frumin (for Gay Sweatshop); *Raising the Wreck*; Pam Gems, *Pasionara*; Maro Green and Caroline Griffin,

More; Joyce Halliday (for W.T.G.), *Anywhere to Anywhere*; Catherine Kilcoyne, *Julie*; Marie Laberge, *Night* (L'Homme Gris); Bryony Lavery, *Origin of the Species* (for W.T.G.) *Witchcraze*; Deborah Levy, *Clam*; *Dream Mamma*; (for W.T.G.) *Ophelia and the Great Idea*; Cheryl Moch, *Cinderella The Real True Story* (American première), Rona Munro, *Ghost Story*; *Piper's Cave*; Christina Reid, *Dissenting Adults*; Jacqueline Rudet, *God's Second in Command*; *Basin*; Timberlake Wertenbaker, *The Grace of Mary Traverse*.

1986: Juliet Aykroyd, *The Clean-up*; Marion Baraitser, *Mr. Bennett and Miss Smith*; Caryl Churchill (and David Lan, for Joint Stock), *A Mouthful of Birds*; Helen Cooper, *Mrs. Gaugin*; Sarah Daniels, *Neaptide* (George Devine Award Winner); Cordelia Ditton and Maggie Ford, *The Day the Sheep Turned Pink*; Andrea Dunbar, *Shirley*; Lisa Evans, *Stamping, Shouting and Singing Home*; Tasha Fairbanks (with W.T.G.), *Fixed Deal*; Jill Flemming, *The Rug of Identity*; Christine Furnival, *The White Headscarves* (unpublished); Annie Griffin, *Blackbeard the Pirate*; Debbie Klein, *Coming Soon*; Deborah Levy, *Heresies* (the only play performed by the R.S.C. Women's Group); *Naked Cake*; (for W.T.G.) *Our Lady*; Eve Lewis, *Ficky Stingers*; Natasha Morgan, *An Independent Woman* (unpublished); Tanya Myers, *Dance for the Girls* (devised with Tamzin Griffin, unpublished); Ayshe Raif, *Fail/Safe*; Christina Reid, *Joyriders* (for Paines Plough); *Last of a Dyin' Race* (radio); Claire Schrader, *Corryvreken*; Heidi Thomas, *Shamrocks and Crocodiles*; Jane Wagner, *The Search for Signs of Intelligent Life in the Universe*; Susan Vankowitz, *Alarms* (for Monstrous Regiment).

1987: Kay Adshead, *Thatcher's Women*; Alison Altman (devised with W.T.G.), *Holding the Reins*; Marion Baraitser, *Mafeking*; Anne Caulfield, *The Ungrateful Dead*; *Cowboys*; Kate Coffey (for The Works), *Bloodward and her Brother*; Sarah Daniels, *Byrthrite*; Claire Dowie, *Adult Child/Dead Child*; Tasha Fairbanks (for Graeae), *A Private View*; Tasha Fairbanks (for Siren), *Hotel Destiny*; Tasha Fairbanks (with Jane Boston and Hilary Ramsden, for Siren) *Bubbles*; Elaine Feinstein (devised with W.T.G.) *Lear's Daughters*; Gilly Fraser, *A Bit of Rough*; Maro Green and Caroline Griffin (for Gay Sweatshop), *Memorial Gardens*; Annie Griffin, *Almost Persuaded*; Jackie Kay, *Chiaroscuro*; Charlotte Keatley, *Waiting for Martin* (a monologue); *My Mother Says I Never Should*; Wendy Kesselman, *My Sister in the House* (Monstrous Regiment version); Deborah Levy (for the R.S.C. Women's Project), *Heresies*; Karen Malpede (N.Y., The Living Theatre), *Sappho and Aphrodite*; Cheryl Moch, Cinderella *The Real True Story* (British première), Jill Posener, *Any Woman Can*; The Raving Beauties, *I Stand in the Land of Roses*; Christina Reid, *Did You Hear the One About the Irishman?* (revival at the King's Head Lunchtime); Heidi Thomas, *Indigo*; Polly Teale, *Fallen*; Anna Wheatley (for The Works), *Cross My Heart and Hope to Die*; *Tasting of Earth*; Valerie Windsor, *Effie's Burning*; Sheila Yeger, *The Lizzy Papers, Self-Portrait* (unpublished).

1988:   Marion Baraitser, *Elephant in a Rhubarb Tree*; Jane Boston and Jude Winter (for Siren), *Les Les*; Carol Bunyan (for Monstrous Regiment), *Waving*; Sarah Cathcart, *The Serpent's Fall*; Helen Cooper, *Mrs. Vershinin*; Sarah Daniels, *Beside Herself (The Power and the Story)*; *The Gut Girls*; Sandra Feeman, *Supporting Roles*; Annie Griffin, *The Deadly Grove*; Juliet Heacock (The Works), *Satis*; Zofia Kalinska (and the Magdalena Project), *Nominatae Filae*; Jackie Kay, *Twice Over*; Bryony Lavery, *Puppet States*; Eva Lewin, *Cochon Flambé*; Peta Lily, *Wendy Darling*; Mary Luckhurst, *Clear Vision*; Sonja Lyndon (Trouble and Strife), *Now and at the Hour of Our Death*; Kathleen McCreery, *The Ballad of Mary Barton*; Clare McIntyre, *Low Level Panic*; Penny O'Connor, *Dig*; *Volley*; *Spike!*; The R.S.C. Women's Group, *Lorca's Women*; Winsome Pinnock (for W.T.G.), *Picture Palace*; Nona Shepphard, *The Adventures of Robyn Hood* (Dramatrix's annual panto); Yana Stanjo (for the Pascal Theatre Co.) *Salt River*; Sue Townsend, *Ear, Nose and Throat*; Michelene Wandor, *Wanted*; Wendy Wasserstein, *The Heidi Chronicles*; Timberlake Wertenbaker, *Our Country's Good*; *The Love of the Nightingale*; Sheila Yeger, *Dancing in the Dark* (unpublished); Eleanor Zeal, *The Tainted Honey of Homicidal Bees*.

1989:   Ruhksana Amhad, *Song for Sanctuary*; Deborah Baddoo and Sally Ridgeworth (devised), *Penalty Fayre*; Peppy Barlow, *Mothering Sunday*; Claire Booker, *A Decision Pure and Simple*; Caryl Churchill, *Ice Cream, Hot Fudge* (rehearsed reading); Lucinda Coxon, *Birdbones*; April de Angelis (for ReSisters), *Iron Mistress*; Helen Edmundson (for The Red Stockings), *Ladies in the Lift*; Siân Evans, *I Sing Myself*; Barbara Ewing, *Alexandra Kollantai*; Tasha Fairbanks (for Siren), *Swamp*; Shirley Gee, *Warrior*; Annie Griffin (with Gloria), *Lady Audley's Secret*; *Ariadne*; Gillian Hanna (translated and adapted from three plays by Franca Rame and Dario Fo, for Monstrous Regiment), *A Common Woman*; Victoria Hardie, *Sleeping Nightie*; Susan Hayes, *BYTE*; Alison Higgins (for Hogwash Theatre Co.), *The Trouble with Mrs. Behn*; Endesha Ida Mae Holland (American playwright — British première directed by Annie Castledine), *From the Mississippi Delta*; Karen Hope, *Foreign Lands*, (with Live Theatre) *Rocking the Cradle*; Catherine Johnson, *Boys Mean Business*; Jackie Kay (for Gay Sweatshop), *Twice Over*; Maureen Lawrence, *Tokens of Affection*;

Liselle Layla (for Second Wave Young Women's Theatre), *Unlucky for Some*; Sharman MacDonald, *When We Were Women*; Miriam Margolyes and Sonia Fraser, *Woman, Lovely Woman*; *What Sex You Are: A Look at the Women in Dickens* (devised); Kathleen McCreery, *Who Cares Wins*; Jenny McLeod (for Monstrous Regiment), *Island Life*; Wendy McLeod, *Apocalyptic Butterflies*; Hattie Naylor, *Monsters*; Eric Overmyer (directed by Anna Furse; starring Juliet Stevenson, Paola Dionisotti, and Gerda Stevenson), *On the Verge*; Winsome Pinnock, *A Rock in Water, A Hero's Welcome*; Gillian Plowman, *Me and My Friend*; Ayshe Raif, *Caving In*; Nina Rapi, *Ithaka*; Bertrice Reading, *Just a W.O.M.A.N.* (One-woman show); Pat Reid, *Atlantas Race*; Nancy Reilly, *The Gangster and the Barmaid and Professional High*; Carol Rumens, *Nearly Siberia*; Nona Shepphard, *The Snow Queen* (for Dramatrix); Alison Smith, *Trace of Arc*; Split Britches (Lois Weaver, et al. — British première of the American play), *Little Women — The Tragedy*; Polly Teale, *What is Seized* (based on the story by Lorrie Moore); Dei Treanor, *Redefining the Whore*; Hannah Vincent, *The Burrow*; Alison West (for Black Theatre Co-op.), *Adam's Dream*; Julie Wilkinson (for Theatre Centre, rewritten for W.T.G.), *Pinchdice and Co.*; Victoria Worsley and Caroline Ward, *Make Me A Statue*; Sandra Yaw (for W.T.G.), *Zerri's Choice*.

1990:   Cindy Artiste, *Meridian* (adaptation of Alice Walker's novel); Black Mime Theatre (Women's Troop), *Mothers* (devised); Claire Booker, *Rainbow Baby*; *Blood so Cheap*; Kathy Burke, *Mr. Thomas*; Marisha Chamberlain, *Scheherezade*; Caryl Churchill, *Mad Forest*; April de Angelis (for Paines Plough) *Crux*; Sheila Dewey, *Wednesday's Child*; Tasha Fairbanks (for Theatre Centre's Women's Company), *Foreign Correspondence*; Maggie Fox and Sue Ryding (Lip Service), *Margaret III*; Sue Glover, *Bondagers*; Lisa Goldman (devised with the University of Essex M. A. in Theatre Group), *The Diaries of Hannah Culwick*; Lisa Goldman and Sarah Tuck (for the Art of Revolution at the Oval House), *On the Bridge*; Maro Green and Caroline Griffin (for W.T.G.), *Mortal*; Annie Griffin, (revival) *Almost Persuaded*; Penny Gulliver (for the Character Ladies), *The Sisters Mysteries*; Debbie Isitt, *Valentino*; *Femme Fatale*; Dillie Keane (ex-member Fascinating Aïda), *Single Again*; Bryony Lavery (for Clean Break) *Wicked*; (for W.T.G.) *Her Aching Heart*; *Kitchen Matters*; Clare McIntyre, *My Heart's a Suitcase*; Paula Milne, *Earwig*; Rona Munro, *Bold Girls*; Eileen Murphy, *Leaving Home*; Sally Nemeth (American playwright's British opening of the new play), *Mill Fire*; Maxine O'Reilly (comedienne), *The Lady's Not for Laughing*; Cindy Oswin, *(R)age*; Gillian Plowman, *Me and My Friend*;

Anna Reading, *Want*; Debbie Shewell (for Monstrous Regiment), *More Than One Antoinette*; Sally Templer, *Antigone*; Marta Tikkane (adapted and directed by Clare Venables, for Monstrous Regiment), *Love Story of the Century.*

1991:   Jean Abbott, *Forced Out*; Black Mime Theatre (Women's Troop), *Total Rethink; Drowning* (both devised); Caryl Churchill, *Lives of the Great Poisoners*; Margaretta D'Arcy, *The Eleanor Mary Show*; Rose English, *Walks on Water; The Double Wedding*; Lisa Evans (for W.T.G.), *Christmas Without Herods*; Marieluise Fleisser (translated by Tinch Minter and Elisabeth Bond-Pablé), *Purgatory in Ingolstadt; Pioneer in Ingolstadt* (German playwright, premièred in London, directed by Annie Castledine); Pam Gems, *The Blue Angel* (adapted from a novel by Heinrich Mann); Debbie Isitt, *The Woman Who Cooked her Husband*; Judith Johnson, *Nowheresville; The Scrappie*; Charlotte Keatley, *The Singing Ringing Tree*; Bryony Lavery, *Flight*; Bryony Lavery and Nona Shepphard, *Peter Pan* (for Dramatrix); Peta Lily, *Hiroshima Mon Amour*; Liz Lochhead, *Quelques Fleurs*; Sharman MacDonald, *All Things Nice*; Monstrous Regiment (adapted from Marivaux, with a second act by Robin Archer), *The Colony*; Louise Page, *Adam Was a Gardener*; Winsome Pinnock, *Talking in Tongues*; Sue Pomeroy and Good Company, *I Bertolt Brecht*; Diana Quick, *A Woman Destroyed* (translation of a monologue by Simone de Beauvoir); Nina Rapi, *Dreamhouse; Johnny is Dead*; Cheryl Robson, *The Taking of Liberty*; Jan Ruppe, *Cut it Out*; Claire Tomalin, *The Winter Wife*; Michelene Wandor, *The Mill on the Floss* (radio adaptation of the novel by George Eliot); *A Summer Wedding* (radio); *Killing Orders* (radio play based on a novel by Sara Peretsky); Timberlake Wertenbaker, *Three Birds Alighting on a Field*; Sheila Yeger, *Variations on a Theme by Clara Schumann.*

1992:   Deborah Baddoo, *Dream Vignette*; Sarah Daniels, *Head-Rot Holiday*; April de Angelis, *Hush*; Helen Edmundson, *Anna Karenina* (adaptation of the novel by Tolstoy); Rose English, *My Mathematics*; Bonnie Greer, *In the Country of the Young*; Debbie Isitt, *You Never Know Who's Out There*; Elfriede Jelinek, *What Happened After Nora Left Her Husband or Pillars of Society*; Ann Jellicoe, *Changing Places*; Judith Johnson, *Los Escombros; Somewhere*; Fiona Knowles, *The Seven Ages of Woman*; Bryony Lavery and Nona Shepphard, *The Sleeping Beauty* (for Dramatrix); *Laying Ghosts* (for television); Deborah Levy, *The Blood Wedding* (adapted from Lorca); *The B File; Call Blue Jane*; Peta Lily, *Beg!; The Lady's Woman*; Claire Luckham, *The Choice*; Claire MacDonald, *Storm from Paradise*; Sharman MacDonald, *Shades*; Phyllis

Nagy, *Weldon Rising* (US playwright, London première); Louise Page, *Like to Live; Hawks and Doves*; Nina Rapi, *Dance of Guns*; Christina Reid, *Les Miserables* (adaptation of the novel by Victor Hugo); Sue Schilperoort, *Mothering Rights*; Ntozake Shange, *The Love Space Demands*; Michelene Wandor, *A Question of Courage* (radio play from the novel by Marjorie Darke); Timberlake Wertenbaker, *The Thebans* (adaptation of three plays by Sophocles); Women's Issues Theatre (experimental piece), *Remodelling Woman*; Sheila Yeger, *A Better Day*.

1993:   Deborah Baddoo, *In Defence of Identity*; Ruth Carter (for Tamasha), *Women of the Dust*; Maya Chowdhri, *Monsoon*; Trish Cooke, *Running Dream*; Helen Edmundson, *The Clearing*; Pam Gems, *Yerma* (adapted from Lorca); *Deborah's Daughter*; Bonnie Greer, *Munda Negra*; Hairy Marys, *Travels on Testos*; Karen Hope, *Foreign Lands*; Debbie Isitt, *Out of the Ordinary*; Jackie Kay; *Twilight Shift*; Fiona Knowles, *Rabby Burns yer tea's oot*; Bryony Lavery, *The Way to Cook a Wolf*; Deborah Levy, *Pushing the Prince into Denmark*; Liz Lochhead, *The Magic Island* (adaptation for children of Shakespeare's *The Tempest*); Sharman MacDonald, *Winter Guest*; Kim Morrissey, *Dora: A Case of Hysteria* (Canadian writer's UK première); Nina Rapi, *Dangerous Oasis*; Sue Schilperoort, *Half a Million Women*; Sophie Treadwell, *Machinal* (revival at Royal National Theatre, London, starring Fiona Shaw); Michelene Wandor, *Deadlock* (radio play from a novel by Sara Peretsky); Women's Issues Theatre (experimental piece), *Judy's Last Punch*; Zindika, *Leonora's Dance*.

1994:   Alma Theatre, *The Belly* (devised piece based on Gertrude Stein's 'Lifting Belly'); Anna O, *Twenty Ways to Learn a Language*; Simi Bloomfield and Fiona Seagrave (devised), *Traces: All the Hands That Have Touched Me*; Marina Carr, *Low in the Dark*; Caryl Churchill, *The Skriker; Thyestes* (translation of Seneca's play); Emilyn Claid, *Laid Out Lovely*; Sarah Daniels, *The Madness of Esme and Shaz*; Anne Devlin, *After Easter*; Helen Edmundson, *The Mill on the Floss* (adaptation of the novel by George Eliot); Christine Entwistle, *Too Much has Fallen in Mine*; Erica Freund, *The Front Door* (Oval House Theatre); Anna Furse, *Wax* (Paines Plough); Anya Gallaccio, Deborah Levy and Kristina Page (for W.P.T.), *Shiny Nylon*; Pam Gems, *The Seagull* (adapted from Chekhov, performed at the Royal National Theatre starring Judi Dench); *Wuthering Heights* (adapted from Emily Brontë); Bonnie Greer, *Dancing on Black Water*; Hairy Marys (choreographed by Emilyn Claid), *Witch Craze*; Shobana Jeyasingh (for W.P.T.), *Answers from the Ocean*; Marie Jones, *The Hamster Wheel*; Fiona Knowles, *Burying Dad*; Claire MacDonald, *Beulah Land*; Sharon

Morgan, *Gobeithion Gorffwyll* (Welsh-language adaptation of a story by Simone de Beauvoir); Maggi Morrison, *My Other Grandmother*; Sue Palmer, *Magdalene*; Sue Townsend, *The Queen and I* (UK tour of play based on her novel); Women's Issues Theatre (experimental piece), *Daisy in Bright Lights*.

1995:   Emilyn Claid, *Fifi La Butch*; Joanna McClelland Glass, *If We Are Women* (Greenwich Theatre); Hairy Marys, *Bitches on Feet*; Charlotte Keatley, *Our Father*; *The Genius of Her Sex*; Deborah Levy, *Honey Baby: 13 Studies in Exile*; Sharman MacDonald, *Borders of Paradise*; Rona Munro, *The Maiden Stone*; Rona Munro and Fiona Knowles, *I Spy Mrs Peery*; Louise Page, *Another Nine Months*; Rebecca Prichard, *Essex Girls* (Sense and Royal Court); Diane Samuels, *Kindertransport*; Emma Thompson, *Sense and Sensibility* (film adaptation of the novel by Jane Austen); Timberlake Wertenbaker, *The Break of Day*.

Forthcoming in 1996:   Lesley Bruce, *Keyboard Skills*; Marina Carr, *Portia Coughlan*; Catherine Johnson, *Boys Mean Business*; Gena Moxley, *Danti-Dan*; Tamsin Oglesby, *Two Lips Indifferent Red*; Winsome Pinnock, *The Rebirth of Robert Samuels*; Naomi Wallace, *Slaughter City* (R.S.C.); *One Flea Spare*.

INDEX

Other titles in the Contemporary Theatre Studies series: